P9-APP-992

Developing Schoolwide Programs
to Prevent and Manage Problem Behaviors

Developing Schoolwide Programs to Prevent and Manage Problem Behaviors

A Step-by-Step Approach

Kathleen Lynne Lane

Jemma Robertson Kalberg

Holly Mariah Menzies

THE GUILFORD PRESS
New York   London

© 2009 The Guilford Press
A Division of Guilford Publications, Inc.
72 Spring Street, New York, NY 10012
www.guilford.com

Printed in the United States of America

This book is printed on acid-free paper.

Last digit is print number: 9   8   7   6   5   4   3   2

Library of Congress Cataloging-in-Publication Data

Lane, Kathleen L.
    Developing schoolwide programs to prevent and manage problem behaviors : a
step-by-step approach / Kathleen Lynne Lane, Jemma Robertson Kalberg, and Holly
Mariah Menzies.
       p.   cm.
    Includes bibliographical references and index.
    ISBN 978-1-60623-032-9 (pbk. : alk. paper)
    1. Problem children—Education—United States.   2. Behavior disorders
in children—United States—Prevention.   3. Problem children—Behavior
modification—United States.   4. School improvement programs—United States.
    I. Kalberg, Jemma Robertson.   II. Menzies, Holly Mariah.   III. Title.
    LC4802.L36 2009
    371.93—dc22

                                                    2008050589

About the Authors

Kathleen Lynne Lane, PhD, is Professor in the Department of Special Education at the University of Kansas. Before earning her master's degree and doctorate in education from the University of California, Riverside, Dr. Lane served as a classroom teacher of general and special education students for 5 years and provided consultation, intervention, and staff development services to five school districts in Southern California for 2 years as a Program Specialist. Dr. Lane's research interests focus on school-based interventions (academic and behavioral) with students at risk for emotional and behavioral disorders (EBD). She has designed, implemented, and evaluated multi-level prevention models in elementary, middle, and high school settings to prevent and respond to EBD. Dr. Lane served as the primary investigator (PI) of several state and federally funded projects, including Project Support and Include (PSI), which provides professional assistance to schools in 17 counties, focusing on the design, implementation, and evaluation of comprehensive, integrated, three-tiered models of prevention; Project WRITE, funded through the Institute for Educational Sciences, which focused on the impact of writing interventions for students at risk for EBD who are also poor writers; an OSEP directed project studying positive behavior interventions and support (PBIS) at the high school level; and an OSEP field-initiated project studying prevention of EBD at the elementary level. She has expertise in school-based intervention and statistical analysis including multivariate analysis of longitudinal data sets. She is the co-editor of *Remedial and Special Education* and an associate editor for *Journal of Positive Behavior Interventions* and *Education and Treatment of Children*. She serves on several editorial boards, including *Exceptional Children*, the *Journal of Special Education*, and *Journal of Emotional and Behavioral Disorders*. Dr. Lane has co-authored six books and published over a hundred refereed journal articles and more than 20 book chapters.

Jemma Robertson Kalberg, MEd, is a special education teacher at Seneca Center in San Leandro, California. Seneca provides both educational and therapeutic services for students with EBD within the context of a day treatment program. Mrs. Kalberg earned her master's degree in special education from Peabody College at Vanderbilt University. In addition, she has met all coursework and experience standards to sit for the exam to become a Board Certified Behavior Analyst. Prior to completing her master's program, she received her bachelor's degree from Vanderbilt with a major in special education and a minor in child development. Mrs. Kalberg's research interest focuses on supporting students who are at risk for, and identified with, EBD, both behaviorally and academically. In addition, she has been involved in designing, implementing, and evaluating schoolwide positive behavior support (SWPBS) plans with academic, behavior, and social components at the elementary, middle, and high school levels. Within the context of SWPBS, Mrs. Kalberg focuses her efforts on using schoolwide screeners to identify students who are nonresponsive to the primary prevention model.

Holly Mariah Menzies, PhD, is Associate Professor in the Charter College of Education at California State University, Los Angeles, and the program coordinator in mild–moderate disabilities in the Division of Special Education and Counseling. She earned her master's degree and doctorate from the University of California, Riverside, and worked as both a general educator and special educator for over 10 years. Dr. Menzies has provided staff development in the areas of assessment, language arts, and SWPBS. Her scholarly interests focus on inclusive education and the role of reform in curricular practices.

Acknowledgments

We extend our sincere thanks to those gentle giants who have shaped our thinking; the districts that supported our research; the project directors and research assistants who participated in this work; room 5116 in San Diego, California, where much of our editing took place; and the personal and professional relationships that provided the foundation for this book. We have conducted multi-tiered interventions for the past 10 years and hope this book will help shape the thinking of the next generation of educators and researchers.

We would especially like to thank Robert Rutherford for the invitation to write this book and Rochelle Serwator for seeing it through to the end. We thank Steven Driscoll and Allison Bruhn for their feedback and support during the writing process. Finally, we thank Lauren M. Magill and Kathryn A. Germer for their edits prior to the second printing.

Contents

Chapter One

Preventing and Managing Problem Behavior in Our Schools
A Formidable Task

Today's administrators and educators are faced with a number of challenges. For example, they are now expected to teach a population that is increasingly diverse not only in terms of unique cultural backgrounds, but also in terms of academic, behavioral, and social skill sets (Lane, Wehby, & Robertson, 2008). Further, teachers are expected to achieve high academic standards for all students (e.g., No Child Left Behind Act [NCLB], 2002); accommodate students with exceptionalities in inclusive settings (MacMillan, Gresham, & Forness, 1996); and serve students who exhibit high levels of violent and antisocial behavior that stem from the growing incivility of our society (Walker, 2003). Furthermore, teachers are expected to address the flood of school violence by preventing the development of antisocial behavior in addition to supporting students who already have these tendencies by promoting prosocial behaviors (Satcher, 2001; Walker, Ramsey, & Gresham, 2004).

Despite some declines in juvenile violence (see Box 1.1), the prevalence of violent crimes continues to be alarming. For example, 28 out of every 1,000 students are victims of crime within or beyond the school walls and, most disturbingly, 6% of all aggressive acts occur on school grounds (DeVoe et al., 2003). Not surprisingly, high school students responding to a national survey in 2003 indicated that fear of school-related crime prompted 5 out of 100 students to miss school at least once during the previous month (Snyder & Sickmund, 2006). In short, school can be a frightening, or at least undesirable, place for many students.

The consequences of school violence affect not only students, teachers, and administrators but society as a whole—particularly when the violence is extreme, as in the cases of school shootings (see Table 1.1). The shocking instances of violence that occurred in our nation's schools during recent years are beyond tragic and have untold costs emotionally, financially, and otherwise (Kauffman, 2005; Lane, 2007; Quinn &

> **Box 1.1.** **Statistics on Juvenile Offenders and Victims: The 2006 National Report**
>
> "While there was a large increase and then a large decline in the murders of male juveniles between 1980 and 2002, the annual number of murdered juvenile females remained relatively constant." (p. 21)
>
> "Between 1980 and 2002, at least 3 of every 4 murder victims ages 15–17 were killed with a firearm." (p. 23)
>
> "In 2002 one in twelve murders in the U.S. involved a juvenile offender. One-third of murders committed by a juvenile offender also involved an adult offender." (pp. 65–66)
>
> "The large decline in the numbers of murders committed by juveniles from the mid-1990s to 2002 stemmed primarily from a decline in minority males killing minority males." (p. 67)
>
> "Thirty-two percent (32%) of youth ages 12 to 17 who reported recently using alcohol also report using marijuana; in contrast, just 2% of youth who report no recent use of alcohol reported using marijuana." (p. 81)
>
> "The violent crime peak in the after-school hours on school days is seen in the crimes committed by male, female, white and black youth." (p. 86)
>
> "In 2003, high school students responding to a national survey reported having property stolen or damaged at school (1 in 3) more often than fighting at school (1 in 8). Fear of school-related crime kept 5 in 100 high schoolers home at least once during the prior month." (p. 73)
>
> "Six percent of high school students said they carried a weapon (e.g., gun, knife, or club) on school property in the past 30 days—down from 12% in 1993. The proportion that carried a weapon to school was about one-third of those who said they had carried a weapon anywhere in the past month. In addition, 6% of high schoolers reported carrying a gun anywhere in the past month, down from 8% in 1993." (p. 74)
>
> "A greater proportion of female arrests (20%) than male arrests (15%) involved a person younger than age 18. (p. 126)
>
> "The juvenile arrest rate for simple assault in 2003 was more than double what it was in 1980." (p. 142)
>
> *Note.* Data from Snyder and Sickmund (2006).

Poirier, 2004). Although many general educators did not imagine they would have to address issues such as violence and antisocial behavior, they are facts of life that must be attended to by our schools (Walker et al., 2004).

Antisocial Behavior Defined

Antisocial behavior may be viewed as the opposite of prosocial behavior. Instead of positive, cooperative, and helpful, a student with antisocial behavior is one who is negative, hostile, and aggressive in his or her interactions across a range of settings (Walker et al., 2004). The term *antisocial behavior* refers to persistent violations of normative

Table 1.1. **School Shootings in the United States of America**

Date	Location	Event
February 2, 1996	Moses Lake, Washington	14-year-old student fired a gun during algebra class, killing two students and a staff member
February 19, 1997	Bethel, Alaska	16-year-old student fired a gun at school, killing another student and a staff member
October 1, 1997	Pearl, Mississippi	16-year-old student fired gun at school, killing two students and a staff member and was later accused of killing his mother
December 1, 1997	West Paducah, Kentucky	14-year-old student shot a gun during prayer circle, killing three other students
December 15, 1997	Stamps, Arkansas	14-year-old student shot at students in the school parking lot, injuring two
March 24, 1998	Jonesboro, Arkansas	13-year-old and 11-year-old shot at classmates during false fire alarm, killing four students and one staff member
April 24, 1998	Edinboro, Pennsylvania	14-year-old student fired a gun during a middle school dance, killing two students and a staff member
May 19, 1998	Fayettesville, Tennessee	18-year-old student killed the boyfriend of an ex-girlfriend
May 21, 1998	Springfield, Oregon	15-year-old student fired shots in the school cafeteria, killing two students and injuring twenty-two others
June 15, 1998	Richmond, Virginia	14-year-old boy fired shots in school hallway, injuring two people
April 20, 1999	Littleton, Colorado	18-year-old and 17-year-old students killed 12 classmates and 1 teacher, injured 23 others, and later killed themselves; they had planned to kill at least 500 and blow up the school
May 20, 1999	Conyers, Georgia	15-year-old student fired a gun, injuring six people
November 19, 1999	Deming, New Mexico	12-year-old student shot a peer at school, killing another student
December 6, 1999	Fort Gibson, Oklahoma	13-year-old student fired a gun at school, injuring four
February 29, 2000	Mount Morris Township, Michigan	6-year-old student killed peer at school

(cont.)

Table 1.1 (*cont.*)

Date	Location	Event
March 10, 2000	Savannah, Georgia	19-year-old student killed two students at a school-sponsored dance
May 26, 2000	Lake Worth, Florida	13-year-old student shot and killed a teacher on the last day of school
September 26, 2000	New Orleans, Louisiana	Two were wounded by gunfire during a fight at a middle school
March 5, 2001	Santee, California	15-year-old student fired a gun in a high school and killed two students
March 7, 2001	Williamsport, Pennsylvania	14-year-old student shot and injured a peer in the school cafeteria
March 22, 2001	Granite Hills, California	18-year-old student fired a gun at school and injured four
March 30, 2001	Gary, Indiana	17-year-old expelled student fired a gun on school campus, killing another student
May 15, 2001	Ennis, Texas	16-year-old killed himself and his girlfriend in a high school English class after taking 17 hostages
November 12, 2001	Caro, Michigan	17-year-old student took two hostages and killed himself
January 15, 2002	New York, New York	Teen shot gun at school and injured two
April 14, 2003	New Orleans, Louisiana	Four teens (not enrolled in the high school) shot at and injured four students and killed one
April 24, 2003	Red Lion, Pennsylvania	14-year-old student killed principal before killing himself
September 24, 2003	Cold Spring, Minnesota	15-year-old shot and killed fellow peer
March 17, 2004	Joyce, Washington	13 year-old student shot and killed himself in school class
December 10, 2004	Nine Mile Falls, Washington	16-year-old high school student committed suicide in school entryway
March 2, 2005	Cumberland City, Tennessee	14-year-old student killed school bus driver
March 21, 2005	Red Lake, Minnesota	16-year-old killed 10 people, 2 at home and 8 on school grounds, then killed himself
November 8, 2005	Jacksboro, Tennessee	15-year-old student fired a gun at school administrators, killing one and wounding two others

Table 1.1 *(cont.)*

Date	Location	Event
August 30, 2006	Hillsborough, North Carolina	High school student opens fire injuring two students
September 29, 2006	Cazenovia, Wisconsin	15-year-old student shot and critically injured the school principal
October 17, 2006	Katy, Texas	16-year-old male high school student committed suicide in school cafeteria
December 12, 2006	Springfield Township, Pennsylvania	16-year-old male high school student killed himself in hallway of school
January 3, 2007	Tacoma, Washington	18-year-old male high school student shot and killed classmate
March 7, 2007	Greenville, Texas	16-year-old male high school student shot himself in band hallway at school

Note. Adapted from "A Time Line of Recent Worldwide School Shootings," *www.infoplease.com/ipa/A0777958.html*, as it appeared on February 13, 2008. InformationPlease® Database © 2007 Pearson Education, Inc. Reproduced by permission of Pearson Education, Inc. publishing as InfoPlease. All rights reserved.

rules and expected behaviors (Simcha-Fagan, Langner, Gersten, & Eisenberg, 1975). Clearly, students with antisocial behavior patterns pose challenges to teachers, parents, and peers. Adding to the complexity of these problems are the different terms used to describe various types of emotional or behavioral disorders (Kauffman, 2005), all of which pose unique difficulties to school systems (Lane, 2004). For example, the psychiatric community uses terms such as *oppositional defiant disorder, conduct disorder,* and *antisocial personality disorder* (American Psychiatric Association, 2000). *Antisocial behavior* is broader than the term *antisocial personality disorder,* as specified in the *Diagnostic and Statistical Manual of Mental Disorders* (4th ed., text revision [DSM-IV-TR]; American Psychiatric Association, 2000). The term *antisocial personality disorder* is used by the mental health community to refer to adults who display extreme patterns of highly aggressive, delinquent behaviors (Lane, Kalberg, Parks, & Carter, 2008). The research community uses terms such as *internalizing* (overcontrolled: anxious, somatic complaints, and depression) and *externalizing* (undercontrolled: delinquency and aggression; Achenbach, 1991). Finally, the educational community uses terms such as *emotional disturbance* (ED) and *social maladjustment.* This wide range of terminology may make it difficult to identify and support students; communicate effectively between educators and mental health professionals; and conduct research with these students (Lane, 2004; Lane, Gresham, & O'Shaughnessy, 2002a).

Many people are under the impression that students with behavior problems do not "belong" in general education classrooms and instead should receive special education services (Individuals with Disabilities Education Improvement Act [IDEIA], 2004). However, according to IDEIA, not all students with behavioral challenges qualify for special education services under the ED category. Therefore, it is important that administrators and teachers are prepared to meet the multiple needs of students with, and at risk for, emotional or behavioral disorders, whether or not they are identified for services. Moving forward, we use the more global term of *emotional or behavioral disorders* (EBD) to refer to students with behavioral patterns that challenge our educational systems.

The Multiple Needs of Students with EBD

Although most often recognized for their behavioral deficits and excesses, students with EBD also have difficulties in social and academic areas. In terms of social-behavioral performance, students with EBD struggle tremendously in their interactions with peers and adults in the classrooms and in unstructured settings (e.g., recess; Walker, Irvin, Noell, & Singer, 1992). For example, they demonstrate high levels of aggression not only toward teachers, peers, parents, and siblings, but also toward property (e.g., arson, vandalism) and themselves (e.g., high-risk behaviors such as drug and alcohol abuse; Walker et al., 2004). These students struggle in their ability to accurately interpret social situations, often misinterpreting neutral social interactions (e.g., being bumped by another student while standing in the lunch line) as confrontational or even hostile (Crick, Grotpeter, & Bigbee, 2002). Due to problems with encoding and interpreting information, students with EBD are quick to respond negatively or inappropriately. During playground time, they exhibit more than twice the amount of negative-aggressive behavior than typical students (Walker, Hops, & Greenwood, 1993), even though their prosocial behavior interactions tend to be comparable. Overall, these maladaptive behavior patterns lead to negative outcomes in their teacher and peer relations, as evidenced by teacher and peer rejection as well as limited social or academic engagement (Walker et al., 1992).

In addition to social and behavioral difficulties, students with EBD show broad deficits in core academic areas. These deficits have been well documented over the past decade (e.g., reading, writing, mathematics: Coutinho, 1986; Greenbaum et al., 1996; Landrum, Tankersley, & Kauffman, 2003; Lane, Barton-Arwood, Rogers, & Robertson, 2007; Mattison, Hooper, & Glassberg, 2002; Nelson, Benner, Lane, & Smith, 2004; Reid, Gonzalez, Nordness, Trout, & Epstein, 2004; Wagner & Davis, 2006). Unfortunately, the academic skill sets of students receiving special education services for behavioral problems tend to remain relatively stable over time—that is, they typically do not improve (Lane, 2004; Mattison et al.) and may even deteriorate (Nelson et al.). In fact, students with EBD typically "experience less school success than any other subgroup of students with or without disabilities" (Landrum et al., p. 148).

Given the deleterious effects of school-based violence and the multiple needs of students with, and at risk for, EBD, it is essential that evidenced-based programs be implemented to prevent and respond to instances of antisocial behavior. Furthermore, because academic, behavioral, and social concerns co-occur and interact with one another, it is important that prevention and remediation efforts address this interconnected relationship (Lane, Wehby, et al., 2002).

A Call for Support

Fortunately, a number of mandates have been issued demanding that schools provide safe, nonviolent learning environments. For example, Title IV of Improving America's Schools Act of 1994, The Safe and Drug-Free Schools and Communities Act (1994), allows state and local agencies to design schoolwide violence and drug abuse prevention programs (Turnbull et al., 2002). Further, this act prompted a zero-tolerance policy for drugs and weapons that is also supported in the Individuals with Disabilities Education Act (IDEA; 1997). The White House called for systematic change to ensure that all schools provide safe, nonviolent environments (Dwyer, Osher, & Warger, 1998; Kern & Manz, 2004). Even the Surgeon General's Report on Youth Violence (Satcher, 2001) offered four recommendations to address antisocial behavior in schools. The specific recommendations included (1) eliminating antisocial groups, (2) improving academic performance, (3) developing positive school climates, and (4) adopting a primary prevention agenda (Satcher). Similar language was included in the reauthorization of Individuals with Disabilities Education Improvement Act (IDEIA, 2004), which provided for "incentives for whole-school approaches, scientifically based early reading programs, positive behavior interventions and supports, and early intervening services to reduce the need to label children as disabled in order to address the learning and behavioral needs of such children" (p. 4).

Many schools have responded to these mandates and concerns surrounding antisocial behavior by moving away from traditional, reactive approaches to schoolwide discipline and shifting toward data-driven, proactive approaches (Horner & Sugai, 2000). Instead of waiting for problems to occur and then responding with a series of increasingly harsh consequences, schools are developing three-tiered models of support that subscribe to a proactive, instructional approach to behavior (Lane, Robertson, & Graham-Bailey, 2006).

Three-Tiered Models of Support

Three-tiered models of prevention, such as response-to-intervention (RTI; Gresham, 2002a; Sugai, Horner, & Gresham, 2002) and positive behavior interventions and supports* (PBIS; Lewis & Sugai, 1999; Sugai & Horner, 2002), contain primary, secondary, and tertiary levels of support. Each level of prevention increases in intensity or magnitude, with a goal of providing more focused interventions for students in need of targeted assistance as determined by schoolwide data (see Figure 1.1). This systematic approach embraces a data-driven method to identify and support students based on their individual needs (Lewis & Sugai). We briefly describe each level of prevention below.

---

*Earlier publications and the first printing of this book refer to this model as Positive Behavior Support. As of 2012, we have adapted to the more current terminology, Positive Behavior Interventions and Supports (PBIS).

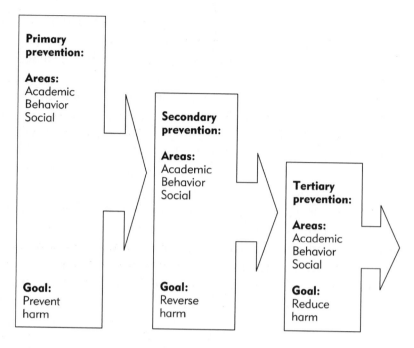

Figure 1.1. **Three-tiered model of prevention: A comprehensive approach.**

Primary Prevention

Primary prevention plans are designed to prevent harm from occurring. Just as parents may decide to have their child vaccinated to decrease the likelihood of his or her getting the flu, primary prevention plans are constructed to prevent certain undesirable academic, behavioral, and social outcomes (e.g., academic failure, school violence, bullying) from occurring. Examples of primary prevention programs include validated literacy curricula, violence prevention, conflict resolution, anti-bullying programs, and schoolwide social skills. All students enrolled in a school are eligible for participation just by virtue of showing up; there are no referral, screening, or eligibility determinations to be made (Lane, Robertson, & Graham-Bailey, 2006).

Thus, primary prevention programs support a large number of students with generally low levels of risk. An anticipated 80% of the students are likely to respond to this level of support (Gresham, Sugai, Horner, Quinn, & McInerney, 1998; Sugai & Horner, 2006). Then, school-wide data are analyzed to identify students who require more targeted levels of support in the form of secondary and tertiary prevention efforts.

Secondary Prevention

Students identified as nonresponsive to the primary prevention plan are placed into secondary prevention programs. Specifically, students with similar academic, behavioral, and social concerns are given more focused interventions to address their acquisition (can't do), fluency (trouble doing), or performance (won't do) deficits (Gresham,

2002b). Examples of these programs include small-group instruction in anger management, self-regulation skills, or reading comprehension strategies. The goal of these programs is to reverse harm by teaching functional skills and adjusting levels of reinforcement (Walker & Severson, 2002).

Approximately 10–15% of the student body is apt to require secondary prevention. Again, data are collected to determine how students are responding to this level of support. If evidence suggests that students are not responding, then they are identified for tertiary prevention.

Tertiary Prevention

Tertiary prevention is the most intensive level of support and is reserved for students who do not respond to primary or secondary efforts and who are exposed to several risk factors (e.g., impoverished living conditions, parents with mental health or addiction problems, chaotic family environments). Typically, students requiring tertiary interventions have complex, long-term, resistant behavioral problems that require intensive approaches (Kern & Manz, 2004). Examples of tertiary prevention efforts include function-based interventions (Umbreit, Ferro, Liaupsin, & Lane, 2007), the multisystemic therapy program (MST; Henggeler, 1998), and highly intensive academic forms of assistance. The goal of this level of support is to reduce harm by addressing the multiple severe difficulties of this population. Approximately 5–7% of the student body may require this intensive level of support. Potentially, schools have the ability to be a strong, positive host setting for coordinating these types of prevention (Walker et al., 1996; Walker & Severson, 2002).

Purpose

In light of the challenges associated with serving an increasingly diverse group of students, coupled with the increased demand for academic accountability while maintaining a safe, nonviolent environment, we offer this book as a tool for administrators, educators, behavior specialists, school psychologists, and researchers alike to help better serve students with, and at risk for, EBD. Although it is quite possible that students with antisocial behavioral tendencies may require and qualify for special education, it is important to note that simply demonstrating emotional or behavioral problems does not mean that the student will be eligible for special education services (Lane, 2007). Accordingly, many student with, and at risk for, EBD spend the better part, if not all, of their educational careers in the general education setting (Lane, 2004).

Unfortunately, many general education teachers have indicated to us personally, and it is also well documented in the literature (Schumm & Vaughn, 1995), that they do not have the skills, resources (personnel, monetary, and time), or support to prevent and respond to the challenging behaviors and academic needs demonstrated by some students (Lane, 2004). We offer this book as one tool to address this concern. Namely, we feel it is critical that we look to the school as an agent of change (Horner & Sugai,

2000) by providing an opportunity for administrators, general education teachers, special education teachers, school psychologists, behavior specialists, and discipline team members to become familiar with strategies that better serve students with, and at risk for, EBD through the support of three-tiered models of prevention. Specifically, this book is a research-based, practical guide for designing, implementing, and evaluating primary prevention programs to (1) prevent the development of EBD in our schools and (2) identify and support students who are nonresponsive to global intervention efforts via secondary and tertiary prevention efforts (Lane, 2007). To this end, we introduce a model containing many of the core elements of PBIS and RTI models. However, rather than focusing predominantly (if not exclusively) on behavioral issues, as in PBIS models, or on academic issues, as in RTI models, the model we introduce provides a primary plan that contains academic, behavioral, and social components to meet students' multiple needs. Below the remaining chapters are briefly described.

Chapter 2, "Primary Prevention across the K–12 Grade Span," begins with an overview of the literature on primary prevention models at the elementary, middle, and high school levels. Next, we address the challenges of conducting schoolwide primary prevention programs, particularly in secondary schools. Finally, we introduce core quality indicators for consideration when designing, implementing, and evaluating the primary plan (Gersten et al., 2005; Horner et al., 2005).

Chapter 3, "A Closer Look at the Positive Behavior Interventions and Supports Model," provides additional information to help further define the PBIS model as conceptualized by Sugai and Horner (2006). Specifically, we (1) introduce four critical elements of schoolwide PBIS, (2) list and describe the four systems constituting comprehensive PBIS models, and (3) illustrate how the progressive continuum of behavior supports functions in the model.

Chapter 4, "Designing and Implementing Primary Prevention Models," provides a step-by-step team-based approach for designing and implementing a comprehensive primary prevention model containing academic, behavioral, and social components. More specifically, this chapter illustrates one method of constructing primary plans that has been used across the K–12 continuum (Lane, Kalberg, Bruhn, Mahoney, & Driscoll, in press; Lane & Menzies, 2003, 2005; Lane, Wehby, Robertson, & Rogers, 2007; Robertson & Lane, 2007).

Chapter 5, "Assessment and Screening at the Primary Level," discusses the importance of conducting a sound evaluation to determine the extent to which the primary program positively impacts student outcomes in terms of academic, behavioral, and social performance. An assessment plan, including tools such as treatment integrity and social validity measures, is introduced. Next, validated screening tools that can be used at both the elementary and secondary levels to identify students with, and at risk for, EBD are discussed; these include the Strengths and Difficulties Questionnaire (SDQ; Goodman, 1997), the Student Risk Screening Scale (SRSS; Drummond, 1994), and Systematic Screening for Behavior Disorders (SSBD; Walker & Severson, 1992). Practical guidelines are provided for selecting feasible, reliable measures to monitor how students respond to the primary intervention program, thereby allowing administrators and teachers to determine whether the primary plan's goals are being met.

Chapter 6, "Determining How Well the Program Is Working: Monitoring Outcomes and Identifying Nonresponsive Students," provides the rationale for, and illustrations of, (1) monitoring how the school as a whole is responding the schoolwide plan; (2) determining how different types of students respond; and (3) identifying students who require additional supports in the form of secondary and tertiary interventions. We also offer recommendations for structuring targeted interventions using schoolwide data, implementing these interventions during the school day using existing resources, monitoring student progress, and determining when the extra support is no longer required. The interventions illustrated include academic, behavioral, and social domains.

Chapter 7, "Getting Started in Your School: Frequently Asked Questions," provides a comprehensive list of frequently asked questions regarding the design, implementation, and evaluation of primary prevention models. The intent of this chapter is to provide concrete information that addresses logistical issues.

In sum, this book provides the tools and procedures necessary to design, implement, and evaluate comprehensive primary prevention programs that recognize the multiple needs of students with EBD. In addition, it illustrates how to use schoolwide data to monitor students' responses to these global intervention efforts and determine which students need additional assistance in the form of secondary or tertiary levels of support. Throughout the book we address concerns and recommendations from practitioners who have implemented comprehensive, primary prevention programs at the elementary, middle, and high school level using the guidelines provided.

Using the tools and procedures included in this text, you can design and implement a comprehensive, data-driven, primary plan that meets the instructional and behavioral goals specified for your school. In addition, using this model will garner the data necessary to inform broad-scale changes and targeted interventions for students who require additional support, as required by No Child Left Behind (2002) and IDEIA (Individuals with Disabilities Education Improvement Act, 2004).

Chapter Two

Primary Prevention across the K–12 Grade Span

Developing a Solid Foundation

As detailed in Chapter 1, at the base of a three-tiered model of prevention, be it a PBIS model or a RTI model, is a primary plan. You may have previously heard the terms *universal*, *tier one*, *schoolwide*, or *primary prevention plan*. To date, many schools have embraced three-tiered PBIS models to prevent the development of EBD and respond to existing cases of EBD, using plans that attend primarily to students' behavioral and social needs. Traditionally, PBIS plans have not included an academic component. As part of the PBIS process, the school-site team develops the primary plan with input from the faculty. In brief, this process involves establishing common expectations for how students should perform behaviorally and socially in order to be successful at a particular school. Once the expectations are established, they are taught to all students in the building using a variety of tools such as lessons, DVDs, and explicit modeling of the expectations. Then, students are given opportunities to practice and receive reinforcement for demonstrating the desired behaviors. Students who demonstrate these identified expectations receive reinforcement from all adults in the building—teachers, paraprofessionals, administrators, secretaries, cafeteria employees, custodians, substitutes, and volunteers. Thus, all students participate in this schoolwide, primary plan. There is no screening or referral to determine eligibility. Just like the measles, mumps, and rubella vaccinations—everyone gets them!

It is important to note that PBIS is a framework, not a curriculum (Scott & Caron, 2005). The PBIS model specifies the provision of progressively more intensive support in the form of targeted interventions based on individual students' needs. The advantage of a framework, as opposed to a specific curriculum, is that a school-site team can develop or choose programs for each of the levels that best addresses the needs of the student body.

There are several stand-alone primary plans that address very specific behavioral and social needs such as violence prevention, anti-bullying methods, drug abuse preven-

Table 2.1. **Primary Prevention Programs**

Name	Description	Representative supporting research	Target group	Cost/contact information
Promoting Alternative Thinking Strategies (PATHS; Greenberg, Kusché, & Mihalic, 1998)	PATHS is intended to reduce aggression and behavior problems. The program focuses on emotional literacy, self-control, social competence, interpersonal problem-solving skills, and positive peer relations.	Greenberg, M. T., Kusché, C. A., Cook, E. T., & Quamma, J. P. (1995). Promoting emotional competence in school-aged children: The effects of the PATHS curriculum. *Development and Psychopathology, 7,* 117–136. Greenberg, M. T., Kusché, C. A., & Mihalic, S. F. (1998). *Promoting alternative thinking strategies (PATHS): Blueprints for violence prevention, book ten.* Blueprints for Violence Prevention Series (D. S. Elliott, Series Editor). Boulder, CO: Center for the Study and Prevention of Violence, Institute of Behavioral Science, University of Colorado. *www.prevention.psu.edu/projects/ PATHSPublications.html*	K–6	Complete PATHS program (Basic Kit and Turtle Unit)—$719 PATHS Basic Kit (grades 1–6)—$629 PATHS Turtle Unit (K)—$189 Channing Bete Company One Community Place South Deerfield, MA 01373-0200 877-896-8532 *custsvcs@channing-bete.com* *www.channing-bete.com/prevention-programs/paths/* *www.prevention.psu.edu/projects/ PATHS.html*
PeaceBuilders (Molina & Molina, 1996)	PeaceBuilders is a violence-prevention program. Programs include lessons to teach violence prevention and additional materials.	Flannery, D. J., Vazsonyi, A. T., Liau, A. K., Guo, S., Powell, K. E., Atha, H., et al. (2003). Initial behavior outcomes for the PeaceBuilders universal school-based violence prevention program. *Developmental Psychology, 39,* 292–308. *www.peacebuilders.com/whatWeDo/research.php*	K–5	Heartsprings, Inc. P.O. Box 12158 Tucson, AZ 85732 800-368-9356 520-298-7670 *www.peacebuilders.com*

(cont.)

Table 2.1 (cont.)

Name	Description	Representative supporting research	Target group	Cost/contact information
Caring School Community (CSC— originally the Child Development Project)	The CSC program focuses on strengthening students' ties to school and aims to reduce drug use, violence, and delinquency. It emphasizes the view of schools as caring communities.	Battistich, V., Schaps, E., Watson, M., & Solomon, D. (2000). Effects of the child development project on students' drug use and other problem behaviors. *Journal of Primary Prevention, 21*(1), 75–99. *www.devstu.org/csc/research.html*	K–6	Costs are approximately $200 per grade level for teacher packages. Each package includes an overview of the program, 30 lessons, and supplementary materials. *www.devstu.org/csc/included.html* Development Studies Center 2000 Embarcadero, Suite 305 Oakland, CA 94606 800-666-7270 *info@devstu.org*
Second Step: A Violence Prevention Program (SSVP; Committee for Children, 2007)	SSVP teaches social and emotional skills for violence prevention. Skills focus on four main areas: empathy, anger management, impulse control, and problem solving.	McMahon, S. D., & Washburn, J. J. (2003). Violence prevention: An evaluation of program effects with urban African-American students. *Journal of Primary Prevention, 24,* 43–62. *www.cfchildren.org/programs/ssp/research/*	Preschool through eighth grade	Grade-level kits range from $169 to $269. Materials include a teacher's guide, lesson plans, posters, academic integration activities, formative knowledge assessments, etc. Committee for Children 568 First Avenue South, Suite 600 Seattle, WA 98104-2804 800-634-4449 x 6223 *clientsupport@cfchildren.org* *www.cfchildren.org/programs/ssp/ overview/*

Program	Description	Grade level	References	Contact
Responding in Peaceful and Positive Ways (RIPP; Meyer & Northup, 1998)	RIPP is a universal violence prevention program designed especially for middle school students. The curriculum develops students' social and cognitive skills to enable them to utilize nonviolent conflict resolution and positive communication.	Middle school	Farrell, A. D., Valois, R. F., Meyer, A. L., & Tidwell, R. P. (2003). Impact of the RIPP violence prevention program on rural middle school students. *Journal of Primary Prevention, 24*(2), 143–167. Farrell, A. D., Meyer, A. L., Sullivan, T. N., & Kung, E. M. (2003). Evaluation of the Responding in Peaceful and Positive Ways (RIPP) seventh grade violence prevention curriculum. *Journal of Child and Family Studies, 12*, 101–120. *www.has.vcu.edu/RIPP/newpage4.htm*	Prevention Opportunities, LLC 12458 Ashland Vineyard Lane Ashland, VA 23005 804-301-4909 *contact@preventionopportunities.com* *www.preventionopportunities.com/index.html* *www.has.vcu.edu/RIPP/*
Bullying Prevention Program (BPP; Olweus, 2001)	BPP is a universal intervention for elementary, middle, or high school students designed to reduce or prevent bullying. It includes schoolwide, classroom, and individual components.	K–12	Black, S. A., & Jackson, E. (2007). Using bullying incident density to evaluate the Olweus bullying prevention programme. *School Psychology International, 28*, 623–638. Olweus, D., Limber, S. P., & Mihalic, S. (1999). *The bullying prevention program: Blueprints for violence prevention, book nine.* Blueprints for Violence Prevention Series (D. S. Elliott, Series Editor). Boulder, CO: Center for the Study and Prevention of Violence, Institute of Behavioral Science, University of Colorado. *www.clemson.edu/olweus/evidence.html*	For cost information, see *www.clemson.edu/olweus/costs.html* Marlene Snyder, PhD Institute on Family and Neighborhood Life Clemson University 158 Poole Agricultural Center Clemson, SC 29634 864-710-4562 *nobully@clemson.edu* *www.clemson.edu/olweus*

(cont.)

Table 2.1 (cont.)

Name	Description	Representative supporting research	Target group	Cost/contact information
Bully-Proofing Your School (BPYS; Garrity, Jens, Porter, Sager, & Short-Camilli, 1994)	BPYS is a comprehensive program designed to reduce and respond to bullying in the school setting. It has multiple components that include staff and student training as well as individual intervention and victim support.	Epstein, L., Plog, A., & Porter, W. (2002). Bully proofing your school: Results of a four-year intervention. *Emotional and Behavioral Disorders in Youth, 2*, 53–80. *www.bullyproofing.org/research2.html*	K–12	Bully Proofing Your School materials are available through Sopris West Educational Services 800-547-6747 *www.sopriswest.com* For training and other information contact: *kathleenkeelan@ bullyproofing.org* *www.bullyproofing.org*
Midwestern Prevention Project (MPP; Pentz, Mihalic, & Grotpeter, 1998)	MPP is a comprehensive program to prevent adolescent drug abuse. It includes school, community, and family based components. The school program uses modeling, role playing, and discussion to provide students with skills that help them avoid drug use.	MacKinnon, D. P., Johnson, C. A., Pentz, M. A., Dwyer, J. H., Hansen, W. B., Flay, B. R., et al. (1991). Mediating mechanisms in a school-based drug prevention program: First-year effects of the Midwestern prevention project. *Health Psychology, 10*, 164–172. Pentz, M. A., Mihalic, S. F., & Grotpeter, J. K. (1998). *The Midwestern prevention project: Blueprints for violence prevention, book one.* Blueprints for Violence Prevention Series (D. S. Elliott, Series Editor). Boulder, CO: Center for the Study and Prevention of Violence, Institute of Behavioral Science, University of Colorado.	Middle through late adolescence	Minimal cost of implementation for 3 years—$175,000. Designed for up to 20 teachers, 20 parent group members (3–4 principals, 4 students, 12 parents), and 1,000 students. *Not commercially available Blueprints for Violence Prevention Center for the Study and Prevention of Violence Institute of Behavioral Science University of Colorado at Boulder 1877 Broadway, Suite 601 Boulder, CO 80302 303-492-1032 *Blueprints@colorado.edu* *www.colorado.edu/cspv/blueprints/*

| Life Skills Training (LST) | LST is a 3-year school-based program targeting middle school students. It is intended to prevent/ameliorate gateway drug use, including tobacco, alcohol, and marijuana. Students learn self-management skills, social skills, and information specific to drug use prevention. | Middle school students | Griffin, K. W., Botvin, G. J., Nichols, T. R., & Doyle, M. M. (2003). Effectiveness of a universal drug abuse prevention approach for youth at high risk for substance use initiation. *Preventive Medicine, 36,* 1–7.

Botvin, G. J., Mihalic, S. F., & Grotpeter, J. K. (1998). *Life skills training: Blueprints for violence prevention, book five.* Blueprints for Violence Prevention Series (D. S. Elliott, Series Editor). Boulder, CO: Center for the Study and Prevention of Violence, Institute of Behavioral Science, University of Colorado. | For cost information, see *www.lifeskillstraining.com/order.php*

National Health Promotion Associates
711 Westchester Avenue
White Plains, NY 10604
800- 293-4969
914-421-2007
lstinfo@nhpamail.com
www.lifeskillstraining.com |
| Project Towards No Drug Abuse (Project TND) | TND provides information about the negative effects of drug use and promotes coping skills, stress management, effective communication, and ways to counteract risk factors. | High school students ages 14–19 | Sun, W., Skara, S., Sun, P., Dent, C. W., & Sussman, S. (2006). Project Towards No Drug Abuse: Long-term substance use outcomes evaluation. *Preventive Medicine, 42,* 188–192.

Sussman, S., Dent, C. W., & Stacy, A. W. (2002). Project Towards No Drug Abuse: A review of findings and future directions. *American Journal of Health Behavior, 26*(5), 354–365. | Program materials include a teacher's manual ($70) and student workbooks ($50/set of 5). Optional materials are available as is a two-day training ($2,500).

Jim Miyano
USC Institute for Prevention Research
1000 South Fremont Avenue, Unit 8
Alhambra, CA 91803
Toll-Free: (800) 400-8461
miyano@usc.edu
www.tnd.usc.edu |

(cont.)

17

Table 2.1 (cont.)

Name	Description	Representative supporting research	Target group	Cost/contact information
Good Behavior Game (GBG)	The GBG is a behavior modification program intended to decrease aggressive or disruptive behaviors. It is introduced as a classroom game that helps to reduce aggressive behavior and promote positive social skills.	Fishbein, J. E., & Wasik, B. H. (1981). Effect of the Good Behavior Game on disruptive library behavior. *Journal of Applied Behavior Analysis, 14,* 89–93. Tingstrom, D. H., Sterling-Turner, H. E., & Wilczynski, S. M. (2006). The Good Behavior Game: 1969–2002. *Behavior Modification, 30,* 225–253.	Early elementary	Hazelden Publishing and Educational Services 15251 Pleasant Valley Road P.O. Box 176 Center City, MN 55012-0176 (800) 328-9000 or (651) 213-4200 *customersupport@hazelden.org* *www.hazelden.org*

Note. See the Center for the Prevention and Study of Violence (2004a) for additional information about the programs above.

tion, social skills, and conflict resolution programs (see Table 2.1 for examples of these programs). Yet, not all of these programs provide additional graduated support, meaning that they do not include additional levels of support for students who fail to respond to the primary plan. It is possible, however, that a school may wish to incorporate a validated primary program into their schoolwide positive behavior support (SWPBS) model to address a specific need at the school site. For example, if office discipline referral (ODR) data indicate that bullying is a key problem on campus, then the PBIS team may want to consider incorporating into their primary prevention program a research-based schoolwide anti-bullying program such as the "Olweus Bullying Prevention Program" (Olweus, 2001) or "Bully-Proofing Your School" (Garrity, Jens, Porter, Sager, & Short-Camilli, 1994).

This book focuses on developing comprehensive primary prevention plans that address behavioral, social, *and* academic needs to prevent the development of EBD as well as to provide *additional* support for students with EBD, given that they struggle in all three areas. Specifically, we focus on how to (1) construct comprehensive, primary plans, and (2) we illustrate how to use data from these plans to monitor student progress and identify students who require more intensive supports in the form of targeted interventions that address acquisition, fluency, and performance deficits in academic, behavioral, and social domains. We also demonstrate how to determine if the core, primary plan could benefit from the inclusion of other validated primary plans based on the school-site needs (e.g., Sprague et al., 2001).

Just in case you are not convinced that primary programs will "work" in your school, let's take a look at how such programs have influenced student performance in elementary, middle, and high schools. In the sections that follow, we describe treatment-outcome studies that illustrate how schoolwide programs that include a behavioral component influenced student behavior as well as academic outcomes.

Primary Prevention at the Elementary School Level

Primary prevention programs have met with demonstrated success at the elementary level. In a recent systematic review of the literature, Lane, Kalberg, and Edwards (2008) identified 19 studies of primary prevention efforts that involved a behavioral component at the elementary level and were published between 1997 and 2007. Except for the studies that employed single-case designs that took place in specific school settings such as playgrounds and hallways (e.g., multiple baseline designs; Colvin, Sugai, Good, & Lee, 1997; Lewis, Powers, Kelk, & Newcomer, 2002; Lewis, Sugai, & Colvin, 1998), most of the studies identified in this review used quasi-experimental, correlational, or descriptive design to evaluate how well the interventions worked (Gay & Airasian, 2000). In brief, the studies reported positive changes in student outcomes. For example, improvements in hallway (Leedy, Bates, & Safran, 2004; Lewis et al., 1998), playground (Lewis et al., 2002; Lewis et al., 1998), and transition (e.g., Colvin et al., 1997) behaviors were reported. Several other studies also reported decreases in ODRs (e.g., Bell, Coleman, Anderson, & Whelan, 2000; Ervin, Schaughency, Goodman, McGlinchey, & Matthews,

2006; George, White, & Schlaffer, 2007; McCurdy, Manella, & Eldridge, 2003; Nelson, 1996; Nelson, Martella, & Galand, 1998; Nelson, Martella, & Marchand-Martella, 2002; Scott & Barrett, 2004; Sprague et al., 2001; Todd, Haugen, Anderson, & Spriggs, 2002) and suspensions (Bell et al.; George et al.; Netzel & Eber, 2003; Scott, 2001; Scott & Barrett, 2004). By decreasing problem behaviors and improving the atmosphere or climate in a school, you can increase instructional time and ultimately improve students' academic performance—a goal of all educators.

In this section we provide examples of primary prevention efforts in elementary schools to illustrate how these programs can influence overall performance in school as well as hallway and recess behavior. We also show how primary prevention programs can target academic, behavioral, and social performance. This three-pronged focus is important to keep in mind, given that academic and behavioral objectives are not separate goals—they interact to influence each other (Hinshaw, 1992; Lane & Wehby, 2002).

Overall Performance at School

Nelson and colleagues (2002) used a pretest–posttest comparison group design to examine the effects of an expanded SWPBS program (see Nelson, 1996, for a complete intervention description). The schools in the treatment condition ($n = 7$) showed consistent declines in administrative disciplinary actions as compared to schools in the comparison condition ($n = 28$). Furthermore, nonparticipating schools actually showed increases in disciplinary contacts. In addition to producing decreases in behavior problems that prompted disciplinary actions, teachers found the intervention to be socially valid (see Chapter 5 for information regarding the assessment of social validity).

McCurdy and colleagues (2003) used a descriptive (pre-post comparison) design to examine the effects of a SWPBS program implemented in conjunction with the Devereaux Foundation. The project included 1 year of initial baseline for comparison purposes followed by 2 years of implementation. Results indicated that the intervention was implemented with a high degree of fidelity, as evidenced by mean schoolwide evaluation tools (SET; Horner et al., 2004) scores of 82%. There was a 46% reduction in ODRs by the end of the second year of implementation. Disruption also decreased by 46.4% and fighting decreased by 55%. As with the Nelson and colleagues (2002) study, there was high staff satisfaction, with an interest in continuing the program.

Ervin and colleagues (2006) also examined the impact of a SWPBS program that spanned a 6-year period, including 2 years of baseline, 3 years of implementation, and 1 year of maintenance. Results of the pre-experimental repeated measures design revealed reductions in ODRs as well as increases in the percentage of students reading at benchmark levels for two of the four schools.

Although this overview is by no means an exhaustive list of all primary prevention programs conducted to date, it is a glimpse into the effectiveness of schoolwide efforts with respect to behavior and academic performance. In addition, these programs also indicated improvements in noninstructional areas.

Hallway Behavior

Given that not all schoolwide problems occur in classrooms, it is important to have programs that address noninstructional settings such as hallways. Leedy and colleagues (2004) conducted a study to improve the hallway behavior of elementary students attending a rural, public elementary school (K–5). This school served 283 students, 99% of whom were European American and 50.5% of whom received free or reduced-fee lunches. They developed an instructional plan using Project Prepare (Colvin, Kame'enui, & Sugai, 1993) as a model. Instructional components included (1) establishing hallway expectations; (2) determining the specific times of day and settings in which the behaviors should be demonstrated; (3) establishing set times to explain the plan; (4) establishing set times to practice the expectations; (5) providing reminders of the procedures at specified times; (6) identifying reinforcers for meeting the expectations; (7) establishing correction procedures in the event that students' hallway behavior did not meet the expectations; and (8) establishing set times and procedures for evaluating how well the program worked. Data on appropriate hallway behavior were collected by the principal and an educational assistant for each class (with two classrooms for each grade level) using event recording. The entire class had to meet the expectations (e.g., use walking feet; walk in a single line; keep hands, feet, and belongings to self in the lunchroom hallway; walk on the right hand side of the hallway; move quietly; and practice self-control) in order to be recorded as a *"yes"* (meaning that appropriate hallway behavior was demonstrated). Results of a quasi-experimental design revealed improved hallway behavior for all students, with an overall increase of 134.9% for whole-class compliance with the six expectations for hallway behavior. In short, it worked!

Recess Behavior

Another setting that often poses significant challenges to educators is recess time. Too often students struggle to behave appropriately in playground settings, particularly when the activities are unstructured. To address this concern, Lewis, Colvin, and Sugai (2000) conducted a study in an elementary school to examine the effects of precorrection and active supervision on recess behavior. The school served 475 students, the majority of whom were European American; 5% were Hispanic. The intervention program included three components: (1) teacher-led review of key recess social skills; (2) precorrections in which teachers prompted the use of recess social skills before students went to recess, and the discipline team members prompted playground monitors to engage in active supervision during recess; and (3) active playground supervision by monitors that included moving around, looking around, and interacting with students. Data were collected on the rate of student problem behavior during structured and unstructured activities and the rate of playground monitor behavior during active and inactive supervision. Results of a multiple baseline design across three target recess periods (recess 1 = fifth grade; recess 2 = fourth grade; and recess 3 = first–third grades) demonstrated decreases in the overall rates of problem behavior during unstructured, but not structured, activities. However, the rate of active supervision by playground monitors did not increase.

Programs with Behavioral and Academic Components

As we mentioned previously, primary prevention efforts can also include academic components. For example, Lane and Menzies (2003) conducted a study to determine the degree to which a multileveled program with academic and behavioral components influenced the reading and behavioral performance of elementary students attending a school with a high at-risk population. The school served students in preschool through grade 6, with 78% of the students receiving free or reduced-free lunches and a 64% transiency rate. The program included a schoolwide behavioral plan (SBP) and a district literacy plan (DLP). The SBP included (1) posting rules, consequences, and rewards; (2) delivering consequences and rewards per the plan; (3) teaching the behavioral expectations to all students; (4) interacting positively with students, consistently and frequently; (5) responding effectively to students who demonstrated problematic behaviors; and (6) assisting students who demonstrated problematic behaviors. The SBP included two additional 1-hour trainings during the year in addition to staff development that occurred prior to intervention onset. The DLP included whole-group, small-group, and individual instruction as part of a district-developed balanced literacy program. The teacher-developed lesson plans adhered to the district standards, and the literacy coach provided ongoing training and in-class demonstrations during the academic year. A number of outcome measures were administered to monitor student responses to the plan: district multiple measures in reading (DMR), curriculum-based measures in reading (CBM-R), state achievement test (Stanford Achievement Test–9; SAT-9), the Student Risk Screening Scale (SRSS; Drummond, 1994), negative narrative comments recorded in school records (Walker, Block-Pedego, Todis, & Severson, 1991), absenteeism, and special education enrollment. Results indicated that regardless of risk status (low, moderate, or high), as measured by the SRSS, students improved on all academic outcomes (DMR, CBM-R, and SAT-9).

Based on the studies provided above, it is clear that primary prevention programs have been successful at the elementary level. Yet, questions arise as to the feasibility and effectiveness of such efforts in secondary schools where behavior challenges become increasingly more resistant to intervention efforts and the consequences of problem behaviors (e.g., aggression) more severe (Lane, Robertson, et al., 2006; Robertson & Lane, 2007).

Primary Prevention at the Middle and High School Levels

A recent review of schoolwide interventions with primary-level efforts targeting behavioral concerns, conducted in secondary schools between 1990 and 1996, found only 14 studies, some of which focused on SWPBS. These studies revealed decreases in ODRs

(Lohrmann-O'Rourke et al., 2000; Metzler, Biglan, Rusby, & Sprague, 2001; Taylor-Greene et al., 1997; Taylor-Greene & Kartub, 2000), decreases in the level of physical and verbal aggression (Metzler et al., 2001), decreases in detentions (Luiselli, Putnam, & Sutherland, 2002), decreases in hallway noise during lunchtime (Kartub, Taylor-Green, March, & Horner, 2000), and increases in the proportion of students that reported receiving praise or rewards (Metzler et al.). In fact, the prototype for what is now called SWPBS was actually developed in middle schools (Gottfredson, Gottfredson, & Hybl, 1993; Mayer, Butterworth, Nafpaktitis, & Sulzer-Azaroff, 1983).

Gottfredson and colleagues (1993) conducted a longitudinal study in eight middle schools (six treatment and two control; suburban and urban) to examine the effects of a program with school-, classroom-, and individual-level components to reduce problem behaviors demonstrated by students in grades 6–8. The intervention included four components: (1) school discipline policy; (2) computerized tracking of behavioral performance; (3) improved classroom organization and management; and (4) positive reinforcement. Some of the specific strategies were (1) decreasing punitive approaches and increasing the use of positive reinforcement; (2) increasing the clarity of expectations regarding school discipline policy; (3) increasing consistency of follow-through; and (4) improving classroom organization and management. In addition to collecting ODR data, the researchers also administered surveys to the teachers and students to assess classroom environment. Further, teachers rated students quarterly. Finally, students completed a questionnaire, the Effective School Battery, and teachers completed another survey to evaluate effectiveness and implementation. A nonequivalent control group design was used to examine differences between schools that implemented the program with high, medium, and low fidelity. Results of student reports of classroom organization showed that both medium- and low-implementation schools had similar results, with slight improvement. Treatment schools showed improved classroom order, organization, and rule clarity, according to student reports. Teacher ratings of student attentiveness increased and disruptive behavior decreased in schools with high levels of fidelity. Teacher ratings of disruptive behavior increased in schools with medium levels of fidelity. However, student reports of rebellious behavior increased for all groups. Yet, students reported lower levels of punishment in the treatment schools.

Since this time, several primary prevention studies in middle schools have been published. Just as in elementary schools, primary prevention programs focusing on behavioral improvement in middle and high schools have influenced overall performance in school as well as positively impacting student behavior in specific settings (e.g., hallways).

Overall Performance at School

Taylor-Green and colleagues (1997) conducted a study in a rural middle school that served 530 students in grades 6–8. The intervention consisted of two features: an opening day support program and ongoing behavioral supports. Opening day components included defining, teaching, and rewarding five expectations (referred to as "high five"

```
┌─────────────────────────────────────────────┐
│  ┌───────────────────────────────────────┐  │
│  │                                       │  │
│  │  Box 2.1.  **High Five Expectations**  │  │
│  │                                       │  │
│  │      1. Be respectful.                │  │
│  │      2. Be responsible.               │  │
│  │      3. Be there—be ready.            │  │
│  │      4. Follow directions.            │  │
│  │      5. Hands and feet to self.       │  │
│  │      ─────────────                    │  │
│  │  *Note.* Data from Taylor-Greene et al. (1997). │
│  └───────────────────────────────────────┘  │
└─────────────────────────────────────────────┘
```

Box 2.1. **High Five Expectations**

1. Be respectful.
2. Be responsible.
3. Be there—be ready.
4. Follow directions.
5. Hands and feet to self.

Note. Data from Taylor-Greene et al. (1997).

expectations; see Box 2.1). Students were taught these five expectations and instructed to apply them across six locations in the school (e.g., classroom, hallway, gym, cafeteria, open common areas, and bus), with 25- to 30-minute lessons conducted in each setting. Ongoing behavior support components included (1) providing reminders and precorrections; (2) rewarding appropriate behavior consistently; and (3) providing corrective consequences, booster procedures, and targeted support, as needed. Two types of data were collected to monitor program outcomes. First, ODR data were collected to determine the average number of ODRs per day per month (i.e., the total number of ODRs given out per month, divided by the number of instructional days for each month). Second, faculty and staff members completed satisfaction surveys to provide their opinions about the program. This study was descriptive, not experimental, which means that causal conclusions cannot be drawn from these findings. However, analysis of ODR data collected during the 1 year of baseline and 2 years of implementation indicate that the average number of ODRs decreased from 15 per day to 8.7 per day (42% reduction). With the exception of April, month-by-month comparisons revealed decreases in ODRs for all months. Survey satisfaction indicated that the faculty thought the program was beneficial.

Metzler and colleagues (2001) examined the effects of a consultative approach to SWPBS at the middle school level using an AB design in one school with a comparison community. Components of their schoolwide effective behavior support system included (1) defining rules and expectations; (2) teaching expected behaviors; (3) providing praise, rewards for desired behaviors; (4) monitoring students' behavior; and (5) using summary data to determine progress and refine intervention plans. They included a wide range of outcome measures, such as a student-completed survey of school climate; number of PBIS tickets awarded to students, good news referrals, and praise notes; ODRs; student reports of perceived safety and harassment; and the Effective Behavior Support (EBS; Sugai, Horner, & Todd, 2003) survey to assess social validity and fidelity. Results revealed increases in (1) the proportion of students at the treatment school who reportedly received praise or reward, (2) tiger tickets awarded per year, and (3) good news referrals. Similarly, a larger proportion of students felt safer at the treatment school compared to the control. In comparing baseline and treatment conditions at the treatment school, the rate of ODRs decreased as did the levels of physical and verbal aggression. The majority of teachers said that the school was safer and that student behavior improved following intervention implementation. Treatment components were implemented with 65–100% integrity.

In summary, primary prevention programs have been associated with decreases in undesirable behaviors that often prompt teachers to write ODRs and increases in access to reinforcement.

Hallway Behavior

As with elementary schools, primary prevention programs aimed at improving behavior in secondary schools have also resulted in improved behavior in hallways. Kartub and colleagues (2000) also published a SWPBS study designed to decrease hallway noise levels during lunchtime in a rural middle school that served 525 students, 62% of whom received free or reduced-fee lunches. Their intervention was implemented during the last 2 months of a school year and contained three components. First, students were given a quick review (7-minute lesson per period) of acceptable and unacceptable noise levels during lunch transition. Second, an environmental change was made to prompt the desired behavior. Specifically, hall lighting was dimmed and a small blinking light was present during lunch transitions. Finally, students could earn a reward of 5 minutes of extra lunchtime for every 3 days with quiet transitions. Thus, the motivation was additional time with peers. Intervention outcomes were measured via median decibel recordings and informal reports from teachers and hall monitors. Data were analyzed using a descriptive, pre–post, nonexperimental design with baseline, intervention, and 10-week follow-up for each grade level. Results revealed that the average decibel levels decreased from baseline to intervention phases and were maintained into the maintenance phase. Further, adults reported reduced noise levels and indicated that students were reminding each other to be quiet.

While such programs are impressive, so are the primary prevention programs that recognize the transactional relationship between academics and behavior. For example, consider the study described in the following section.

Programs with Behavioral and Academic Components

Luiselli and colleagues (2002) implemented a program that included both academic expectations and behavioral markers in a rural middle school. For example, students received recognition cards for improved academic performance, attendance, the absence of detentions or expulsions, or for improvements in these areas. Thus, students could receive these cards for academic, social, or behavioral reasons. The cards were then entered into weekly drawings. Results of this descriptive study revealed decreases in detention slips issued for disruptive or antisocial behavior, substance abuse, or vandalism. The researchers also reported improvements in attendance.

It is encouraging to see this combined attention to academic and behavioral concerns. Another positive development within the existing framework of SWPBS programs is the inclusion of validated schoolwide programs targeting violence prevention (e.g., Second Steps Violence Prevention; Sprague et al., 2001).

Incorporating Validated Programs into SWPBS Programs

As we mentioned at the beginning of the chapter, primary prevention programs can also be supplemented with other validated programs (e.g., Second Steps Violence Prevention; Sprague et al., 2001) to address additional behavioral concerns (e.g., violence). Sprague and colleagues (2001) conducted such a study to determine the effects of a primary intervention package designed to improve the safety and social behavior of students in elementary and middle schools. In this program they implemented the Second Steps Violence Prevention curriculum in conjunction with their Effective Behavior Support program. Results indicated that students at the treatment schools increased their knowledge of violence prevention as measured by the Second Steps Knowledge Test. In addition, treatment schools showed a reduction in ODRs compared to baseline years and greater improvements in ODRs than did comparison schools.

As with primary prevention studies conducted at the elementary level, studies conducted in middle and high schools have yielded a range of positive outcomes. Moving forward, we hope to see additional investigations at the high school level due to the unique challenges associated with implementing primary prevention programs with older students.

Challenges of Conducting Primary Prevention Efforts in Secondary Schools

To date, the majority of primary prevention studies aimed at improving behavior have been conducted at the elementary level, with fewer investigations at the middle school level and still fewer published studies at the high school level. You may wonder why there are fewer studies of primary prevention in secondary schools when the consequences of problem behavior become increasingly more severe as students grow older. In this section we discuss five of the unique challenges of working in secondary schools that may lead to the limited number of studies conducted in this area (Lane, Robertson, et al., 2006).

First, whereas elementary-age students tend to spend their school days in but a few settings such as their homeroom class, specials (e.g., music or physical education), and the cafeteria, middle and high school students are far more transient throughout the day. Secondary school students attend as many as seven or eight classes per day, requiring them to interact with several teachers and literally hundreds of their peers. Thus, these students must negotiate a range of academic, behavioral, and social expectations held by their teachers and peers over the course of the school day (Isakson & Jarvis, 1999). This task is particularly challenging because teachers often have different expectations of how students need to perform to be successful in school (Kerr & Zigmond, 1986; Lane, Pierson, & Givner, 2004; Walker & Rankin, 1980). A critical component of primary prevention programs is that clear expectations for student behavior in instructional and noninstructional settings are taught and reinforced consistently. Yet, many middle and high schools struggle to achieve consensus about behavioral expectations, perhaps due in part to the large number of faculty and staff employed. Not surprisingly, if faculty and staff do not establish schoolwide behavioral expectations, it is not possible for adults to achieve consistency in teaching and reinforcing these expectations.

Second, some faculty and staff do not subscribe to an instructional approach to discipline and are of the opinion that adolescents should "already know how to behave" and that teachers should not have to teach middle and high school students how to behave. These views are often highly salient in high school settings where the curricular demands become increasingly more precise, leaving teachers feeling very pressed for time to cover the required material. Yet, the reality is that some students are not clear on how to "play the school game," and their skill deficits result in lost instructional time for not only themselves but for other students when teachers are forced to stop instruction to respond to inappropriate behavior. Therefore, rather than getting angry or frustrated with students who exhibit undesirable behavior, primary prevention plans encourage an instructional approach in which desired behaviors are defined, taught, practiced, and reinforced. In this model, behavior problems are reduced by eliminating the excuse that students were unaware of desired behaviors, ultimately resulting in increased instructional time—a goal of most teachers.

Third, it is possible that primary prevention programs become more challenging in secondary schools due to the difficulties associated with identifying desirable (and appropriate!) reinforcers for this age group. Whereas teacher attention and adult recognition may be popular types of reinforcers at the elementary level, these may actually be punishing for secondary students. For example, as students transition from middle to high school, the peer group may be more likely to influence student behavior than adults (teachers, paraprofessionals, and administrators) (Alspaugh, 1998; Morrison, Robertson, Laurie, & Kelly, 2002). Thus, identifying reinforcing activities/tasks, tangibles, or sensory experiences may become more difficult than at the elementary level.

Finally, another difficulty associated with conducting primary prevention efforts in middle and high schools is the challenging nature of behavior problems for this age group. While some students engage in overt behaviors such as verbal and physical aggression (Walker et al., 2004) that pose severe consequences as students increase in age and size, other types of discipline problems tend to occur during adolescence that also make it particularly difficult to intervene. For example, internalizing behavior patterns (e.g., eating disorders, suicidal tendencies, somatic complaints; Morris, Shah, & Morris, 2002) and covert acts of aggression (e.g., stealing, threats; Loeber, Green, Lahey, Frick, & McBurnett, 2000) tend to typify older students.

As a whole, these issues may offer some insight into the unique challenges of designing, implementing, and evaluating primary prevention programs in middle and high schools. They may also explain the small body of literature examining primary prevention in secondary schools (Lane, Robertson, et al., 2006). Yet, despite these challenges, it is essential for researchers and practitioners to identify feasible and effective methods for facilitating primary prevention programs in secondary schools, given the negative consequences associated with academic underachievement and school violence (Lane, Gresham, & O'Shaughnessy, 2002a; Lane & Wehby, 2002; Walker et al., 2004). In the section that follows, we discuss some of the core indicators you should consider when designing, implementing, and evaluating primary prevention programs across the K–12 continuum.

Core Quality Indicators for Primary Prevention Programs

When designing primary prevention programs, we encourage you to build a strong, defensible program that will allow you to draw accurate conclusions about whether or not the primary prevention program is achieving the desired outcomes (Gersten et al., 2005; Horner et al., 2005). Specifically, we encourage you to do the following: (1) Design a program based on the needs of your school. (2) Describe clearly both your school's characteristics and the program's so that others can replicate what you've done and make accurate decisions about the circumstances under which this program "worked." (3) Include a range of outcome measures that are reliable, valid, and sensitive to change. (4) Include a method for monitoring the degree to which the plan is implemented as designed (referred to as *treatment integrity*; Gresham, 1989; Lane & Beebe-Frankenberger, 2004, see Chapter 5) and the consumers' opinions about the program's goals, procedures, and outcomes (referred to as *social validity*; Kazdin, 1977; Lane & Beebe-Frankenberger, 2004; Wolf, 1978). (5) Employ an experimental design that allows you to draw accurate conclusions about how the program influenced student behavior, using caution not to draw causal conclusions if the design did not include a true experimental test (Gay & Airasian, 2000). (6) Use data analysis procedures that are appropriate to the design. (7) The program should provide very clear guidelines and procedures for identifying students who require more intensive intervention that can be provided within the context of secondary and tertiary levels of prevention (Walker & Severson, 2002).

As a practitioner, adhering to core quality indicators will allow you to create and implement a primary prevention program that is well documented and defensible, should the need arise. Further, by designing a well-defined primary plan that is more comprehensive because it includes an academic emphasis in addition to the behavioral and social domains, you are more apt to (1) meet the instructional goals you set for your school as the instructional leader and (2) inform broad-scale changes and targeted interventions for students with additional needs, as mandated by the No Child Left Behind Act (2001) and the Individuals with Disabilities Education Improvement Act (2004). As a researcher, including these core quality indicators will allow valid inferences to be drawn about the internal and external validity of your study and enable others to determine whether the practices employed are truly evidence-based (Crockett, Gerber, & Landrum, 2007).

Summary

In this chapter our goal was to provide you with information on how primary prevention programs with behavioral components have influenced student performance in elementary, middle, and high schools. We also wanted to highlight the possible challenges associated with conducting primary prevention programs in middle and high schools. Finally, we wanted to introduced some of the core quality indicators for defensible primary prevention programs as they apply to practitioners and researchers. These are the basic building blocks of primary prevention programs. Now that the foundation has been poured, so to speak, if your school is ready to design and implement a primary prevention model to prevent and respond to students' needs, read on!

In the next chapter we provide additional information to help further define the PBIS model as conceptualized by Sugai and Horner (2002, 2006). This model serves as the foundation for the comprehensive primary prevention planning process that we then describe in Chapter 4.

Chapter Three

A Closer Look at the Positive Behavior Interventions and Supports Model

In this chapter we further describe the PBIS model as conceptualized by Sugai and Horner (2002, 2006). Namely, we (1) introduce four critical elements of schoolwide positive behavior support (SWPBS); (2) list and describe the four systems constituting comprehensive PBIS models; and (3) illustrate how the progressive continuum of behavior support functions in the model

As illustrated in Chapter 2, SWPBS models have produced desired changes in student behavior at the elementary level (Lane, Kalberg, & Edwards, 2008), and to a lesser extent at the middle and high school levels (Lane, Robertson, & Graham-Bailey, 2006). By focusing on the school rather than an individual student as the unit of analysis, schools are able to shift their thinking and approaches to managing problem behaviors. Within the context of three-tiered models of support, schools are able to construct database problem-solving programs that contain *proactive components* for preventing the development of problem behaviors that may lead to EBD as well as *reactive components* for responding to existing instances of EBD with more intensive, evidenced-based supports (Lane, 2007). Such models include the full range of systematic and individualized strategies that schools need to implement if they are to achieve the socially significant learning and social outcomes that prevent the development of problem behaviors (Sugai & Horner, 2002; Sugai et al., 2005). The base of the model—SWPBS—as defined by Sugai and Horner includes (1) four critical elements, (2) a multiple-systems perspective; and (3) a progressive continuum of behavior support.

Four Critical Elements

As schools move away from a reactive approach to managing behaviors that interrupt instruction, they are integrating effective practices composed of four "critical elements" (Sugai & Horner, 2002). First, SWPBS is guided by a consideration of student outcomes that are valued by significant stakeholders (e.g., teachers, parents, students). For example, if two goals are to decrease physical aggression and improve attendance, then these goals must be used to select evidenced-based curriculum, conduct meaningful assessments to monitor student progress in these areas, allocate resources, and develop positive school climates that support these goals.

Second, SWPBS is predicated on the use of evidence-based practices and curricula that maximize student and teacher outcomes. Rather than simply adopting a practice or curricula that someone heard about at an inservice training, adoption decisions should be data-based. Recently a number of guidelines have been proposed to operationally define a practice as "evidence-based" (Gersten et al., 2005; Horner et al., 2005). For example, when evaluating a body of literature evaluated using single-case methodology, Horner and colleagues recommended five standards for documenting a practice as evidence-based:

1. The practice must be operationally defined.
2. Authors must define the context for use of the practice.
3. The practice must have been implemented with treatment fidelity, meaning that it was put in place as originally planned (see Chapter 5).
4. Results document the introduction of the practice as functionally related to change in the dependent variables.
5. Experimental effects are replicated across a sufficient number of peer-reviewed studies ($n = 5$) published in refereed journals; across three different researchers at three different geographical locations; and include at least 20 participants from five or more studies.

In addition, it is important that the practices be feasible within the context of an applied setting. That is, it has to be practical and viewed as socially valid (Kazdin, 1977; Wolf, 1978; see Chapter 5). If the people responsible for implementation view an evidence-based practice as feasible—meaning that the procedures are acceptable and the goals likely to be obtained—they will be far more likely to put the intervention in place as designed. Consequently, it is more likely to produce the desired results (Lane & Beebe-Frankenberger, 2004).

Third, SWPBS is grounded in data-based decision making. Data are used to guide all components, including the selection of practices and strategies as well as the implementation of core program features. In addition, schoolwide data are used to determine which students require more intensive supports, such as secondary and tertiary levels of prevention (Lane, 2007; Sugai & Horner, 2002; see Chapter 6).

Fourth, SWPBS pays close attention to operating procedures, processes, and administrative supports that are required to ensure that (a) student outcomes are achieved, (b) evidence-based practices and curricula are employed, and (c) data-based decision making transpires (Sugai & Horner, 2002). In short—systems are created in order to put the primary plan into action.

Collectively these four elements focus on supporting student behavior in an efficient, effective manner within the SWPBS plan. Clearly, this is a formidable task—one that challenges administrators, teachers, and researchers with the best of intentions. One method of facilitating the development of these elements within schools is to structure efforts within a multiple-systems perspective (Sugai & Horner, 2002).

A Multiple-Systems Perspective

Sugai and Horner's (2002) model of multiple systems has been widely accepted across the country. The model includes four foci or systems: schoolwide, classroom, nonclassroom, and individual student (see Table 3.1 for a description of each system).

Schoolwide

The schoolwide system contains six common features. First, schools develop a purpose statement containing the objectives of, and rationale for the SWPBS program. When constructing the purpose statement, it should (1) be phrased in positive terms; (2) focus on students and staff in all settings; and (3) provide a link between behavioral and academic outcomes (Sugai & Horner, 2002).

Table 3.1. **Multiple Systems Perspectives**

Systems	Common features
Schoolwide	1. Purpose statement. 2. Explicitly defined behavioral expectations for all settings. 3. Procedures for teaching behavioral expectations. 4. Procedures for reinforcing behavioral expectations. 5. Procedures for preventing problem behavior. 6. Procedures for monitoring and evaluating data.
Classroom	1. Behavioral expectations and routines to facilitate instruction. 2. Validated behavior management practices. 3. Evidence-based, culturally and developmentally appropriate curriculum.
Nonclassroom	1. Behavioral expectations for nonclassroom settings (e.g., hallways, recess, lunch, cafeterias, parking lots, buses). 2. Instruction in expectations, with opportunities to practice. 3. Overt, active, and efficient supervision. 4. Precorrections in situations where rule violations are likely to occur. 5. Reinforcement for meeting behavioral expectations.
Individual student	1. Individualized, comprehensive, and high-intensity interventions. 2. Team-based approach for intervention design and implementation. 3. Function-based interventions. 4. Person-centered approach to intervention and service delivery. 5. Explicit connection to schoolwide academic and behavioral expectations.

Note. Data from Sugai and Horner (2002).

Second, schools develop five or fewer positively stated behavioral expectations that are defined and illustrated for each setting. The expectations should be customized to the specific school site, recognizing that middle and high schools settings are different than those at elementary schools (see Boxes 4.5 and 4.6 in Chapter 4 for specific examples at the elementary and secondary school levels). The goal of the feature is to provide a common set of expectations and language to allow teachers, students, and parents to communicate more easily. For example, if a student earns a PBIS ticket for demonstrating respect in the cafeteria, the student can share this information with his or her parent, which in turn provides the student with an opportunity to receive additional reinforcement beyond the school setting. This is very important if a goal is to encourage students to use these new behaviors in another setting (i.e., generalization; Cooper, Heron, & Heward, 2007).

Third, schools develop specific procedures for teaching expectations in all settings (Sugai & Horner, 2002). In general, teaching expectations is just like teaching an academic skill: (a) Use a direct instruction approach to delivery (i.e., tell, show, do, practice, and test; Scott & Barrett, 2004); (b) provide students with opportunities to practice and receive positive and/or corrective feedback when they do/do not demonstrate the desired behaviors (Lewis et al., 1998); and (c) actively supervise and provide students with reminders, also called precorrections, about the expectations before transition to a new setting (e.g., recess; Leff, Costigan, & Power, 2003; Lewis et al., 2000; Todd et al., 2002). Explicitly teaching students the schoolwide behavioral expectations as well as the routines (e.g., hallway behavior; Leedy et al., 2004) eliminates the "I didn't know I wasn't supposed to …" type of problem. In other words, this process creates a level playing field for students (Lane, Robertson, et al., 2006; Lane, Wehby, et al., 2007). Now, if students violate a rule or expectation, it is because they chose to (performance deficit; "won't do"), not because they did not know the rule or expectation (skill deficit; "can't do" problem; Gresham, 2002b).

Fourth, schools establish procedures for prompting and reinforcing expected behaviors. It is important to remember that what is reinforcing or motivating for one student is not necessarily motivating for another student. For example, some students thrive on public praise from their teacher (Anne Louise!), whereas other students view this attention to be a fate worse than death! You will know what is reinforcing to students by observing how their behavior changes *after* you give them what you believe to be a reinforcer (Umbreit et al., 2007). For example, if a teacher reads Chris's story aloud to the class and Chris starts writing more stories, then receiving peer and teacher attention in the form of having his story read aloud is reinforcing (because it increased the likelihood of the behavior occurring in the future; Cooper et al., 2007). However, if Chris refuses to write any more stories after that experience, then having his story read aloud was not reinforcing—it was actually punishing because the behavior decreases (Cooper et al.).

Fifth, schools develop procedures for preventing problem behaviors (Sugai & Horner, 2002). These procedures should be developed along two continuums: (a) minor to major violations and (b) low to high intensity. For example, if one of the problems (minor) is tardiness to class, then a low-intensity, proactive procedure to prevent tardiness is to have all teachers in their rooms 5 minutes before the bell rings. Teachers should greet students at the door and be prepared with a starter activity that students can complete easily. Many teachers make this an "A or an F" assignment, meaning that if students are on time and complete the entry activity, they earn an A; otherwise, they get an F. The goal here is to develop a procedure that will make "being to class on time" behavior more reinforcing than "being in the hallways after the tardy bell" behavior (Horner & Billingsley, 1988; Umbreit et al., 2007). But, if students, particularly those in middle and highs schools, know that teachers are not in classrooms waiting with a mandatory entry activity (with an A tied to it!), and there is no negative consequence (e.g., detention) for being late—why should they be in class on time? In this case time with their friends in the hallway is more reinforcing than arriving to class on time. It is important that these procedures clearly state rule-violating behaviors and are accompanied by examples. Further, it is important for everyone to be clear on which rule-violating behaviors will be managed in the classroom by teachers and which behaviors warrant sending a student to the office.

The final component of the schoolwide plan is to create or identify procedures that can determine how well the plan is being implemented (i.e., treatment integrity; Gresham, 1989; Lane & Beebe-Frankenberger, 2004; see Chapter 5), including how much reinforcement students receive. In addition, it is important for the school to use data on student performance (e.g., ODRs, tardiness, grades, referrals for extra support services) to make decisions about how well the schoolwide plan is working and what to modify. Data should be collected on all components of the schoolwide plan so that questions like the following can be answered: To what extent do we have fewer behavior problems in the cafeteria? To what extent is tardiness decreasing? To what extent are we seeing fewer fights on the playground? Chapter 5 discusses the issues of monitoring and assessing in more detail.

Once the schoolwide perspective is considered and developed, the next systems need to be considered. These are classroom, nonclassroom, and individual student systems. We only briefly discuss each system below because the main focus of this book is the schoolwide perspective. However, given that these systems are interrelated, all should be understood before learning how to construct a schoolwide prevention program.

Classroom

As you see in Table 3.1, the behavior management and routines specified as common features of the classroom setting compliment the six features constituting the school-wide system (Sugai & Horner, 2002). In short, it is important that teachers establish routines and procedures in their classroom that are aligned with the behavior expectations delineated in the schoolwide plan. Why? Because doing so allows teachers to organize their classroom to facilitate instruction. Classrooms that are well organized and well managed afford increased instructional time because teachers need to spend less time addressing behavior problems and can therefore spend more time instructing. In particular, it is important that the classroom setting provide (1) clear structure, (2) appropriate curriculum, (3) effective strategies for delivering instruction, and (4) consistent procedures for intervening during instruction (Walker et al., 2004).

Structure

Classrooms should be structured to include physical room arrangements that support independent work, group work, free-time activities, and have classroom materials available as appropriate (e.g., storage of materials; access to required materials). In addition, teachers need to establish a checklist of operating procedures to ensure that the classroom events are as predictable as possible. For example, there should be procedures for turning in assignments, picking up assignments when absent, and making requests for help or permission (e.g., how to access teacher support, how to ask for permission to use the restroom).

Appropriate Curriculum

Of the utmost importance is the recognition that behavior and learning are linked (Lane & Wehby, 2002). What we teach directly influences how students behave and, in turn, student behavior influences teacher behavior (Hinshaw, 1992; Lane, Gresham, & O'Shaughnessy, 2002b; Wehby, Lane, & Falk, 2003). Consequently, it is critical that teachers select curriculum and instructional materials that are appropriate to the students' skill sets—neither "too hard" nor "too easy." It is not surprising that students often act out or withdraw if the instructional tasks are either too difficult (e.g., being asked to read a passage from a fifth-grade science book when the student reads at a first-grade level) or too easy (e.g., being asked to do 50 math problems with regrouping when the student is capable of performing more advanced skills; Umbreit, Lane, & Dejud, 2004).

Delivering Instruction

In addition to establishing a well-structured classroom and selecting appropriate curricula (Sugai & Horner, 2002), it is also essential that teachers maximize their use of validated strategies for delivering instruction. Some of these features include providing students with (1) instructional objectives so that they understand both the purpose and importance of a given lesson (Hunter, 1991); (2) continuous monitoring of student performance to ensure high rates of success (Walker et al., 2004); (3) appropriate pacing across the curriculum (Miller, 2002); (4) planned variation of instruction (e.g., whole-class, small-group, and individual instruction; Lane & Menzies, 2003); (5) frequent, positive teacher–student interactions, with a goal of six to eight positive interactions for every one negative interaction (Walker et al.); (6) high rates of opportunities to respond to increased academic engagement time (Gunter & Denny, 1998; Sutherland, Adler, & Gunter, 2003; Wehby & Lane, in press); and (7) timely feedback that includes appropriate strategies for managing student errors (Colvin, 2002; Walker et al.). Collectively, using these strategies will facilitate the instructional delivery process and minimize behavioral difficulties (Lane, Falk, & Wehby, 2006; Walker et al.).

Intervening during Instruction

Finally, teachers must have a classroom management program that includes specific strategies for preventing problem behaviors from occurring and for responding to problem behaviors that do arise. Some specific strategies include (1) high rates of positive reinforcement for students who are cooperative and productive (Maag, 2001); (2) entry and exit activities to limit downtime (Walker et al., 2004); (3) effective routines that facilitate smooth transitions between activities (Mastropieri & Scruggs, 2007); and (4) consistent delivery of consequences when students violate expectations (Lane, Falk, et al., 2006; Walker et al.).

In sum, well-organized and appropriately managed classrooms facilitate instruction. This is important because a predictable classroom is a safe, productive classroom for all students (Lane, 2007).

Nonclassroom

Nonclassroom settings include common areas in the building such as hallways (Kartub et al., 2000; Leedy et al., 2004), cafeterias (Colvin et al., 1997), playgrounds (Leff et al., 2003; Lewis et al., 2000; Lewis et al., 2002; Todd et al., 2002), and parking lots (Sugai & Horner, 2002). Despite the fact that these areas are frequented by large numbers of students, they are often overlooked. It is imperative that these nonclassroom settings are included in the schoolwide plan, given that interactions and unresolved problems that occur in these settings often cause frustration, agitation, and other emotions that spill over into instructional time. For example, the tenth grader who is mocked in the cafeteria for dropping a lunch tray or the second grader who is threatened on the playground by a group of older students does not leave these experiences and feelings at the classroom door (personally, I [K. L.] am *still* traumatized!). Consequently, it is important to develop plans to ensure that *all* settings—nonclassroom and classroom alike— are predictable and safe. The five common features of nonclassroom settings include established expectations, instruction in behavioral expectations, adequate supervision, precorrections, and reinforcement.

Behavioral Expectations

First, students need to understand that the schoolwide expectations *do* apply to nonclassroom settings. Therefore, the behavior expectations contain explicit guidelines for how respect, responsibility, and/or care of property *look* in noninstructional areas. For example, in elementary school hallways, respect is defined as (1) following directions, (2) using kind words and actions, (3) controlling tempers, (4) cooperating with others, and (5) using an inside voice. Then these specific expectations and routines are taught explicitly to all students. As noted, this teaching can be done in the same way you would teach an academic skill: tell, show, and do. Additionally, students need opportunities to practice and receive reinforcement for demonstrating these expectations.

Adequate Supervision

Next, faculty and staff must actively supervise students in nonclassroom areas to give praise when students meet the desired expectations and redirection when they do not do so. Active supervision involves three components: (1) watching or scanning to see how students are behaving; (2) moving about the target setting; and (3) interacting with students in a prosocial manner, with a goal of having positive interactions with as many students as possible. It is important that faculty and staff perform all three components.

Precorrections

Precorrections can be thought of as "gentle reminders" or practice sessions in the desired behavior before students enter a noninstructional setting where problems may occur. For example, before walking a group of seventh-grade students to an assembly, teachers can remind them of the expectations for walking in the hallway. This is a preventive approach that is designed to pre-empt problems.

Reinforcement

A third feature of nonclassroom systems involves reinforcement. As we discussed previously, if the goal is to increase the likelihood of students demonstrating the desired expectations it is essential that they receive reinforcement when they do demonstrate the desired behavior. Otherwise, students will "do" whatever gets them the most reinforcement (Colvin et al., 1997). Unfortunately, some faculty and staff members acknowledge only the undesirable behavior. We need a shift in thinking here: Reinforce what you want to see by giving students behavior-specific praise and deliver negative consequences consistently when students violate a given rule.

Consistent implementation of established practices in these three systems (schoolwide, classroom, and nonclassroom) will prevent a substantial number of problem behaviors from occurring. However, some students will still require additional, more intensive supports: the final system.

Individual Student

This final system, individual student supports, is reserved for students who are nonresponsive to the primary plan. How is nonresponsiveness defined? Ideally, nonresponsiveness is determined by analyzing schoolwide data to see how students are progressing academically, behaviorally, and socially. In Chapter 5 we provide specific instruction on how to use systematic screening tools as well as existing schoolwide data to monitor students' progress.

Once identified, students are placed in secondary prevention or tertiary prevention programs based on their level of need. In Chapter 2, we showed you how to determine (1) secondary and tertiary prevention supports already in place in your school and (2) additional supports that you may need based on the data.

In brief, individual systems include the following features: (1) focused, intensive intervention efforts; (2) a team-based approach to designing, implementing, and evaluating intervention efforts; (3) interventions linked to the reason *why* behavioral excesses and deficits occur (Umbreit et al., 2007); (4) a comprehensive, child-centered approach to intervention; and (5) interventions connected explicitly to schoolwide expectations (Lane & Wehby, 2002; Sugai & Horner, 2002).

As schools shift toward proactive, integrated, data-based service delivery within the context of three-tiered models of supports, it is important to recognize the features that constitute the four systems: schoolwide, classroom, nonclassroom, and individual students. In addition, it is important to understand the continuum of behavior supports constituting three-tiered models of support.

Continuum of Behavior Support

As we mentioned in Chapters 1 and 2, three-tiered models contain primary, secondary, and tertiary levels of prevention. Primary plans focus on preventing problem behaviors from occurring. Secondary plans focus on reversing harm by providing additional supports for students not responding to primary prevention efforts. Tertiary plans are reserved for students exposed to multiple risk factors who require the most intensive levels of support.

You may now see how the critical elements of PBIS, the multiple-systems perspective, and the continuum of behavior supports are interrelated. We encourage you to keep this information close at hand as we shift to describing a team-based process for developing a model that embraces these critical elements, multiple systems, and the continuum of supports. There are number of approaches that can be used to help schools develop, implement, and evaluate three-tiered models of support. The model we describe next has been used to assist elementary (Lane, Kalberg, Bruhn, Mahoney, & Driscoll, in press; Lane & Menzies, 2003, 2005), middle (Robertson & Lane, 2007), and high schools (Lane, Wehby, et al., 2007) to design three-tiered models of support in both rural (Lane et al., 2008; Lane, Wehby, et al., 2007) and suburban (Lane & Menzies, 2003, 2005) communities.

Summary

In Chapter 3, we have taken a closer look at the PBIS model, as conceptualized by Sugai and Horner (2002, 2006). First, we introduced four critical elements of SWPBS. Second, we examined the four systems constituting the PBIS model. Third, we explained how the progressive continuum of behavior support functions in the model.

In Chapter 4, we offer a step-by-step approach to designing and implementing a comprehensive primary prevention model that incorporates behavioral, social, and academic domains specific to your school's purpose statement. The process is a year-long training series for school-site PBIS or site-leadership teams that requires the input of faculty, staff, parents, and teachers. To this end, we describe our (1) team-based processes for training and developing the model, (2) implementation procedures, and (3) strategies for teaching and reinforcing the desired student expectations. You'll find forms for use during this process as well as a list of other resources for implementing primary interventions. So, grab a diet soda (or a French-brew coffee) and a piece of dark chocolate and read on!

Chapter Four

Designing and Implementing Primary Prevention Models

As we have noted, this book is designed to help you construct a comprehensive, primary prevention program to prevent the development of EBD and to provide additional support for students with EBD. Specifically, this chapter focuses on providing one method of constructing primary plans that has been used across the K–12 continuum. The process we illustrate is a team-based approach for developing a program that is closely tied to the model posed by Sugai and Horner (2002, 2006), but is broader in scope in that it includes (1) an academic emphasis, (2) a data-based process for constructing expectations, and (3) parental feedback. In the remaining chapters we use the terms *positive behavior interventions and supports* (PBIS) *team* and the *schoolwide positive behavior support* (SWPBS) model. However, we encourage you to keep in mind that we are designing a PBIS program that includes academic, behavioral, and social components in primary, secondary, and tertiary levels of prevention (see Figure 4.1, which repeats Figure 1.1 in Chapter 1).

We introduce a step-by-step, team-based approach for designing, implementing, and evaluating a primary prevention model that integrates academic, behavioral, and social components, based on the work of Lane, Menzies, Kalberg, and colleagues (Lane, Kalberg, Bruhn, et al., in press; Lane & Menzies, 2003, 2005; Lane, Wehby, et al., 2007; Robertson & Lane, 2007). We begin by providing a detailed description of how to use a team-based approach with input from faculty, staff, parents, and students to construct a context-sensitive, customized primary prevention program that addresses the core values held by the community. Next we explain specific procedures for implementing the primary prevention program at the school site. We conclude by discussing specific procedures for teaching and reinforcing the desired expectations. In next section we provide suggestions on how to "kick-off" or introduce the program to the entire student body as well as how to continue teaching and reinforcing expectations throughout the school year. We end the chapter with a brief summary of the content and a preview of the next steps: monitoring student progress.

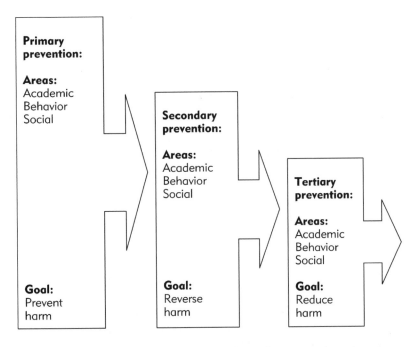

Figure 4.1. **Three-tiered model of prevention: A comprehensive approach.**

A Team-Based Process for Training and Developing the Model: A Focus on the Schoolwide System

Determine Faculty Interest

Whereas some researchers and practitioners begin the training process by securing a PBIS or school-site leadership team, we begin our training process in a slightly different way (see Table 4.1). First, we begin by meeting with a school's entire faculty and staff to provide an overview of the three-tiered model of support, with an emphasis on the importance of developing a comprehensive, primary plan (see Table 4.1 for a description of a full faculty meeting). During this 1-hour faculty meeting we emphasize that the primary prevention plan needs to meet the school's unique needs (academically, behaviorally, and socially) and cultural values. We also emphasize that we are not asking or suggesting that the school do "one more thing." Instead of working "harder," we are suggesting that schools work "smarter" (Sugai & Horner, 2006) by developing a three-tiered model of support to better serve all students. As such, this model should be customized to include the school's specific goals for improvement and the supports that the school already has in place. This latter point of emphasis is particularly important, given that many teachers have been victims of what we call "hit and run" research and/or staff development. That is, many teachers have attended staff development sessions that recommend a new strategy or curriculum, only to find that 6 months, 1 year, or 2 years later, the district now recommends or mandates some other new strategy or curriculum. However, PBIS is not a curriculum. It is a multilevel model whose design is based on the

Table 4.1. **Overview of the Training Process**

Training title	Date and length	Content	Participants
Full Faculty Meeting	November 2010 1 hour	Introduction Overview of PBIS: A Customized Approach	All teachers
Team Training 1: Introduction and Overview	December 2010 2 hours	Introductions Current Concerns Overview of PBIS Students: PBIS Overview	All PBIS team members
Faculty Assessment 1	January 2011 1 hour	Teacher Expectation Survey	All teachers
Team Training 2: Designing Your Primary Intervention	January 2011 8 hours	Introduction Review of Background Information Teacher Expectation Survey Results Designing Your Primary Intervention Plan and Expectation Matrix Procedures for Teaching Procedures for Reinforcing	Adult PBIS team members
Faculty Assessment 2	February 2011 1 hour	Effective Behavior Support (EBS) Self-Assessment Survey Version 2	All teachers
Team Training 3: Data-Based Decision Making for Secondary and Tertiary Interventions	February 2011 2 hours	Introduction EBS Survey Results Primary Intervention Plan: Revisions Data-Based Decision Making Secondary Intervention Illustrations Students: Expectation Matrix	All PBIS team members
Team Training 4: Monitoring Outcomes and Meeting with Your Faculty	February 2011 2 hours	Introduction Primary Plan Revisions Review Data Requirements Draft Procedures for Monitoring Assessment Schedule Prepare Faculty Presentations Students: Reinforcers	All PBIS team members
Faculty Presentation 1	March 2011 1 hour	Introduce the Revised PBIS Plan Administer Social Validity Survey to Faculty and Staff	Full faculty + PBIS team members
Consumer Feedback	March 2011 1 hour	Administer Social Validity Surveys to Randomly Selected Parents and Students	Randomly selected parents and students

Table 4.1 *(cont.)*

Training title	Date and length	Content	Participants
Team Training 5: Designing Your Secondary and Tertiary Plans	March 2011 8 hours	Introduction Revise Procedures for Monitoring and Assessment Schedule Review Behavioral Principles Draft Secondary and Tertiary Plans Schedule Date for Faculty Vote	Adult PBIS team members
Team Training 6: Revising the Plan and Preparing for Implementation	April 2011 2 hours	Introduction Post-Training Survey Review Feedback from Faculty, Parents, and Students Polish Secondary and Tertiary Plans Review Implementation Logistics	All PBIS team members
Faculty Presentation 2	April 2011 1 hour	Present Polished PBIS Plan Faculty Vote	Full faculty + PBIS team members
Team Training 7: Implementation Steps	May 2011 2 hours	Introduction and Overview Review Faculty Votes Implementation Logistics: Teaching the Plan, Reinforcing the Plan, Monitoring the Plan, Participation Requirements, Summer Preparation	Adult PBIS team members

needs of the school, and it changes as the needs of the school change. Thus, it is comparable to a constitution—a living document that accommodates and allows for change.

The next step in our approach is to explain the training activities that occur in Year 1 and ask the school to form a PBIS team (discussed below). We explain that a PBIS approach may improve the school's ability to meet the needs of all students, with a particular emphasis on better supporting students with, or at-risk for, learning and behavior problems.

Then, if teachers and staff agree to implementing a PBIS approach, we explain that the time commitment includes attendance at two monthly trainings (1 hour each), beginning in late fall or early winter, to be held as part of their regular faculty meetings. In these trainings faculty and staff learn more about how teachers and students will benefit from PBIS plans as well as an overview of how to design, implement, and evaluate the PBIS plans. During these trainings teachers complete two anonymous questionnaires: (1) one about their expectations for student behavior (see Table 4.1 for Faculty Assessment 1) and (2) one about systems currently in place and those in need of improvement in their schools (the Effective Behavior Support Self-Assessment Survey 2 [EBS]; Sugai et al., 2003; see Table 4.1 for Faculty Assessment 2). Next, teachers and staff review the PBIS plan drafted by their team during the training program and provide feedback by completing a social validity survey (Lane, Kalberg, Bruhn, et al., 2008) to determine faculty and staff opinions about the goals, procedures, and potential outcomes of the primary plan (see Table 4.1 for Faculty Presentation 1). To obtain their opinions about the PBIS plan, randomly selected parents and their children also complete a similar social validity survey (see Table 4.1 for Consumer Feedback). Finally, teachers and staff vote on whether or not they would like to implement the PBIS plan as part of regular school practices during the next year (see Table 4.1 for Faculty Presentation 2). For any faculty and staff members who indicate that they do not wish to implement the plan, we ask them if they are willing to agree to a "no sabotage" clause, meaning that although they are not in favor of the plan, they are willing to refrain from saying anything derogatory about it. If more than a simple majority of the faculty and staff agrees to these components—(1) attend two presentations, (2) complete the specified assessments (teacher expectation and EBS survey) to inform plan development, and (3) offer opinions about the proposed plans by completing a social validity measure and vote on plan implementation—then we move forward with the training activities.

We think it best to avoid forcing a PBIS program on a faculty. As long as a simple majority of teachers and staff is willing to contribute to the year-long planning process, we view it reasonable—and worthwhile—to work with the PBIS teams to design a plan for their school. Once the plan has been designed, somewhere near the end of spring, then we return to the faculty (Faculty Presentation 2) and ask them to decide via an anonymous ballot as to whether or not they want to implement the program. For this vote, we recommend a goal of 80% participation to move forward with implementation.

Establish a School-Site Team

Once initial participation from faculty and staff is secured, a PBIS team is selected to design a comprehensive plan that includes schoolwide, classroom, nonclassroom, and individual systems (Sugai & Horner, 2002), based on the resources available at the school. Clearly, establishing a solid PBIS team is an important step in this process. When we work with schools, we recommend that teams include a minimum of one administrator, three teachers, one to two parents, and one to two students. Ideally, the administrator should be the principal. If not, it is imperative that the administrator be someone with decision-making authority. We have seen instances where an administrative designee has been asked to serve as the administrator in this process, only to later have his or her decisions overturned by the principal. Such an occurrence can be disheartening not only to the administrative designee but to the PBIS team as a whole.

When selecting PBIS team members, it is important to ensure that the various groups of teachers have a voice in the planning process. Therefore, we recommend recruiting at least one teacher to serve students with special needs. At the elementary level, we recommend at least one teacher from the primary and upper elementary grades. For middle and high schools, we encourage representation from the different departments to ensure adequate representation for all participants. When selecting parents and students, we strongly suggest choosing people who will return the following year. Parental involvement can be a tremendous asset not only in the planning process, but also when it comes time to implement the plan.

If you are conducting PBIS as part of a research project, you'll need to obtain separate consents and assents for the following PBIS team members: (1) a team consent form for adult members of the PBIS team (teachers and parents); (2) a parental consent form for the student PBIS team members; and (3) a child assent form for the student PBIS team member. Remember, if you are collecting data as part of a study, you'll need to get permission to conduct research from both the district and the university with whom you're working.

As part of this planning process, the PBIS team members commit to the following activities that are beyond the regular school program responsibilities. First, the team members agree to participate in two full-day trainings (for all adult members) and five 2-hour meetings held after school. We recommend that the students not attend the full-day trainings to avoid missing instructional time. However, all PBIS team members participate in the after-school trainings. See Table 4.1 for an overview of what takes place in each of these training sessions—as well as what happens back at the school in-between these training sessions. Second, PBIS team members, with the help of those conducting the training, agree to design and give a presentation to their entire school staff (including *everyone*—teachers, paraprofessionals, administrators, office staff, cafeteria staff, and custodians) to introduce the proposed PBIS plan. Third, the team members agree to participate in a 20- to 30-minute interview to share their thoughts about the plan—referred to as a *social validity interview*. The interview, which is audiotaped either after school or during a planning period, is confidential and typically conducted by trained personnel when done as part of a research study. Fourth, the team members agree to complete two rating scales (approximately 20 minutes each) before and after the training to determine what has been learned during the training process. These instruments are delivered to each team member and then picked up one week later. This information is used to identify how participants' views change over time. Fifth, team members, teachers, and some randomly selected parents and their students (approximately 100 of each, depending on the school size) share their opinions about the PBIS plan. A copy of the PBIS plan and a rating scale, the Primary Intervention Rating Scale (PIRS; Lane, Robertson, & Wehby, 2002; a revised version of the Intervention Rating Profile–15; Witt & Elliott, 1985; discussed in Chapter 5), is mailed with a postage-paid envelope to each person who was asked to evaluate the proposed primary prevention plan (approximately 15 minutes). Finally, team members agree to conduct a vote at their school to see if the vast majority (80%) of their faculty and staff are willing to implement the PBIS plan as designed.

In selecting the PBIS team members, remember that not all members need to be enthusiastic, bubbly people. The goal is to get input from all major groups or constituencies in the school. Now that you've selected your PBIS team members, it's time to begin the planning process.

Develop a Data-Based Action Plan

At the onset of the training, it is important to achieve clarity on the answers to three questions: What are the main concerns? What are the main objectives for participating in the training series? What do the faculty and staff value in terms of student behavior?

In this section, we clarify these questions and explain how we collect information to help answer them.

Concerns

We encourage PBIS teams to bring available data from their schools to help determine their main concerns. Schools collect a substantial amount of data in the form of (1) academic performance scores on standardized measures; (2) academic performance scores on curriculum-based measures; (3) ODRs; (4) suspension and expulsion records; (5) referrals to the prereferral intervention team, special education, and alternative learning centers; and (6) absentee and tardiness records. Some schools even conduct systematic screening procedures (discussed in Chapter 6) to identify students who are not responding academically and/or behaviorally to their primary prevention programs. Still other schools conduct self-assessments or surveys to collect information from teacher, parent, and/or student perspectives as to how the school is functioning. We also ask the schools to complete the Effective Behavior Support (EBS) survey (Sugai, Todd, & Horner, 2003) to determine the extent to which key practices and processes in the four systems (schoolwide, classroom, nonclassroom, and individual systems) are "in place" or need "to be improved." The EBS survey can be used as an annual assessment to examine the goal for and status of improvement of each system. All school staff should complete the survey independently, which typically takes between 20 and 30 minutes. Questions are related to one of the four systems. Each question is rated first on current status (in place, partially in place, or not in place) and then on priority for improvement (high, medium, or low). The aggregated results will allow you to examine the status of each system to guide the development of the PBIS plan and support you in prioritizing areas in need of attention. This validated tool can also be used to determine which systems need improvement.

It is wonderful that school personnel have become more concerned with addressing instructional and behavioral programming from a data-driven perspective. But, too often, schools do not have a system for regularly examining their data to determine what is and is not working in their building. One of the goals in this training is to help PBIS teams find reasonable, efficient systems for viewing their data on a monthly basis to inform practice. During the first training session, we encourage the schoolwide team to review their current data (e.g., items 1–6 above) to identify areas of concern (see Box 4.1).

Objectives

Once areas of concern are identified, we clarify the main objectives for the training session. The goals are to develop (1) a mission statement; (2) a purpose statement; (3) clear expectations for students' performance in all key instructional settings; (4) schoolwide procedures for teaching and reinforcing desired student expectations; (5) secondary prevention supports; (6) tertiary prevention supports; (7) procedures for monitoring plan implementation; and (8) procedures for monitoring how students respond, with an emphasis on explicit procedures for identifying students in need of more focused support (secondary and tertiary prevention efforts).

Box 4.1. **Examples of Concerns Identified Using Schoolwide Data**

Data source	Concern identified
Office discipline data	• Five eighth-grade boys generated 80% of the ODRs during the month of December. • 60% of the ODRs occurred during the morning recess. • During the 2010–2011 academic year, the rate of ODRs per instructional day increased by 50% during second semester compared to the first semester.
Behavioral screeners: Student Risk Screening Scale (SRSS; Drummond, 1994)	• 30% of students fall in the moderate-risk category. • 15% of students fall in the high-risk category. • The high-risk category (total scores 9–21) has grown (increased) since previous fall assessment. • 45% of students earned a 1 or more on the item regarding cheating and stealing at school.
Report cards	• Ten seventh graders received failing grades in more than one class. • 10% of high school seniors have two or more failing grades.
Attendance data	• 75% of primary grade students have been late to school more than three times per month. • 95% of high school seniors have three or more tardies each month.
Curriculum-based measurement (CBM) reading probes	• Seven second graders continue to read below grade-level benchmark. • Five third graders obtained scores significantly above grade-level benchmark.
ACT scores	• 20% of juniors did not complete ACT test during spring administration. • 60% of students received below-state average on the ACT test.
Writing assessment	• 25% of sixth graders are performing below the 25th percentile. • 30% of students are at or above grade level according to a writing assessment.
Bully referrals	• 50% of bully referrals are concerned with behavior in the bathrooms. • Seven eighth-grade boys make up 85% of bully referrals in the school.
Positive behavior interventions and support (PBIS) ticket turn-in rates	• There was a 50% decrease in the rate of tickets turned in per instructional day during the month of October. • Ninth-grade teachers decreased the number of tickets they handed out by 70%.

We think it is important to clarify what the training *will* and *will not* address, just to make sure that the participants' and trainers' expectations are aligned. Also, we emphasize that the training process is designed to develop a three-tiered plan that is customized for the community it serves; that is, it should be culturally sensitive. The goal is not to introduce a "canned" program specific to all. As we've indicated previously, PBIS is not a program, per se, but a process.

Student Behavior

Finally, we encourage faculty and staff to formally determine what they value in terms of student behavior (Kerr & Zigmond, 1986; Lane, Givner, & Pierson, 2004; Lane, Pierson, et al., 2004; Lane, Wehby, & Cooley, 2006; Walker & Rankin, 1983). In other words, which student behaviors are essential for success?

Rather than trying to arrive at the desired expectations and specific student behaviors through committee discussion, we encourage the team to administer a formal survey in which all adults rate the importance of specific skills (e.g., attends to instruction; resolves conflicts with peers). In our projects (e.g., Lane, Kalberg, Bruhn, et al., in press; Lane, Wehby, Robertson, & Barton-Arwood, 2008) we encourage faculty to complete the social skills items of the Social Skills Rating System (SSRS; Gresham & Elliott, 1990) by rating the importance of each item in terms of school success. Teachers rate each of 30 items on a 3-point Likert-type scale ranging from 0 (*not important*), to 1 (*important*), to 2 (*critical*). These 30 items are equally distributed across three factor-analytically derived domains: cooperation, assertion, and self-control. This information allows the team to determine (1) the domain that is most important (and, may I [K. L.] say that in my 10 years of studying teacher expectations, I have yet to come across a school that selects assertion skills as more important than either the cooperation or self-control domains!) and (2) specific skills within the domain that most teachers view as essential for success. This information can be used to help identify common expectations and specific student behaviors that are most likely to be reinforced by faculty and staff (Lane, Pierson, Stang, & Carter, 2007). This step is *very* important because it is essential that students receive more praise (and other types of reinforcement) for demonstrating the desired behaviors (e.g., arriving to class on time) than they previously received for demonstrating less desirable behaviors (e.g., arriving to class 5 minutes after the bell rings).

Once information is collected regarding the school's key concerns, the main objectives for participating in the training series, and faculty and staff members' views on student behavior, it is time to construct the schoolwide plan. It is important to collect this information prior to developing the plan to ensure that it addresses the key concerns and incorporates the core values shared by the faculty and staff. In the next section, we describe this process.

Construct the Primary Plan

There are many different approaches to developing primary plans that can include a range of components. In general, such plans focus on improving systems-related objectives, one at a time, by developing specific action plans. To this end, action plans are developed that include (1) a 1- to 3-year time frame for design, implementation, and evaluation; (2) faculty and staff commitments; (3) specific activities that lead to measurable outcomes; (4) staff development activities; (5) measurable outcomes; and (6) required resources and supports (Sugai & Horner, 2002).

During our training programs, we support teams in designing a comprehensive three-tiered model with primary, secondary, and tertiary levels of prevention using research-based practices. Although many schools are eager to begin with tertiary prevention efforts for the students with the most intensive needs, we recommend that schools begin by implementing and refining their primary prevention plan. By designing and implementing a solid base program, it is possible to prevent problems from occurring, thereby reducing the proportion of students who require secondary and tertiary levels of prevention (Walker & Severson, 2002).

In the SWPBS plans, we acknowledge the connection between academic and behavior performance, as noted previously, by constructing schoolwide plans that include procedures for teaching expectations in the behavioral, social, and academic domains (see Boxes 4.2 and 4.3). By embedding skills that promote academic performance into the behavior plan, we provide a framework for unifying the features of schoolwide and classroom settings.

When developing the academic and social domains of the program, we encourage teachers and administrators to select curricula that are culturally sensitive, developmentally appropriate, and evidence-based (meaning that studies have been conducted to make sure that it "works" for students with similar characteristics or at least provides a promising approach to that end; Gersten et al., 2005; Horner et al., 2005). In other words, avoid incorporating curricula or strategies that you might have heard about at an inservice (no matter how inspiring!), unless the validity of the curriculum or strategy is well documented.

In the sections that follow, we describe the components of the comprehensive, three-tiered model that we have helped schools to construct. In each section we illustrate the following components of the schoolwide, primary prevention plan: (1) mission statement (see Box 4.4); (2) purpose statement; (3) expectation matrix (see Boxes 4.5 and 4.6); (4) student, teacher, parent, and administrator responsibilities and activities; (5) procedures for teaching expectations; (6) procedures for reinforcing expectations; (7) procedures for monitoring program fidelity and student progress; and (8) procedures for soliciting and incorporating consumer feedback. In addition, we explain how ongoing staff development and resource needs can be addressed. See Boxes 4.2 and 4.3 for illustrations of three-tiered models designed for an elementary and high school, respectively.

Mission Statement

First, a mission statement is designed to provide direction and focus. Specifically, a mission statement is a clear, succinct declaration to help guide the school. It typically contains socially meaningful concepts, goals, and ambitions (Business Resource Software, 2007). For example, in Box 4.2, Orange Elementary School's mission is to "facilitate the learning experience while developing a kind and caring environment in which to build character." As you may recall from Chapter 3, a mission statement is worded positively;

Box 4.2. **Orange Elementary School's Primary Intervention Plan**

Mission statement	The mission of Orange Elementary School is to facilitate the learning experience while developing a kind and caring environment in which to build character.
Purpose statement	All of the Orange Elementary community, including administrators, faculty, staff, parents, and students, will work together to design and implement a variety of programs that support the specific academic, behavioral, and social needs of the students served.
Schoolwide expectations	1. Show respect. 2. Be responsible. 3. Give best effort. *See expectation matrix (Box 4.5)

Responsibilities

Area I: Academics	Area II: Behavior	Area III: Social skills
Students will: • Meet schoolwide expectations stated in the expectation matrix • Arrive on time and stay all day • Participate in class activities • Complete all work to the best of their ability • Bring all materials, including daily planners	**Students will:** • Meet schoolwide expectations stated in the expectation matrix • Take responsibility for own actions and the impact on others • Tell an adult about any unsafe behaviors	**Students will:** • Meet schoolwide expectations stated in the expectation matrix • Participate in monthly social skills lessons • Participate in the anti-bullying program
Faculty and staff will: • Provide engaging lessons, linked to the district standards • Differentiate instruction • Include starter and closing activities as part of lesson plan • Support students who miss instruction • Engage in positive teacher–teacher and teacher–student interactions • Encourage the use of daily planners	**Faculty and staff will:** • Display schoolwide expectations • Model schoolwide expectations • Teach schoolwide expectations • Provide praise and reinforcement to students who display schoolwide expectations • Follow the reactive (consequence-based) discipline plan consistently when infractions of expectations occur • Foster a safe environment for all students	**Faculty and staff will:** • Teach social skills curriculum: Character under Construction • Model social skills in the schoolwide plan • Provide praise and reinforcement to students who demonstrate social skills • Teach and support anti-bullying program

Box 4.2 (cont.)

Responsibilities		
Area I: Academics	**Area II: Behavior**	**Area III: Social skills**
Parents will: • Provide a place, materials, and assistance to complete homework • Sign daily planner • Follow attendance policies • Communicate with schools as requested (e.g., review progress notes and return to school) • Encourage students to give their best effort	**Parents will:** • Post expectation matrix at home • Communicate with teachers and administrators when necessary • Review and support proactive and reactive disciplinary components	**Parents will:** • Post expectation matrix at home • Support social skills program • Support anti-bullying program
Administrators will: • Provide faculty and staff with materials to facilitate instruction	**Administrators will:** • Implement the proactive and reactive behavioral components of the schoolwide plan	**Administrators will:** • Implement social skills and anti-bullying programs consistently

Procedures for teaching	
• Display posters and expectations matrix • Model schoolwide expectations • Participate in the first day of school assembly • Lead students during the first week of school on the schoolwide expectations tour • Teach the expectations for each setting using provided lesson plans and power points • Allow students to attend monthly schoolwide assemblies • Allow students to listen to morning and afternoon announcements, including the PBIS instructional videos	• Send home the parent letters and supporting PBIS materials • Post the school mission statement/vision • Attend to e-mails to faculty and staff prompting PBIS during the first week of school on setting, social skills, and anti-bullying lessons • Listen to staff announcements during faculty meetings • Teach monthly social skills curriculum: Character under Construction • Teach and support anti-bullying program

(cont.)

Box 4.2 *(cont.)*	
Procedures for reinforcing	
• When staff observe students displaying schoolwide expectations, staff will provide verbal praise paired with a PBIS ticket • Provide photos and nominations for the "You Caught Me" wall (upon entering school building the wall contains student pictures displaying expectations) • Allow students to participate in PBIS drawings (prizes from reinforcer menu for staff, parents, and students) • Allow students to attend PBIS assemblies	• Participate in the "lunch with a favorite staff" reinforcer option • Allow students to redeem "lunch with a peer" reinforcer option • Allow students to redeem "special seating during lunch" reinforcer option • Mail home "You Caught Me" Postcards • Post reinforcer menu • Post student-made PBIS posters • Conduct weekly surprise drawings

Monitoring procedures: Student measures

Academic:	**Discipline:**	**Social skills:**
Report card Progress reports Writing assessment Curriculum-based measures (CBM) State assessments	Office discipline referrals (ODRs) Behavior screenings: Student Risk Screening Scale (SRSS; Drummond, 1994) and Systematic Screening for Behavior Disorders (SSBD; Walker & Severson, 1992) Attendance	Behavior screenings (SRSS, SSBD) Office discipline referrals (ODRs) Counseling referrals Bullying referrals

Monitoring procedures: Program measures

Social validity:	**Treatment integrity:**	**Program goals:**
Primary Intervention Rating Scale (PIRS; Lane, Wehby, & Robertson, 2002)	School-wide Evaluation Tool Version 2.1 (SET; Sugai, Lewis-Palmer, Todd, & Horner, 2005) Monthly self-report forms Direct observations by outside observers Rate of access to reinforcement (# of tickets received or distributed/ instructional day)	Effective Behavior Support Self-Assessment Survey Version 2 (EBS; Sugai, Horner, & Todd, 2003)

Box 4.3. **Contra Costa High School's Primary Intervention Plan**

Mission statement	The mission of Contra Costa High School is to provide a safe and secure learning environment that allows students to engage in academics and act respectfully and responsibly to both peers and adults.
Purpose statement	All of the Contra Costa community will work together to design and implement a variety of programs that include primary, secondary, and tertiary levels of prevention to support the specific academic, behavioral, and social needs of all students.
Schoolwide expectations	• Be on time and ready to learn. • Show respect for yourself, peers, and all adults. • Be proud of your school. *See expectation matrix

Responsibilities

Area I: Academics	Area II: Behavior	Area III: Social skills
Students will: • Arrive at and leave school on time • Participate in starting and closing activities • Produce quality work • Complete all work • Bring all materials, including daily planners, to class	**Students will:** • Meet schoolwide expectations stated in the expectation matrix • Follow the reactive and proactive components of the behavior plan	**Students will:** • Meet schoolwide expectations stated in the expectation matrix • Participate in monthly social skills lesson plans
Faculty and staff will: • Provide engaging lessons, linked to the district standards • Differentiate instruction • Include starter and closing activities as part of lesson plan • Support students who miss instruction • Engage in positive teacher–teacher and teacher–student interactions • Encourage the use of daily planners • Create clear routines within the classroom	**Faculty and staff will:** • Display posters of schoolwide expectations • Model schoolwide expectations • Teach schoolwide expectations • Provide praise and reinforcement to students who display schoolwide expectations • Follow the reactive (consequence-based) discipline plan consistently when infractions of expectations occur • Foster a safe environment for all students	**Faculty and staff will:** • Teach social skills curriculum • Model social skills in the schoolwide plan • Provide praise and reinforcement to students who demonstrate social skills *(cont.)*

Box 4.3 (*cont.*)

Responsibilities

Area I: Academics	Area II: Behavior	Area III: Social skills
Parents will: • Provide a place, materials, and assistance to complete homework • Sign daily planner • Read newsletters from school • Check websites for announcements • Follow attendance policies • Communicate with school-site personnel as requested • Encourage students to give their best effort	**Parents will:** • Be familiar with and post schoolwide expectations • Communicate with teachers and administrators when necessary • Review and support proactive and reactive disciplinary components • Support students in problem solving by discussing issues at home in a positive manner	**Parents will:** • Enforce expectations consistently • Support social skills program
Administrators will: • Provide faculty and staff with materials to facilitate instruction	**Administrators will:** • Implement the proactive and reactive behavioral components of the schoolwide plan consistently	**Administrators will:** • Implement social skills consistently

Procedures for teaching

• Display posters and expectations matrix • Participate in the first day of school assembly • Teach the expectations for each setting using provided lesson plans and power points • Allow students to attend monthly schoolwide assemblies • Allow students to listen to morning and afternoon announcements, including the PBIS instructional videos	• Send home the parent letters and supporting PBIS materials • Post the school mission statement/vision • Attend to e-mails to faculty and staff prompting PBIS setting, social skills lessons • Listen to staff announcements during faculty meetings • Teach monthly social skills lessons

Procedures for reinforcing

• When staff observe students displaying schoolwide expectations, staff will provide verbal praise paired with a PBIS ticket • One-on-one time with adults • Preferred parking • PBIS drawings (prizes from reinforcer menu for staff, parents, and students) • PBIS assemblies • PBIS tickets	• Lunch with a favorite staff • Lunch with a peer • Grade-level rewards • Postcards home • Weekly surprise drawings • Recognize teachers with Teacher of the Week • Teacher reinforcements—gift certificates for Parent–Teacher Store, coffee shop, etc. • Large-scale seasonal prizes (e.g., prom package, sporting events)

Box 4.3 (*cont.*)		
Monitoring procedures (measurement)		
Academic: Grade-point average (GPA) Course failures Writing assessment ACT scores State-wide assessments	**Behavior:** Office discipline referrals (ODRs) Student Risk Screening Scale (SRSS; Drummond, 1994) Strengths and Difficulties Questionnaire (SDQ; Goodman, 1997) Attendance	**Social skills:** Office discipline referrals (ODRs) Students taking a right stand (STARS) Counseling referrals Student Risk Screening Scale (SRSS; Drummond, 1994) Strengths and Difficulties Questionnaire (SDQ; Goodman, 1997)
Program measures:		
Social validity: Primary Intervention Rating Scale (PIRS; Lane, Robertson, & Wehby, 2002)	**Treatment integrity:** School-wide Evaluation Tool Version 2.1 (SET; Sugai, Lewis-Palmer, Todd, & Horner, 2005) Monthly self-report forms Direct observations by outside observers Rate of access to reinforcement (# of tickets received or distributed/ instructional day)	**Program goals:** Effective Behavior Support Self-Assessment Survey Version 2 (EBS; Sugai, Horner, & Todd, 2003)

focuses on the relation between academic and behavioral outcomes; and involves all adults (faculty, staff, administrators, etc.), the entire student body, and all key settings. In our work (Lane, Kalberg, Bruhn, et al., in press; Lane, Wehby, et al., 2007) we also encourage parent and student participation in the development of the mission statement, purpose statement, and expectations (the latter two are described below). The intent is to enhance the home–school partnerships and increase the likelihood that students will be reinforced with verbal praise both in the home and school settings.

Purpose Statement

Next, the team members generate a statement as to the purpose of their three-tiered model. This is done to clarify to all parties—administrators, faculty, staff, parents, and students—how the proposed plan aligns with the school's mission statement. For example, Orange Elementary School's purpose statement reflects the spirit of its mission

---

Box 4.4. **Sample Mission Statements**

School	Mission
Roosevelt Elementary School	Roosevelt Elementary School, in a collaborative effort with parents, families, students, and the community, seeks to cultivate the unique potential and ability of each student by providing an enriched, supportive environment that addresses the needs of all learners.
Mountain Vista Middle School	The Mountain Vista Middle School community is committed to providing an intellectually engaging environment where students learn to become responsible citizens and independent thinkers.
North High School	North High School provides a safe and orderly setting in tandem with rich educational experiences that promote common respect and understanding. We advocate for our students as we help them reach our high expectations so that they will be ready to meet the challenges of future work, continued learning experiences, and participation in a democratic society.

---

statement while adding specificity: "All of the Orange Elementary community, including administrators, faculty, staff, parents, and students, will work together to design and implement a variety of programs that supports the specific academic, behavioral, and social needs of the students served."

Expectation Matrix

When constructing the expectation matrix, we encourage team members to first identify the major common areas in their school, such as classrooms, cafeteria, hallways, playground or outdoor areas, bus loading and unloading areas, and bathrooms. Once these areas are identified, the next major goal is to identify three to five expectations that will be operationalized across these key common areas.

We then encourage the teams to review data from the expectation survey to see which types of behaviors are reported as most critical by their faculty and staff. As part of this survey, the faculty and staff complete the 30 social skills items from the SSRS (Gresham & Elliott, 1990) by rating the degree to which these skills are important for school success.

First, note the reported mean scores for each of the three sets of skills. For example, in Table 4.2 you can see that most faculty and staff members view cooperation and self-control skills as more important for school success as compared to assertion skills. Specifically, you can see that the average importance scores are highest for self-control skills ($M = 15.61$, $SD = 2.80$), with cooperation skills following closely ($M = 13.04$, $SD = 2.78$). Assertion skills are rated as the least important ($M = 10.48$, $SD = 2.28$).

Second, we look at the specific items in each skill area to determine the percentage of teachers who rated a given skill as critical for success. In Table 4.2 we have illustrated the

Box 4.5. **Expectation Matrix for Orange Elementary School**

	Settings					
	Classroom	Hallway	Cafeteria	Playground	Bathroom	Bus
Respect	• Follow directions • Use kind words and actions • Control your temper • Cooperate with others • Use an inside voice	• Use a quiet voice • Walk on the right side of the hallway • Keep hands to yourself	• Use an inside voice • Use manners • Listen to and follow adult requests	• Respect other people's personal space • Follow the rules of the game	• Use the restroom and then return to class • Stay in your own bathroom stall • Little talking	• Use kind words toward the bus driver and other students • Listen to and follow the bus driver's rules
Responsibility	• Arrive to class on time • Remain in school for the whole day • Bring your required materials • Turn in finished work • Exercise self-control	• Keep hands to yourself • Walk in the hallway • Stay in line with your class	• Make your choices quickly • Eat your own food • Choose a seat and stick with it • Clean up after yourself	• Play approved games • Use equipment appropriately • Return equipment when you are done • Line up when the bell rings	• Flush toilet • Wash hands with soap • Throw away any trash properly • Report any problems to your teacher	• Talk quietly with others • Listen to and follow the bus driver's rules • Remain in seat after you enter the bus • Use self-control
Best effort	• Participate in class activities • Complete work with best effort • Ask for help politely	• Walk quietly • Walk directly to next location	• Use your table manners • Use an inside voice	• Include others in your games • Be active • Follow the rules of the game	• Take care of your business quickly • Keep bathroom tidy	• Listen to and follow the bus driver's rules • Keep hands and feet to self

Note. Adapted from Walker, Ramsey, and Gresham (2004). Copyright 2004 by Wadsworth, a part of Cengage Learning, Inc. Reproduced by permission. www.cengage.com/permissions.

Box 4.6. Sample Expectation Matrix for Middle and High School Levels

	Settings				
	Classroom	**Hallway**	**Cafeteria**	**Bathroom**	**Bus**
Be on time ready to learn	• Be seated in assigned seat before tardy bell • Bring all necessary materials, including the school planner • Make up work when absent • Participate in all activities • Complete all assignments to the best of your ability	• Use a quiet voice • Walk on the right side of the hallway • Keep hands to yourself	• Know your order when walking through lunch line • Have money ready • Find a seat quickly and stay in it	• Use facility quickly and quietly • Return to class promptly	• Be ready when bus arrives • Carry on all personal belongings needed
Show respect for yourself, peers, and all adults	• Follow the dress code • Use kind words toward others; avoid gossip • Use appropriate ways to show affection to others • Listen to and follow directions • Be truthful	• Keep hands to yourself • Use appropriate ways to show affection to others • Walk in the hallway	• Share lunch tables with others • Follow directions first time asked • Keep food on your plate • Eat your own food • Clean up area	• Take care of your own business • Remain in own stall • Minimize chatting • Keep water in the sink	• Share seating on the bus • Listen to and follow the bus driver's directions the first time given • Speak in a quiet inside voice • Remain seated after entering the bus
Be proud of your school	• Keep desk area clean • Use classroom supplies and books appropriately	• Respect materials (e.g., posters in the hallways) • Keep the hallways clean	• Keep lunch tables clean • Clear any trash • Recycle	• Keep bathroom clean • Throw away any trash properly	• Keep bus clean • Take off all personal belongings

Note. Adapted from Walker, Ramsey, and Gresham (2004). Copyright by Wadsworth, a part of Cengage Learning, Inc. Reproduced by permission. *www.cengage.com/permissions.*

Table 4.2. **Teacher Expectations for Orange Elementary School**

Item no.	n	%
Self-Control		
1	24	100.00
11	13	54.17
12	18	75.00
22	10	41.67
25	19	79.17
Importance score $M(SD) = 15.61(2.80)$		
Assertion		
6	9	37.50
7	7	29.17
10	3	12.50
19	3	12.50
23	2	8.33
Importance score $M(SD) = 10.48(2.28)$		
Cooperation		
8	12	50.00
9	14	58.33
15	8	33.33
16	11	45.83
20	22	91.67
Importance score $M(SD) = 13.04(2.78)$		

Note. See wording of individual items on the Social Skills Rating System—Elementary version completed by teachers (Gresham & Elliott, 1990).

information provided for a few items from each domain. In actuality, you would provide the PBIS teams with results of all 30 items. Based on the information provided, you'll see that 100% of the teachers rated item 1 (*controls temper when experiencing conflict with peers*) as critically important; 79% of the teachers also rated the item 25 (*responds in an appropriate manner when hit or pushed by another child*) as critically important.

Collectively, information on the domains of importance and the specific skills in each domain can help the team construct the schoolwide expectation matrix. For example, in the elementary school illustration, self-control is presented as the most important domain. This led to the team's selection of *respect* and *responsibility* as two of their three expectations (see Box 4.5). The *best effort* expectation stemmed from the second highest rated domain: cooperation. Next, the specific items constituting these domains are used to help identify specific behaviors or skill sets to be placed in the appropriate "boxes" or "cells" in the expectation matrix. For example, in Box 4.5 you'll see the following state-ment in the Respect: Classroom intersection: (1) follow directions (cooperation item 20: *follows directions when given by a teacher*); (2) use kind words and actions; (3) con-trol your temper (self-control items 1 and 12: *controls temper when experiencing conflict with peers* and *controls temper when experiencing conflict with an adult*); (4) cooperate with others (cooperation item 22: *cooperates with peers without prompting*), and (5) use inside voice. Taken collectively, these entries indicate that students will be respectful in the classroom if they perform these five behaviors.

One goal of an expectation matrix is to level the playing field for all students. Now, no matter where students are in the school building, they'll know what is expected of them. This eliminates the "I didn't know that I wasn't supposed to …" or "No one ever told me that I was supposed to …" types of problems. Now, if students decide to use an "outside voice" in the hallway, they are doing so because they chose to break the rule. This is a performance problem ("I can do what you're asking, but I don't want to"; Gresham, 2002b). Students will no longer be in a situation in which they do not have or know the expected skills; that is, they cannot claim skill deficits ("I don't know how to or what to do"). This is important because performance deficits and skill deficits require different types of intervention supports. Performance deficits require changes in reinforcement rates to motivate students to want to meet the expectations, whereas skill deficits require explicit instruction to make sure that students know how to do the expected task or behavior (Gresham). The primary prevention plan contains specific responsibilities for teachers and parents to make sure that the environment and the adults' behavior sets the stage for the desired student behaviors to occur. The plan also contains strategies for teaching all students the required skills and then reinforcing students for demonstrating these skills.

Student, Faculty, Parent, and Administrator Responsibilities and Activities

We further operationalize expectations by explicitly stating student, faculty, parent, and administrator responsibilities in academic, behavioral, and social domains. For example, students are expected to demonstrate the behaviors listed in the expectation matrix. In addition, if schools incorporate an "anti-bullying," "character," or "conflict resolution" program, these expectations are also specified under the social skills component of the primary plan, and students are expected to meet these expectations as well.

Faculty responsibilities are stated explicitly for the three areas constituting the pri-mary plan: academics, behavior, and social skills. For example, as specified in Box 4.2, as part of the academic component of the primary plan, faculty and staff are expected to (1) provide engaging lessons linked to the district standards, (2) differentiate instruc-tion, (3) include starter and closing activities as part of lesson plan, (4) support students who miss instruction, (5) engage in positive teacher–teacher and teacher–student inter-actions, and (6) encourage the use of daily planners. As part of the behavioral com-ponent of the primary plan, teachers are expected to (1) display schoolwide expecta-tions posters, (2) model schoolwide expectations, (3) teach schoolwide expectations, (4) provide praise and reinforcement to students who demonstrate schoolwide expectations, (5) follow the reactive (consequence-based) discipline plan consistently when infractions of expectations occur, and (6) foster a safe environment for all students. As part of the social skills component of the primary plan, teachers are expected to (1) teach social skills curriculum, (2) model social skills in the schoolwide plan, (3) provide praise and reinforcement to students who demonstrate social skills, and (4) teach and support anti-bullying program.

In addition, students, parents, and administrators have responsibilities as part of the schoolwide plan to support each of the three components: academic, behavioral, and social. Refer to Boxes 4.2 and 4.3 for sample responsibilities at the elementary and high school levels, respectively.

Thus, all key players—students, faculty, parents, and administrators—have clearly defined responsibilities that support the three components of the primary plan: academics, behavior, and social skills. Once the responsibilities are clarified for all parties, the next step is to decide what procedures will be used to teach all components of the plan. In other words, how do we teach everyone these expectations?

Procedures for Teaching

When we think about teaching the expectations, we often only think about teaching the schoolwide expectations to the students. However, it is just as important that *all* people involved, including teachers, staff, paraprofessionals, custodians, and parent volunteers, as well as parents and students, be familiar with the components of the primary plan. So, how do you do that? We recommend that you plan for an initial program kick-off training as well as ongoing training to keep the plan in the forefront of everyone's mind.

In terms of program kick-off activities, we encourage the PBIS team to introduce the plan to their faculty (who will have already provided feedback when constructing the plan) with a presentation that involves modeling of the core components. For example, one of the high school teams with which we worked developed a PowerPoint presentation to introduce the PBIS plan. While presenting the plan, they passed out tickets paired with behavior-specific praise (e.g., "Thank you for asking questions about when to give out PBIS tickets"). At the end of the presentation, after all questions were addressed, they collected the tickets they had distributed during the presentation and raffled off some prizes (reinforcers) that had been displayed in the front of the library. These prizes included an extra 45-minute planning period, a free car wash pass, and a preferred parking space (right next to the principal's spot) for 1 week.

To introduce the program to parents, the team mailed home a letter (see Box 4.7) along with a copy of the primary plan (including the expectation matrix). Among other things, the letter states that this new plan focuses on "catching students being good." Now, the school would have a comprehensive plan with proactive strategies for preventing problem behaviors from occurring as well as reactive strategies for responding to problems that do occur. In the letter we encourage parents to post the expectation matrix on their refrigerator (the site of most important things in a household!) to serve as a prompt for expected behavior and as a communication tool to facilitate the home–school partnership. For example, when a student receives a PBIS ticket, the parent can

---

Box 4.7. **Sample Parent Letter**

Dear Parent(s) or Guardian(s),

As the school year begins, we want to share some important information with you regarding a new program that began at Orange Elementary School last year called *positive behavior interventions and supports*, or PBIS. PBIS is a program that we believe will allow our student body to grow and strengthen and will encourage the development of academic, social, and behavioral skills of each individual student. As part of our community, we hope that the parent group will be in support of our PBIS plan. We have included a brief description of our PBIS program for you to review. In addition, we will be hosting a discussion session on Wednesday August 18th at 7:00 P.M. to clarify any details before school starts. We are certain that you will hear more about the program from your children over the next several weeks and months, as we will be introducing the plan during our kick-off assembly on Wednesday. Please don't hesitate to contact any Orange Elementary School staff or faculty if you have any questions or comments regarding our PBIS plan.

What is PBIS?

Positive behavior interventions and supports (PBIS) refers to a three-tiered model to support all students. The first part of PBIS is a schoolwide component—a primary prevention program designed to prevent any harm from occurring. **Each and every student is impacted by this program just by virtue of showing up to school**. The goal of this schoolwide plan is to level the playing field by identifying schoolwide expectations for each setting, teaching these expectations, reinforcing them through the use of positive reinforcement, and providing ample opportunities to practice. In addition to just telling students they did a great job (academically, socially, or behaviorally) through verbal praise, we will be introducing *orange tickets*, which are tickets that are given out when a student is caught performing an expected behavior. Tickets can be turned in for drawings that will occur monthly (and sometimes there will be weekly surprise drawings!).

However, if the primary plan that every student receives just by showing up each day is not enough, there will be additional levels of support. Some students may require small focus groups to support their needs; this is called *secondary support*. Others may benefit from one-on-one instruction and other customized supports—tertiary prevention efforts. Whatever the level of support, our PBIS program will help us identify students who may need a little more and support than those doing the right thing.

What is the goal of PBIS?

The purpose of Orange Elementary School's PBIS program is to teach and reward students for displaying our three schoolwide expectations or Orange Expectations: (1) Show respect, (2) be responsible, and (3) give best effort. The expectation grid (attached; please post this on your refrigerator at home!) defines what each expectation looks like in various school locations. For example, what does responsibility look like in the cafeteria, in the hallway, on the bus, in the classroom?

Who is involved in the PBIS program?

EVERYONE! All adults and students at Orange Elementary School are encouraged to participate in the PBIS plan (please see the attached PBIS plan to find everyone's roles and responsibilities for this plan).

The Orange Elementary School community is grateful for the tremendous amount of support received from our parents and families! Upon reading the PBIS primary plan and schoolwide

---

Box 4.7 (*cont.*)
===

expectations matrix attached, please sign the signature of support form at the bottom of this sheet and return by Friday August 20th.

   Again, thank you for your unwavering time and support to our school, our students, and our staff. We look forward to a wonderful school year!

Sincerely,

Loretta Jackson
Orange Elementary Principal

Attachments:
   School's Primary Intervention Plan
   School's Expectations Matrix

- -

Please detach, complete, and return the "Signature of Support" form to the school office by Friday August 20th.

I, _____, have thoroughly read Orange's PBIS plan and school expectations.

_____ I will support and participate in implementing the PBIS plan each time I am at Orange Elementary.

_____ Although I am not in favor of this PBIS plan, I agree to not sabotage the plan.

Signature _____   Date _____

---

say "Oh, what did you get it for?" If the child does not recall, then the parent can say, "Well, *where* did you get it? … Oh, in the hallway for using a quiet voice. Well, that's great!" In this way, a positive parent–child conversation is prompted and the child/adolescent receives additional reinforcement for demonstrating the desired behavior. Similarly, if the student receives an ODR, then the parent can use the information on the expectation matrix to help facilitate a conversation as to how he or she should have behaved and what was expected of him or her. The goal of involving the parent in the primary plan is not to impose values on the family, but to strengthen the home–school partnership by facilitating communication (Lane, Stanton-Chapman, Roorbach, & Phillips, 2007). Parent letters can also be used to clarify the purpose and scope of the PBIS programs (see Box 4.8)

   To introduce the program to the students, one elementary school opened the doors on the first day of school and began passing out PBIS tickets paired with verbal praise

Box 4.8. **Sample Parent Letter Clarifying the Plan**

Dear PBIS Team,

I thought it was time to re-educate parents on PBIS, so I included the article below in tomorrow's newsletter. I had a few of my most well-educated, highly involved Orange Elementary parents make comments to other parents (who promptly told me!) that these tickets were only for "problem" children and were silly, and that children should do what's right because it's right. So I took that as an opportunity for enlightenment. Hope I expressed the program satisfactorily.

> Loretta Jackson
> Principal, Orange Elementary School

PRINCIPAL'S MESSAGE 2/20/2011

I thought I would take this week's message to update you (or inform you) about our positive behavior and interventions support (PBIS) program at Orange Elementary.

PBIS is a schoolwide plan for promoting positive, appropriate behaviors at school. The PBIS program was developed at the Vanderbilt Kennedy Center under the direction of Dr. Kathleen Lane. A team of teachers, a parent, and I studied the program and created a plan personalized to the needs of Orange Elementary students over a 6-month period last spring. *Respect, responsibility,* and *best effort* and participation were chosen as our key expectations. We trained the remainder of the teachers and support staff during the spring semester and at the fall inservice. The Vanderbilt team, with OES teacher and staff approval, committed to a 2-year support plan and to evaluate our plan's effectiveness by using the information we collect as part of regular school practices. In addition, we provide teacher counseling from graduate students in behavior specialist programs as part of a different project, Project FUNCTION, to help our most challenged (and challenging students) improve their behavior.

The PBIS program involves three tiers of support for students. The Orange tickets are the main component of the first tier and positively affect 80–90% of the students. Your children love PBIS and their terrific Orange tickets. Their self-esteem grows each time they receive one and, though we want children to do the right thing because it's the right thing, that doesn't always happen. Your initial PBIS team meets once a month to evaluate program components, though we do not change anything in the first year in order to gather reliable data. The team recently decided that it was time to "up the ante" on criteria for receiving an Orange ticket in our school. In other words, students have been taught the expectations and now they will have to really demonstrate meeting them in extraordinary ways to receive a ticket. The second tier involves planning and conducting small-group interventions for students with similar behavior issues, such as anger management, being a good friend, etc. This tier heavily engages Mr. Hughes's expertise. The third tier is for those 2–5% of our students who display significantly disruptive behavior. This tier is supported by the Vanderbilt experts who spend weeks observing and providing counseling to the individual students' teachers so that, not only can they improve behavior for their current students, but they will learn very valuable skills to use with future students.

Your child may, at one time or now, be in class with a child who has severe behavior issues. We are thrilled to have the PBIS program and the Vanderbilt researchers' expertise so that we can turn the lives of these children around while they are still so young AND truly improve the climate of learning for all other children in the class. We feel fortunate to have this research-based intervention program in our school because, as one teacher put it, "It works!"

Please feel free to ask questions about PBIS any time, and thank you for your support and creative home plans that encourage what we do at school.

> Loretta Jackson
> Principal, Orange Elementary School

Note. Reprinted with permission from a school-site principal. School name and principal's name are fictitious at the request of the principal.

(e.g., "Thanks for coming to school on time!" "Great job taking your hat off when coming in the building!"). Students immediately asked questions such as "What is this?", "What's this for?", and "What do I do with this?" Students were then ushered into an assembly (one assembly for students in grades 1–3, and one assembly for students in grades 4 and 5) that introduced the program. As students walked into the assembly, they were asked to place their tickets into a large trash can, again prompting lots of questions. The assembly included PBIS cheerleaders, skits introducing the expectations for each setting, and then a drawing. At the end of the assembly, the principal conducted a drawing during which three students received prizes ranging from homework passes, cash, and even a bicycle! Displayed throughout the school were posters illustrating the expectations (see Figures 4.2, 4.3, and 4.4), PBIS tickets (see Figure 4.5 and 4.6), and slogans (see Figure 4.7). These visual reminders were present in all key locations: classrooms, hallways, cafeteria, library, and even bathroom stalls. No matter where a student was and whether or not he or she was sitting or standing, the expectations were present!

To provide ongoing training for all individuals in the building, various combinations of the following strategies can be used:

Figure 4.2. **Sample PBIS poster—elementary level.**

Figure 4.3. **Sample PBIS poster—elementary level.** Designed by Kylie Beck, Vanderbilt University Kennedy Center/National Institute of Child Health and Human Development Grant No. P30 HD15052.

CONTRA COSTA HIGH SCHOOL

Student:_____   Date: _____
Adult Name: _____
Location: ☐ Classrooms ☐ Hallways ☐ Cafeteria
                ☐ Bathroom   ☐ Bus

Circle skill that was observed

EXPECTATIONS
☐ Be on time and ready to learn
☐ Show respect for yourself, peers, and all adults
☐ Be proud of your school

GET YOURS TODAY

Figure 4.4. **Sample PBIS poster—high school level.**

Orange Elementary School

Student Name: _____ Date: _____

Adult name: _____ Location: ☐ Classroom ☐ Hallway

Grade: _____   ☐ Cafeteria ☐ Playground ☐ Bathroom ☐ Bus

Mark the schoolwide expectation that was shown.

Respect!

Responsibility!

Best Effort!

Figure 4.5. **Orange Elementary School's PBIS ticket.**

CONTRA COSTA HIGH SCHOOL

Student:_____ Date:_____

Adult Name:_____

Location: ☐ Classroom ☐ Hallway ☐ Cafeteria ☐ Bathroom ☐ Bus

Circle the skill that was observed

EXPECTATIONS

☐ Be on time and ready to learn

☐ Show respect for yourself, peers, and all adults

☐ Be proud of your school

Figure 4.6. **Contra Costa High School PBIS ticket.**

Middle School:

PBIS: That's the Ticket!

Elementary School:

PBIS PAWS: Follow the Path!!!

Figure 4.7. **Sample school slogans.** Reprinted with permission from school-site principals. School names omitted to protect anonymity.

1. Morning announcements with a primary plan pledge.
2. Introduction of new posters to increase interest.
3. Monthly teacher-led lessons to teach the character traits or social skills identified as part of the social skills component of the primary plan.
4. Daily student-developed videos illustrating expectations (including examples and "nonexamples").
5. Teacher led-lessons (30 minutes) to reteach expectations for each setting specified in the expectation matrix.
6. Bookmarks for substitutes and parent volunteers that contain essential information about the PBIS plan, including how and when to give out PBIS tickets. We encourage these bookmarks to be distributed along with a pack of tickets when these adults sign in and enter the building.
7. E-mails to teachers to provide reminders about teaching the setting lessons and monthly social skills lessons (see Box 4.9).
8. E-mails to all adults—employees and volunteers—in the building to provide suggestions about when to give out tickets and the importance of pairing the ticket with behavior-specific praise (see Box 4.9).

As we mentioned previously, it is important to provide initial and ongoing training for all parties involved: all adults in the building, parents, and teachers. By training broadly and diversely, we promote generalization of the desired skills (Cooper et al., 2007; Dunlap, 1993; Lane & Beebe-Frankenberger, 2004), which in turn increases the probability of students demonstrating similar behaviors in new environments and in the presence of a variety of people (stimulus generalization).

Also critical to keeping the newly acquired behaviors evident over time (maintenance) and in new situations (stimulus generalization) is reinforcement. It is important that the desired behaviors receive higher rates of reinforcement than the previously undesirable behavior (Umbreit et al., 2007). In the next section we describe a range of procedures for reinforcing behavior.

Box 4.9. **Sample E-Mails to Adults Regarding Ticket Distribution**

Reminder regarding pairing ticket with specific verbal praise	Faculty, staff, and volunteers,
	Thank you for supporting PBIS this year. When you give a student a PBIS ticket, be sure to pair it with specific verbal praise! For example, "Gary, I noticed that you showed responsibility when you knew your lunch order right away in the cafeteria. Way to go!"
	Keep up the good work,
	Coach Hughes
Focus on a specific skill	Hello PBIS-ers,
	This month try to reward those students who arrive to class on time and are prepared. Give the first five students in their desks ready to begin class a PBIS ticket!
	Thanks for all you do,
	Ms. Suzanne
Last month's ticket total	PBIS Supporters,
	After counting night and day the grand total has arrived ... 658 tickets were passed out during the month of October (twice the rate distributed in September!). Keep on catching them in the act!
Emphasize the month's focus social skill	PBIS-ers,
	Remember that the character trait for the month of February is sharing/cooperation. Be sure to keep an eye out for those students demonstrating this important skill!
	Mr. Steve

Procedures for Reinforcing

When we think about reinforcement, it is important to remember that all people with responsibilities need to receive reinforcement. You might remember that there are two types of reinforcement: positive reinforcement and negative reinforcement. Positive reinforcement occurs when a behavior (e.g., following a teacher's direction) is followed by the introduction of a stimulus (e.g., a PBIS ticket paired with verbal praise and a smile) that increases the likelihood that the same behavior (e.g., following a teacher's direction) will occur in the future under similar conditions (Cooper et al., 2007). Negative reinforcement also increases the probability of a behavior occurring in the future, but involves the removal of a stimulus that is aversive.

When selecting reinforcers, we recommend incorporating mainly positive reinforcement, although negative reinforcement can also be useful at times. Whereas many people are trying to "get" or "seek" social attention, activities, or tangible items (positive reinforcement; see Table 4.3), others will try to "avoid" or "escape" social attention, activities, or tangible items (Umbreit et al., 2007). So, we encourage you to develop a reinforcement system that appeals to a range of people, such as the attention-seeking elementary student (or in some instances, graduate students) and the escape-motivated high school student. And, remember that sources of reinforcement change over time. Whereas teacher attention may be highly reinforcing to early-elementary students, peer attention tends to become more meaningful as students transition into middle and high school grades. Adults, too, are motivated in different ways. In Table 4.3, you'll see a range of reinforcers that can be used in elementary, middle, and high schools to reward those students, faculty, staff, and parents who are either trying to "seek" or "avoid" attention, tasks, or tangibles. Some schools have done a great job of combining a range of reinforcers. See Box 4.10 for a description of how one middle school designed a reinforcement system to appeal to its students.

Box 4.10. **Description of One Middle School's Reinforcement System**

One middle school developed a monthly "awards assembly" that was designed to appeal to all different types of students—both the seekers and the avoiders. In other words, there was something for everyone. See below how each type of reinforcement was met by this assembly.

	Seekers (positive reinforcement)	Avoiders (negative reinforcement)
Attention	Opportunities for students to win prizes and names called out in front of entire grade. In addition, teachers were on duty and could engage in activities with students. Students could gain attention from peers. Students who earn A's and B's on their report card are posted on the High Flyer Wall.	Students who wanted to avoid attention from teachers in class could find quiet space to read, listen to music, and hang out with peers.
Activity	Variety of activities available to engage in (e.g., basketball, ping-pong, dancing, chatting, movie watching, outside sports)	Avoid class by attending this assembly. Avoid dressing for P.E.
Tangible/ sensory	Prizes were drawn from the large bucket of PBIS tickets every 10 minutes. A variety of prizes (see reinforcer menu for examples) were on display. Students could put PBIS tickets in a box placed in front of the desired prize to be raffled. Additionally, snacks were on sale for tickets (guaranteed reinforcement!—no "chance" of not getting what you want!).	Students who didn't want to engage in social activity or hear the load noise of the music and raffles could go to a quiet classroom to watch a movie.

Table 4.3. **Reinforcer Menu: Suggested Reinforcers Based on the Function of the Behavior**

Function	Persons		
	Students	Faculty and staff	Parents
	Seeking positive reinforcement		
Social attention	• Lunch with friend • Lunch with staff of choice • Preferential seating • Reading time with adult • Meeting with the principal • Tutor/mentor younger class • Award given in front of class/school • Featured in a PBIS video/skit • Praise postcard sent home	• Preferential parking spot • Award given during faculty meeting • Recognition during assembly • Featured in a PBIS video/skit	• Student featured on school webpage • Student featured in newsletter or bulletin board • Phone call home from principal/teacher • Praise postcard sent home • Featured in a PBIS video/skit
Activity/task	• Lunch with a friend • Lunch with staff of choice • Movie (on-campus) • Preferential seating • Class helper • Extra reading time • PBIS assembly • Additional computer time • Additional recess time • Game of choice • Ticket to school event (e.g., sporting, dance, play) • Extra basketball time • Feature spot in PBIS video	• Draws winning PBIS ticket during assemblies • Ticket to school event (e.g., sporting, play, dance) • Feature spot in PBIS video	• Ticket to school event (e.g., sporting, dance, play) • Feature spot in PBIS video
Tangible items	• School supplies • Food coupon • School T-shirt or sweatshirt • Bike, radio, iPod • Candy, soft drinks • Gift cards (e.g., movie, stores, restaurants) • Discounted yearbook, dance ticket, sporting event	• Free yearbook • Gift certificate to local restaurant • Gift cards (e.g., movies, stores, restaurants) • Candy, soft drinks • School T-shirt or sweatshirt • School supplies • Car wash coupon	• Gift certificate (e.g., movies, stores, restaurants) • Postcard sent home regarding student's exemplar behavior • Bumper sticker for car • School T-shirt or sweatshirt *(cont.)*

Table 4.3 *(cont.)*

Function	Persons		
	Students	Faculty and staff	Parents
	Avoiding negative reinforcement		
Social attention	• Lunch in private area with peer and staff of choosing • Extra computer time • Quiet time in the library pass • Get out of class participation pass • Get out of P.E. • Preferential seating during school event	• Relief from supervision duty at the PBIS assembly • Relief from before/after school supervision duty • Relief from hallway monitor duty	• Phone conference instead of on-campus conference • Get out of classroom support duty
Activity/task	• Extra computer time (avoid class time) • Homework pass • Front of the lunch line pass • Additional free time • Extra library time • Preferred parking (avoid the long walk to class!)	• Extra planning period • Relief from bus duty • Relief from lunch duty	• Phone conference instead of on-campus conference • Get out of classroom support duty
Tangible items	• Certificate to drop lowest grade	• Certificate to avoid walkie-talkie duty in the hallway	• Certificate to avoid supervision duty at extracurricular activities

Note. Adapted from Umbreit, Ferro, Liaupsin, and Lane (2007, p. 81). Copyright 2007 by Pearson Education, Inc., Upper Saddle River, NJ.

As you consider how to develop your reinforcement system, keep in mind that the rate of reinforcement is important. For example, if your initial goal is to teach students the desired behaviors, then it is important to have a rich, thick schedule of reinforcement (for you behaviorists, we're talking about a *variable ratio schedule*) to make sure that students receive reinforcement for demonstrating the desired behaviors. Once the students have learned the desired expectations, we want to make sure that these newly acquired behaviors are sustained over time. At that point, the team will most likely want to introduce a leaner schedule of reinforcement, moving to a more intermitted reinforcement schedule (Cooper et al., 2007).

A few other points to consider are the following. First, not everyone supports the use of tangible reinforcers. If people are opposed to tangible reinforcers, then focus on using social attention and activity reinforcers (see Table 4.3). Social reinforcers such as time with friend, working with a peer, and behavior-specific praise are very convenient, practical, and inexpensive. Second, if you are using primary reinforcers such as edibles (e.g., food or beverages) and sensory stimulation (e.g., music), be careful to remember that many students have food allergies and everyone will eventually satiate on food (yes, even dark chocolate). If you do use edible reinforcers, also make sure to pair food with social reinforcers such as a smile and/or behavior-specific praise (e.g., "Katie Scarlett, you did a great job of _____!"). Third, if you are using secondary reinforcers such as preferred activities and privileges, make sure to vary the choice of reinforcers as the novelty often wears off. Fourth, by using tickets, cards, or tokens that can later be traded for reinforcers, such as time with friends during assemblies, activities, or tangibles, you are also encouraging delayed gratification—another essential skill (Alberto & Troutman, 2003).

Over the years we have often heard faculty and staff register concerns that giving reinforcement is nothing less that bribery. We respectfully remind people that all behavior is maintained by consequences (Cooper et al., 2007). You do what you do because of what you get or avoid (Umbreit et al., 2007). Whereas bribery is using strategies to increase the likelihood of people doing things that are *not* in their best interest, positive reinforcement is a behavioral principle that involves the contingent introduction of any stimuli to increase the probability of the desired behavior occurring in the future. As adults, it is easy to forget how difficult school can be for some. It is an environment that offers few opportunities for choice and provides real challenges for many students. Helping teachers to remember to pay attention to positive behaviors and rewarding students for displaying them helps fosters an environment where these behaviors are performed for the intrinsic satisfaction they provide.

Procedures for Monitoring Fidelity and Student Progress

Another important component of a PBIS program is data collection to determine (1) if the plan is being put in place as planned (i.e., treatment integrity; Gresham, 1989; Lane, Bocian, MacMillan, & Gresham, 2004) and (2) how students are responding to the plan. We discuss these concepts and procedures in detail in Chapter 5.

Procedures for Soliciting and Incorporating Consumer Feedback

Once the primary prevention plan has been drafted, it is important to get feedback from all key consumers (e.g., teachers, staff, parents, and students) before moving forward with implementation. Why? By seeking input and informing all parties about the expectations of the plan, procedures for teaching, procedures for reinforcing, and data to monitor outcomes, you can determine whether or not these participants have taken ownership of the goals, procedures, and intended outcomes. In other words, you're seeking information about people's perceptions of social validity (see Chapter 5). The reasoning is as follows: If people view the schoolwide primary plan as addressing socially significant goals, socially acceptable procedures, and socially important outcomes, then it is possible that the intervention will (1) be implemented with fidelity and (2) produce meaningful, lasting change (Baer, Wolf, & Risley, 1968; Kazdin, 1977; Lane & Beebe-Frankenberger, 2004; Wolf, 1978).

One method of assessing social validity is through the use of rating scales. Several rating scales are validated for use with secondary and tertiary levels of intervention efforts. These include the Treatment Acceptability Rating Form—Revised (TARF-R; Reimers & Wacker, 1988, Form 4.1); the Intervention Rating Profile–15 (IRP-15; Witt & Elliott, 1985, Form 4.2) for obtaining teacher opinions, and the Children's Intervention Rating Profile (CIRP; Witt & Elliott, 1985, Form 4.3) for obtaining student options. In our work with schoolwide primary prevention efforts, we have adapted the IRP-15 to evaluate teacher, parent, and student perspectives of the goals, procedures, and outcomes of the prevention efforts. We refer to this adapted version of the IRP-15 as the Primary Intervention Rating Scale (PIRS; Lane, Robertson, et al., 2002; see Forms 4.4, 4.5, and 4.6 for elementary, middle, and high school versions, respectively). Initial reliability studies of the PIRS indicate that the instrument has strong internal consistency at the elementary, middle, and high school levels, with alpha coefficients estimates ranging from 0.97 to 0.98 (Lane, Kalberg, Bruhn, et al., 2008).

Data gleaned from these perspectives can be used to shape the intervention plan, ensure that the behavioral expectations are consistent with cultural values held by the community, or at least identify where teachers, parents, and students may converge and diverge in their expectations and opinions (Lane, Stanton-Chapman, et al., 2007).

Staff Development

Once the schoolwide primary plan has been revised using feedback provided by consumers, the next step is to offer sufficient staff development opportunities to ensure proper understanding and implementation. To facilitate these staff development offerings, we encourage you to develop an implementation manual that (1) describes the plan, including all components previously outlined; (2) includes copies of the expectation matrix, PBIS tickets, and other related implementation materials (e.g., lesson plans to teach schoolwide expectations, posters, bookmarks, postcards); (3) the assessment schedule, including a corresponding list of PBIS team members responsible for each piece of information monitored; and (4) a list of frequently asked questions and their answers (see Chapter 7). This manual should be distributed to all adults in the building, so that everyone is familiar with the plan (including procedures for teaching, reinforcing, and monitoring desired behaviors).

As previously stated, primary prevention is a program, not a curriculum in isolation. Consequently, it is important to recognize that the primary prevention plan should be modified based on the needs of the people (in this case, the teachers, administrators, parents, and students). However, revisions should occur *between* academic years, not during the academic year. If revisions are made during the academic year, then the school-site PBIS team cannot examine the impact of the primary prevention program

Treatment Acceptability Rating Profile—Revised (TARF-R)

Please complete the items listed below. The items should be completed by placing a check mark on the line under the question that best indicates how you feel about the psychologist's treatment recommendations.

1. How clear is your understanding of this treatment?

   _____   _____   _____   _____   _____
   Not at all   Neutral   Very clear
   clear

2. How acceptable do you find the treatment to be regarding your concerns about your child?

   _____   _____   _____   _____   _____
   Not at all   Neutral   Very acceptable
   acceptable

3. How willing are you to carry out this treatment?

   _____   _____   _____   _____   _____
   Not at all   Neutral   Very willing
   willing

4. Given your child's behavioral problems, how reasonable do you find the treatment to be?

   _____   _____   _____   _____   _____
   Not at all   Neutral   Very reasonable
   reasonable

5. How costly will it be to carry out this treatment?

   _____   _____   _____   _____   _____
   Not at all   Neutral   Very costly
   costly

6. To what extent do you think there might be disadvantages in following this treatment?

   _____   _____   _____   _____   _____
   Not at all   Neutral   Many are likely
   likely

7. How likely is this treatment to make permanent improvements in your child's behavior?

   _____   _____   _____   _____   _____
   Unlikely   Neutral   Very likely

8. How much time will be needed each day for you to carry out this treatment?

   _____   _____   _____   _____   _____
   Little time will   Neutral   Much time will
   be needed   be needed

9. How confident are you that the treatment will be effective?

   _____   _____   _____   _____   _____
   Not at all   Neutral   Very confident
   confident

10. Compared to other children with behavioral difficulties, how serious are your child's problems?

    _____   _____   _____   _____   _____
    Not at all   Neutral   Very serious
    serious

(cont.)

Form 4.1 (cont.)

11. How disruptive will it be to the family (in general) to carry out this treatment?

_____	_____	_____	_____	_____
Not at all disruptive		Neutral		Very disruptive

12. How effective is this treatment likely to be for your child?

_____	_____	_____	_____	_____
Not at all effective		Neutral		Very effective

13. How affordable is this treatment for your family?

_____	_____	_____	_____	_____
Not at all affordable		Neutral		Very affordable

14. How much do you like the procedures used in the proposed treatment?

_____	_____	_____	_____	_____
Do not like them at all		Neutral		Like them very much

15. How willing will other family members be to help carry out this treatment?

_____	_____	_____	_____	_____
Not at all willing		Neutral		Very willing

16. To what extent are undesirable side effects likely to result from this treatment?

_____	_____	_____	_____	_____
No side effects are likely		Neutral		Many side effects are likely

17. How much discomfort is your child likely to experience during the course of this treatment?

_____	_____	_____	_____	_____
No discomfort at all		Neutral		Very much discomfort

18. How severe are your child's behavioral difficulties?

_____	_____	_____	_____	_____
Not at all severe		Neutral		Very severe

19. How willing would you be to change your family routine to carry out this treatment?

_____	_____	_____	_____	_____
Not at all willing		Neutral		Very willing

20. How well will carrying out this treatment fit into the family routine?

_____	_____	_____	_____	_____
Not at all well		Neutral		Very well

21. To what degree are your child's behavioral problems of concern to you?

_____	_____	_____	_____	_____
No concern at all		Neutral		Great concern

From Reimers and Wacker (1988). Reprinted with permission from Thomas M. Reimers.

Form 4.2

Intervention Rating Profile—15

The purpose of this questionnaire is to obtain information that will aid in the selection of classroom interventions. These interventions will be used by teachers of children with behavior problems. Please circle the number which best describes your agreement or disagreement with each statement.

	Strongly Disagree	Disagree	Slightly Disagree	Slightly Agree	Agree	Strongly Agree
1. This would be an acceptable intervention for the child's problem behavior.	1	2	3	4	5	6
2. Most teachers would find this intervention appropriate for behavior problems in addition to the one described.	1	2	3	4	5	6
3. This intervention should prove effective in changing the child's problem behavior.	1	2	3	4	5	6
4. I would suggest the use of this intervention to other teachers.	1	2	3	4	5	6
5. The child's behavior problem is severe enough to warrant use of this intervention.	1	2	3	4	5	6
6. Most teachers would find this intervention suitable for the behavior problem described.	1	2	3	4	5	6
7. I would be willing to use this intervention in the classroom setting.	1	2	3	4	5	6
8. This intervention would *not* result in negative side effects for the child.	1	2	3	4	5	6
9. This intervention would be appropriate for a variety of children.	1	2	3	4	5	6
10. This intervention is consistent with those I have used in classroom settings.	1	2	3	4	5	6
11. The intervention was a fair way to handle the child's problem behavior.	1	2	3	4	5	6
12. This intervention is reasonable for the behavior problem described.	1	2	3	4	5	6
13. I liked the procedures used in this intervention.	1	2	3	4	5	6
14. This intervention was a good way to handle this child's behavior problem.	1	2	3	4	5	6
15. Overall, this intervention would be beneficial for the child.	1	2	3	4	5	6

From Witt and Elliott (1985). Reprinted with permission from Joseph C. Witt and Stephen N. Elliott.

Form 4.3

Children's Intervention Rating Profile (CIRP)

	I agree					I do not agree

1. The method used to deal with the behavior
   problem was fair.   + —— + —— + —— + —— + —— +

2. This child's teacher was too harsh on him.   + —— + —— + —— + —— + —— +

3. The method used to deal with the behavior
   may cause problems with this child's friend.   + —— + —— + —— + —— + —— +

4. There are better ways to handle this child's
   problem than the one described here.   + —— + —— + —— + —— + —— +

5. The method used by this teacher would be a
   good one to use with other children.   + —— + —— + —— + —— + —— +

6. I like the method used for this child's behavior
   problem.   + —— + —— + —— + —— + —— +

7. I think that the method used for this problem
   would help this child do better in school.   + —— + —— + —— + —— + —— +

From Witt and Elliott (1985). Reprinted with permission from Joseph C. Witt and Stephen N. Elliott.

---

accurately. In short, you cannot evaluate a program that is changed during the middle of year.

If the data suggest that the primary plan needs to include components to address specific areas such as anti-bullying or conflict resolution components, then we encourage schoolwide teams to ensure that the practices (i.e., the intervention and procedures) are evidence-based or, at a minimum, are promising practices. As previously mentioned, guidelines are now available for determining whether a specific practice is indeed evidence-based or promising (Gersten et al., 2005; Horner et al., 2005). In brief, treatment-outcome studies are evaluated against a set of quality indicators (e.g., description of participant settings, participant selection criteria, intervention features, external validity, internal validity, and social validity) to determine if the given study testing a practice is a "good-quality" study. Then, the studies that meet these standards are evaluated to determine if this body of literature establishes a practice as "evidence-based." For studies conducted using single-case methodology, this means that at least five studies conducted by three separate research groups with 20 participants must demonstrate experimental control. These same criteria should be used to evaluate the extent to which secondary- and tertiary-level prevention efforts are also evidence-based practices.

Form 4.4

Primary Intervention Rating Scale—
Preimplementation, Elementary Teacher Version

The purpose of this survey is to obtain information that will aid in determining the effectiveness and usefulness of the primary PBIS plan components for your elementary school. The PBIS plan components are to be used by all teachers. Please read the following statements regarding the primary PBIS plan developed by your school and circle the number which best describes your agreement or disagreement with each statement.

	Strongly Disagree	Disagree	Slightly Disagree	Slightly Agree	Agree	Strongly Agree
1. This would be an acceptable intervention for the elementary school.	1	2	3	4	5	6
2. Most teachers would find this intervention appropriate.	1	2	3	4	5	6
3. This intervention should prove effective in meeting the purposes.	1	2	3	4	5	6
4. I would suggest the use of this intervention to other teachers.	1	2	3	4	5	6
5. The intervention is appropriate to meet the school's needs and mission.	1	2	3	4	5	6
6. Most teachers would find this intervention suitable for the described purposes and mission.	1	2	3	4	5	6
7. I would be willing to use this intervention in the school setting.	1	2	3	4	5	6
8. This intervention would *not* result in negative side effects for the students.	1	2	3	4	5	6
9. This intervention would be appropriate for a variety of students.	1	2	3	4	5	6
10. This intervention is consistent with those I have used in school settings.	1	2	3	4	5	6
11. The intervention is a fair way to fulfill the intervention purposes.	1	2	3	4	5	6
12. This intervention plan is reasonable to meet the stated purposes.	1	2	3	4	5	6
13. I like the procedures used in this intervention.	1	2	3	4	5	6 (cont.)

Form 4.4 (cont.)	Strongly Disagree	Disagree	Slightly Disagree	Slightly Agree	Agree	Strongly Agree
14. This intervention is a good way to meet the specified purpose.	1	2	3	4	5	6
15. The monitoring procedures are manageable.	1	2	3	4	5	6
16. The monitoring procedures will give the necessary information to evaluate the plan.	1	2	3	4	5	6
17. Overall, this intervention would be beneficial for elementary school students.	1	2	3	4	5	6

Open-Ended Questions

1. What do you feel is most beneficial about this primary intervention? What is least beneficial part?

2. Do you think that your and your students' participation in this intervention will cause your students' behavior problems to improve/decrease?

3. What would you change about this intervention (components, design, implementation, etc.) to make it more student-friendly and teacher-friendly?

4. What other information would you like to contribute about this intervention?

Form 4.5

Primary Intervention Rating Scale—
Preimplementation, Middle School Teacher Version

The purpose of this survey is to obtain information that will aid in determining the effectiveness and usefulness of the primary PBIS plan components for your middle school. The PBIS plan components are to be used by all teachers. Please read the following statements regarding the primary PBIS plan developed by your school and circle the number which best describes your agreement or disagreement with each statement.

	Strongly Disagree	Disagree	Slightly Disagree	Slightly Agree	Agree	Strongly Agree
1. This would be an acceptable intervention for the middle school.	1	2	3	4	5	6
2. Most teachers would find this intervention appropriate.	1	2	3	4	5	6
3. This intervention should prove effective in meeting the purposes.	1	2	3	4	5	6
4. I would suggest the use of this intervention to other teachers.	1	2	3	4	5	6
5. The intervention is appropriate to meet the school's needs and mission.	1	2	3	4	5	6
6. Most teachers would find this intervention suitable for the described purposes and mission.	1	2	3	4	5	6
7. I would be willing to use this intervention in the school setting.	1	2	3	4	5	6
8. This intervention would *not* result in negative side effects for the students.	1	2	3	4	5	6
9. This intervention would be appropriate for a variety of students.	1	2	3	4	5	6
10. This intervention is consistent with those I have used in school settings.	1	2	3	4	5	6
11. The intervention is a fair way to fulfill the intervention purposes.	1	2	3	4	5	6
12. This intervention plan is reasonable to meet the stated purposes.	1	2	3	4	5	6
13. I like the procedures used in this intervention.	1	2	3	4	5	6 (cont.)

Form 4.5 (*cont.*)

	Strongly Disagree	Disagree	Slightly Disagree	Slightly Agree	Agree	Strongly Agree
14. This intervention is a good way to meet the specified purpose.	1	2	3	4	5	6
15. The monitoring procedures are manageable.	1	2	3	4	5	6
16. The monitoring procedures will give the necessary information to evaluate the plan.	1	2	3	4	5	6
17. Overall, this intervention would be beneficial for middle school students.	1	2	3	4	5	6

Open-Ended Questions

1. What do you feel is most beneficial about this primary intervention? What is least beneficial part?

2. Do you think that your and your students' participation in this intervention will cause your students' behavior problems to improve/decrease?

3. What would you change about this intervention (components, design, implementation, etc.) to make it more student-friendly and teacher-friendly?

4. What other information would you like to contribute about this intervention?

Form 4.6

Primary Intervention Rating Scale— Preimplementation, High School Teacher Version

The purpose of this survey is to obtain information that will aid in determining the effectiveness and usefulness of the primary PBIS plan components for your high school. The PBIS plan components are to be used by all teachers. Please read the following statements regarding the primary PBIS plan developed by your school and circle the number which best describes your agreement or disagreement with each statement.

	Strongly Disagree	Disagree	Slightly Disagree	Slightly Agree	Agree	Strongly Agree
1. This would be an acceptable intervention for the high school.	1	2	3	4	5	6
2. Most teachers would find this intervention appropriate.	1	2	3	4	5	6
3. This intervention should prove effective in meeting the purposes.	1	2	3	4	5	6
4. I would suggest the use of this intervention to other teachers.	1	2	3	4	5	6
5. The intervention is appropriate to meet the school's needs and mission.	1	2	3	4	5	6
6. Most teachers would find this intervention suitable for the described purposes and mission.	1	2	3	4	5	6
7. I would be willing to use this intervention in the school setting.	1	2	3	4	5	6
8. This intervention would *not* result in negative side effects for the students.	1	2	3	4	5	6
9. This intervention would be appropriate for a variety of students.	1	2	3	4	5	6
10. This intervention is consistent with those I have used in school settings.	1	2	3	4	5	6
11. The intervention is a fair way to fulfill the intervention purposes.	1	2	3	4	5	6
12. This intervention plan is reasonable to meet the stated purposes.	1	2	3	4	5	6
13. I like the procedures used in this intervention.	1	2	3	4	5	6 (cont.)

Form 4.6 (cont.)

	Strongly Disagree	Disagree	Slightly Disagree	Slightly Agree	Agree	Strongly Agree
14. This intervention is a good way to meet the specified purpose.	1	2	3	4	5	6
15. The monitoring procedures are manageable.	1	2	3	4	5	6
16. The monitoring procedures will give the necessary information to evaluate the plan.	1	2	3	4	5	6
17. Overall, this intervention would be beneficial for high school students.	1	2	3	4	5	6

Open-Ended Questions

1. What do you feel is most beneficial about this primary intervention? What is least beneficial part?

2. Do you think that your and your students' participation in this intervention will cause your students' behavior problems to improve/decrease?

3. What would you change about this intervention (components, design, implementation, etc.) to make it more student-friendly and teacher-friendly?

4. What other information would you like to contribute about this intervention?

Resources and Supports

Once the plan is solidified and inclusive of evidence-based practices, the next step is to secure the necessary resources and support to ensure proper implementation. In particular, we encourage schools to consider personnel and fiscal resources. We have had the privilege of working with incredibly creative schools that have secured financial support in some unique ways. One elementary school charged $10 to park cars in their school parking lot for people eager to attend local college football games. A middle school hosted a "lock-in" during which time parents could drop off their student at the school on a weekend evening for a fixed period of time and a nominal amount of money (e.g., $20 for 5 hours of child care!). In addition, schools have solicited donations from local businesses and have conducted PBIS silent auctions (see Box 4.11 for PBIS fundraising ideas).

Box 4.11. **PBIS Fundraising Ideas**

Lock-in	One school hosted a schoolwide "lock-in" that cost $20 per student. Students would be dropped off on a weekend evening about 5 P.M. and school staff would support and supervise (closely!) various activities (e.g., pizza, basketball, movies, arts & crafts, music) in the school gymnasium and cafeteria until parents picked them up at 10 P.M.
PBIS silent auctions	One PBIS team member paired up with the PTA and organized a silent auction on a weekday evening at which various items were auctioned (e.g., dinners, donated items) for parents of students. Parents were charged a fee to attend the auction, which went toward PBIS funds.
Donations	PBIS team members received donations from local businesses to support the school. Items varied from fast-food coupons, to NFL tickets, to overstock items at Target and Wal-Mart, to gift certificates.
Car wash	One high school student council group hosted a car wash in which all proceeds went to the PBIS funds.
Holiday-grams	One school collected various items (e.g., carnations for Valentine's Day, Halloween candy, candy canes, etc.) to be purchased by students and faculty and delivered to others in the school during the schoolday for various holidays/occasions (e.g., Valentine's Day, Halloween, finals week, homecoming).
Parking	One elementary school located near the local university charged $10 per car to park and walk to the university sporting events.
Mall quest	One middle school hired a bus to transport a group of teachers to the mall to solicit tangible items and gift certificates from all the stores.

Construct the Secondary and Tertiary Plans

Although beyond the scope of this text, PBIS teams also design secondary and tertiary levels of preventions based on the needs of the students in the school. For example, if the schoolwide data suggest that kindergarten students are struggling with decoding skills; fifth-grade students are generating high rates of referrals due to conflicts with peers during recreational times (e.g., recess and lunch); and students with internalizing behavior problems are showing high rates of absenteeism, then secondary-level supports can be designed for these groups of students. In Chapter 5 we introduce secondary intervention grids that illustrate this level of prevention. The secondary intervention grid includes the following: a program description, implementation logistics, entry and exit criteria, procedures for monitoring fidelity, and additional measures to monitor student outcomes for each secondary support. The same procedures are illustrated for identifying and implementing tertiary prevention efforts as well. This final level of supports is even more intensive and costly because tertiary interventions are designed for students with multiple risk factors and for those who were nonresponsive to primary and secondary prevention efforts.

Summary

In this chapter we carefully detailed a step-by-step approach to designing and implementing a primary prevention model that fits your particular school. To this end, we described our (1) team-based process for preparing schools to develop a customized model, (2) implementation procedures, and (3) strategies for teaching and reinforcing the desired student expectations. In the next chapter you'll find guidelines and forms for use in monitoring the implementation of the PBIS program as well as recommendations for monitoring student response to your primary prevention efforts.

Chapter Five

Assessment and Screening at the Primary Level

In this chapter we discuss procedures for monitoring program implementation (treatment integrity), assessing consumer feedback (social validity), monitoring student progress, and implementing procedures that systematically screen all students for possible behavior and academic concerns. First, we define treatment integrity, explain its importance, introduce a variety of ways to monitor it, and then offer suggestions as to who should monitor this part of your program. Second, we define social validity, explain why it should be considered when designing your plan, offer suggestions about whose opinions should be consulted, introduce a few ways of monitoring social validity, as well as make recommendations about who might conduct these assessments. Third, we present a practical assessment plan for monitoring how students respond to the primary-level program. Easy-to-follow guidelines are provided for selecting schoolwide intervention outcomes and monitoring student progress (academically, behaviorally, and socially). We emphasize the selection of reliable, valid measures to monitor student progress and allow administrators and teachers to determine whether the goals of the primary plan are being met. Finally, we explain the importance of conducting systematic screenings, describe current tools available for use across the kindergarten through 12th-grade span, and offer recommendations for how to put the screenings in place.

Monitoring Program Implementation: Is the Program Being Put in Place as Originally Planned?

Treatment Integrity Defined

Once an intervention plan has been designed, the next step is to put the plan in place. Rather than just assuming (remember what your high school teacher said about assuming!) that the program is working the way you intended it to, it is important to collect information to see if it is being implemented as originally designed—that is, ascertain the degree of *treatment integrity* (Gresham, 1989; Yeaton & Sechrest, 1981). In research terms, treatment integrity is a measure of the accuracy with which the independent variable (intervention) is instituted as planned. Without treatment integrity data, it would be difficult, if not impossible, to draw accurate conclusions regarding intervention outcomes (Peterson, Homer, & Wonderlich, 1982). In other words, you would not be able to tell if the plan is working.

The Importance of Monitoring Treatment Integrity

It is very important to measure treatment integrity in order to determine whether the plan is in place and how well it is being used. In the past, interventions were often implemented but not monitored for fidelity (Lane, Bocian, et al., 2004). This omission was a critical problem because without treatment integrity data, you cannot draw accurate conclusions about *why* a program did or did not produce the desired outcomes. For example, it could be that ODRs did not decrease because the program did not work (poor program), or it could be that not all program components were put in place as originally designed (poor treatment integrity). Similarly, if ODRs decreased but treatment integrity data was not monitored, you couldn't be sure if the decrease was attributable to the plan you designed or because the teachers changed the current program or perhaps even introduced a new program.

Methods of Monitoring Treatment Integrity

Treatment integrity can be measured—and hence monitored—in a variety of ways and from different perspectives. For example, it can be monitored by using behavior checklists that contain key components of the plan. These checklists can be completed by the people at the school site who are responsible for program implementation (e.g., teachers, administrators, office workers). This type of information is referred to as *self-report data*, and it can be less than accurate in some cases, although still useful (some people tend to rate themselves somewhat higher than their actual performance so that they look good to others; Lane, Beebe-Frankenberger, Lambros, & Pierson, 2001). Behavior checklists can also be completed by outside observers to obtain a more objective perspective on how the plan is being implemented.

   In Box 5.1 you'll see an example of a completed form. In this case, components 1, 4, 5, 6, 7, 8, 9, 10, 12, 13, 15, 16, and 17 were done *"all of the time,"* receiving a rating of 2. Yet, the teacher received a 0 on component 11 because the mission and vision statements were not posted, and a 1 on component 3 because the teacher only had a starting activity and not a closing activity. An overall percentage of the score was computed by adding up all the points earned (29) and dividing by the number of points possible (40), to receive an overall score of 73%. You can also compute the treatment fidelity for each domain—Academic Responsibilities: Procedures for Teaching ($10/12 \times 100 = 83\%$; see Box 5.1), Behavioral and Social Responsibilities: Procedures for Teaching ($12/14 \times 100 = 86\%$) and Academic, Behavioral, and Social Responsibilities: Procedures for Reinforcing ($7/14 \times 100 = 50\%$)—if you would like to see where some teachers could benefit from coaching. In our work we have created average component and session scores for teachers and for the school as a whole. Component integrity allows you to see

Box 5.1. **Sample Completed Treatment Integrity Form**

Teacher ____Sam Smith____   Teacher ID Number __17__   School ____Fanning____

Subject Taught ____Literature Circle_____   Grade Level(s) ____2nd____

Date Completed ____8/31/10____   Observation: Start Time __9:15__   End Time: __9:45__

Rater: ☐ Teacher Perspective   ☐ Outside Observer Perspective

Academic Responsibilities: Procedures for Teaching	#	**Not at All (0)**	**Part of the Time (1)**	**All of the Time (2)**
Provide engaging lessons, linked to the district standards.	1			2
Differentiate instruction.	2		1	
Include starter and closing activities as part of the lesson plan.	3		1	
Support students who miss instruction.	4			2
Engage in positive teacher–teacher and teacher–student interactions.	5			2
Encourage the use of daily planners.	6			2
Behavioral and Social Responsibilities: Procedures for Teaching	#	**Not at All (0)**	**Part of the Time (1)**	**All of the Time (2)**
Display posters and expectations matrix.	7			2
Teach and model schoolwide expectations.	8			2
Allow students to attend monthly schoolwide assemblies.	9			2
Allow students to listen to morning and afternoon announcements, including the PBIS instructional videos.	10			2
Post the school mission statement and vision.	11	0		
Teach monthly social skills curriculum: Character under Construction.	12			2
Teach and support anti-bullying program.	13			2

(cont.)

Box 5.1 (*cont.*)				
Academic, Behavioral, and Social Components: Procedures for Reinforcing	**#**	**Not at All (0)**	**Part of the Time (1)**	**All of the Time (2)**
Use verbal praise paired with a PBIS ticket to reinforce appropriate student behaviors.	14		*1*	
Provide photos and nominations for the "You Caught Me" Wall	15			*2*
Allow students to participate in PBIS drawings, assemblies, and various reinforcer options.	16			*2*
Participate in various reinforcer options and post reinforcer menu.	17			*2*
Mail home "You Caught Me" postcards.	18	*0*		
Post student-made PBIS posters.	19	*0*		
Conduct weekly surprise drawings.	20	*0*		
Overall percentage score				*73%*

how a certain program component (e.g., "*Use verbal praise paired with a PBIS ticket to reinforce appropriate student behaviors*") is implemented over the course of a school year. Session integrity allows you to evaluate how a teacher is implementing the program components overall during a certain period of time (e.g., monthly or quarterly). Both pieces of information can be used to determine how the primary prevention program is being implemented. Then this information can be used to shape the program for next year. For example, if you find that teachers are not taking the students to the award assemblies (component 16), then the team can meet with those teachers to find out what it is about the assemblies (e.g., the time of day? the day of the week? content?) that is prompting them not to take their class.

In addition to behavior checklists, standardized measures such as the School-wide Evaluation Tool Version 2.1 (SET; Sugai et al., 2005) are available to monitor the implementation of the primary prevention level of a three-tiered PBIS plan. The SET contains 28 items constituting seven subscales to evaluate the seven key features of SWPBS (Horner et al., 2004). The key features evaluated on the subscales include: (1) schoolwide behavior expectations are defined, (2) schoolwide expectations are taught to all students in the school, (3) rewards are provided for following schoolwide behavior expectations, (4) a consistently implemented continuum of consequences for problem behavior is in place, (5) problem behavior patterns are monitored and the information is used to inform ongoing decision making, (6) an administrator actively supports and is involved in the SWPBS program, and (7) the school district provides support to the school (e.g., functional policies, staff training opportunities, and data collection; Horner et al., 2004). Each item on the SET is scored on a 3-point Likert-type scale ranging from 0 (*not implemented*), to 1 (*partially implemented*), to 2 (*fully implemented*). Next, summary scores for each subscale are computed by determining the percentage of possible points for each of the seven key features. Then, an overall total summary score is computed by taking the average of the seven subscale scores. The SET has strong psychometric properties with an overall alpha coefficient of 0.96 and test–retest reliability of 97.3% (Horner et al., 2004).

In our work we complete the SET at the beginning (6 weeks into the school year) and end (6 weeks prior to the end of the school year) of the school year. In Box 5.2 you'll see a summary report for a hypothetical elementary school. The school had a high level of fidelity during fall 2010, with an overall SET score of 89.29%. During the following fall, the level of fidelity as measured by the SET was even higher, with a total SET score of 98.21%. During fall 2010, the school scored 100% on four components: expectations defined, behavioral expectations taught, ongoing system for rewarding behavioral expectations, and monitoring and decision making. These same four components were also fully present during fall 2011. In addition, the school improved in the three remaining areas, with only one component—system for responding to behavioral violations (87.5%)—with less than 100%.

In our work we rely on a combination of methods to monitor treatment fidelity (see Lane, Kalberg, Bruhn, et al., in press). First, each teacher completes monthly component checklists to self-report his or her implementation of the program (see Form 5.1). Second, outside observers watch each teacher for a 20- to 30-minute period to examine implementation during a randomly selected time period. At the end of this time period, the teacher is also asked to complete a separate checklist on how he or she viewed his or her implementation during the same observation period. These perspectives are compared to see if the outside observers and the teachers' self-ratings are comparable. For example, in Figure 5.1, you can see that teachers, on average, rated themselves with higher fidelity as compared to outside observer ratings, with both raters reporting similar levels of fidelity in April and May. This information can be used to provide feedback to teachers and help shape the design of the PBIS plan.

As you can see, treatment integrity ratings may vary according to who completes the ratings or which rating system is used (Lane, Kalberg, Bruhn, et al., in press). As noted above, teacher self-report scores tend to be somewhat higher than outside observer ratings. This is not to suggest that faculty and staff should not self-evaluate the degree to which they are implementing the plan as designed. The self-monitoring literature suggests that the simple act of recording and evaluating one's own behavior can actually change and/or improve behavior (DuPaul & Hoff, 1998; Jones, Wickstrom, & Friman, 1997; Peterson, Young, Salzberg, West, & Hill, 2006). From a behavioral perspective, the act of completing the monthly treatment integrity forms may serve as a prompt for

92   *Chapter Five*

Box 5.2. **Hypothetical Results from School-wide Evaluation Tool Data (SET; Sugai, Lewis-Palmer, Todd, & Horner, 2005)**

	Category	Fidelity scores					
		Total points earned fall 2010	Total points possible fall 2010	Percent earned fall 2010	Total points earned fall 2011	Total points possible fall 2011	Percent earned fall 2011
Schoolwide components	Expectations defined	4	4	100%	4	4	100%
	Behavioral expectations taught	10	10	100%	10	10	100%
	Ongoing system for rewarding behavioral expectations	6	6	100%	6	6	100%
	System for responding to behavioral violations	5	8	62.5%	7	8	87.5%
	Monitoring and decision making	8	8	100%	8	8	100%
	Management	14	16	87.5%	16	16	100%
	District-level support	3	4	75%	4	4	100%
	Total *(average of percentages)*			89.29%			98.21%

program participation (e.g., "Oh yeah, I need to remember to give behavior-specific praise when giving out the PBIS tickets"). However, it is important to consider the potential discrepancy between self-report and outside observer ratings (Lane, Kalberg, Bruhn, et al., in press).

Deciding Who Will Monitor Treatment Integrity

When deciding who will monitor treatment integrity, we strongly encourage schools to measure it from more than one perspective. For example, the PBIS team members might complete the SET at the beginning and end of each school year and conduct classroom

Form 5.1

Monthly Treatment Integrity Rating Scale (Teacher Completed)

Teacher _____ Teacher ID Number _____ School _____

Subject Taught _____ Grade Level(s) _____

Date Completed _____ Month Evaluated _____

Academic Responsibilities: Procedures for Teaching	#	Not at All (0)	Part of the Time (1)	All of the Time (2)
Provide engaging lessons, linked to the district standards.	1			
Differentiate instruction.	2			
Include starter and closing activities as part of the lesson plan.	3			
Support students who miss instruction.	4			
Engage in positive teacher–teacher and teacher–student interactions.	5			
Encourage the use of daily planners.	6			
Behavioral and Social Responsibilities: Procedures for Teaching	#	Not at All (0)	Part of the Time (1)	All of the Time (2)
Display posters and expectations matrix.	7			
Teach and model schoolwide expectations.	8			
Allow students to attend monthly schoolwide assemblies.	9			
Allow students to listen to morning and afternoon announcements, including the PBIS instructional videos.	10			
Post the school mission statement and vision.	11			
Teach monthly social skills curriculum: Character under Construction.	12			
Teach and support anti-bullying program.	13			

(cont.)

Form 5.1 (cont.)

Academic, Behavioral, and Social Components: Procedures for Reinforcing	#	Not at All (0)	Part of the Time (1)	All of the Time (2)
Use verbal praise paired with a PBIS ticket to reinforce appropriate student behaviors.	14			
Provide photos and nominations for the "You Caught Me" Wall	15			
Allow students to participate in PBIS drawings, assemblies, and various reinforcer options.	16			
Participate in various reinforcer options and post reinforcer menu.	17			
Mail home "You Caught Me" postcards.	18			
Post student-made PBIS posters.	19			
Conduct weekly surprise drawings.	20			
Overall Total				

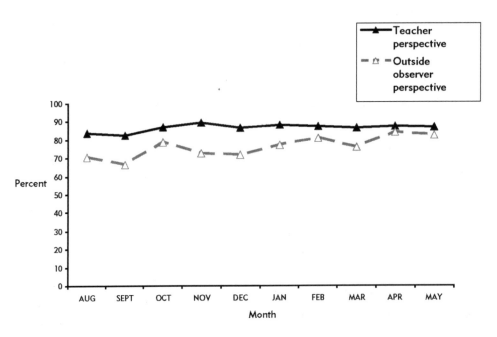

Figure 5.1. **Treatment integrity data: Teacher and outside observer ratings.**

observations of each teacher once per semester or as part of annual teaching evaluations. In addition, a PBIS team may ask teachers to complete self-report checklists monthly or quarterly both to monitor implementation and to prompt teachers to participate actively in the program (Lane, Kalberg, Bruhn, et al., in press).

For the reasons mentioned above, it is essential that implementation be measured and not assumed. Once you have decided who will monitor treatment integrity, make sure to provide the raters with (1) training in how to conduct the evaluations and provide formative feedback to the persons rated, (2) time to conduct the evaluations, (3) assistance with the analysis of the information acquired, and (4) time to share feedback with the entire faculty staff in a manner that informs but does not embarrass anyone.

When doing any type of intervention work, it is important to measure treatment integrity—the extent to which the intervention plan was put in place as designed (Gresham, 1989). If treatment integrity is not assessed, then it is not possible to draw accurate conclusions regarding intervention outcomes. Consequently, it is imperative that treatment integrity data be collected using research-based approaches (e.g., the SET or direct observation procedures) and, ideally, from multiple perspectives.

Assessing Consumer Feedback: What Do People Think about the Program?

Social Validity Defined

When conducting any type of intervention, it is important to obtain input from the persons involved regarding the intervention goals, procedures, and outcomes to establish their *social validity*. More specifically, social validity refers to the social significance of the intervention goals, the social acceptability of intervention procedures, and the social importance of effects produced by the intervention (Kazdin, 1977; Lane & Beebe-Frankenberger, 2004; Wolf, 1978).

Social validity can be measured before an intervention begins, during implementation, and following intervention completion. We recommend assessing social validity of schoolwide programs prior to intervention onset and then again at the end of each academic year.

The purpose of assessing social validity before getting started is to make sure that all parties involved (e.g., faculty, staff, parents, and, in some cases, students) are "on the same page." Namely, do all parties view the program goals (e.g., improving attendance, decreasing behaviors that lead to ODRs) to be important? Are the procedures viewed as acceptable? For example, do the required components, such as using tickets paired with verbal praise to acknowledge students who meet expectations, "fit" with teachers' instructional styles? Is the program likely to produce the desired outcomes; meaning, do people think the program will "work"? If the people involved do not think that the program is targeting the right goals; if the procedures are viewed as too labor intensive or in conflict with cultural or personal values (e.g., if people do not believe in giving tangible rewards; Lane, Kalberg, Bruhn, et al., in press); or if people do not think the program is likely to work, then it is quite possible that the program will be implemented with low levels of integrity—which *is* apt to influence programs in a negative way (Gresham & Lopez, 1996; Lane & Beebe-Frankenberger, 2004). In short, if the people do not "buy in" to the program, the program either needs to be modified or additional training is needed to help staff reach consensus on the program components. Persons involved must be in agreement that the educational experiences of students and the school climate are apt to improve if the program is implemented as planned, and that program implementation will provide students with more reliable, efficient strategies for experiencing academic, social, and behavioral success in the school setting (Gresham & Lopez; Lane et al., 2001; Noell & Gresham, 1993).

Further, the participants need to view the intervention procedures as worth the investment (Reimers, Wacker, & Koeppl, 1987). Teachers working in chaotic, violent, or apathetic environments may be more willing to implement the required intervention procedures than teachers working in predictable, safe, productive environments. In general, the type and severity of a problem; the time, effort, and cost associated with conducting the intervention; the level of training and support provided during implementation; and the extent to which the intervention procedures will influence the environment are all highly predictive of treatment acceptability (Gresham & Kendell, 1987). Finally, to invest the time in implementing the intervention as designed, participants need to view the program as likely to meet the intervention goals, some of which may be immediate (e.g., less disruption and more instructional time) and others that may be more distal (e.g., improved academic outcomes for students; Fawcett, 1991). By assessing social validity prior to intervention onset, it is possible to later determine if the intervention met, fell short, or even exceeded initial expectations (Lane, Little, et al., 2007). It also provides a method with which to determine whether the intervention was "worth it" in terms of time, money, personnel, and other costs (Noell & Gresham). Additionally, social validity measures gathered prior to onset of the program can be used as a baseline and later compared to subsequent time points (e.g., months, years). This information may also allow comparisons to be drawn regarding the level of social acceptability as the PBIS plan is modified.

We recommend collecting social validity data at the end of each year to evaluate the extent to which these initial expectations were met and to inform the following year's school plan. The point of the data is to determine if the intervention targeted worthy goals (social significance of the goals) and if those goals were met (social importance of effects). Were there meaningful lasting changes evident, also referred to as *habilitative validity* (Baer et al., 1968, 1987; Hawkins, 1991)? Did the school see improvements in attendance and decreases in ODRs? Over a few years, were there improvements in grade-point averages (GPAs)? In addition, we again assess social acceptability of intervention (treatment) procedures to determine if the steps and components were satisfactory to the people involved. For example, it may have been that teachers who initially thought it would be burdensome to pass out tickets and pair them with verbal praise to recognize students who met desired behaviors (e.g., using a quiet voice in the hallway) later found that it was quite simple to do so in their classrooms and in noninstructional areas (e.g., cafeteria, hallway). This information can be ascertained from assessing social validity. Once acquired, the information obtained from assessing the social acceptability of the treatment procedures can be used by teams to (1) provide a forum for discussions about the schoolwide plan; (2) inform future intervention efforts (e.g., what components to keep or to revise); and (3) predict treatment integrity of similar plans (Lane & Beebe-Frankenberger, 2004).

The Importance of Assessing Social Validity

In recent years, many secondary and tertiary level intervention studies have begun to assess social validity from various perspectives (Lane, Barton-Arwood, et al., 2007), but relatively few studies of schoolwide intervention efforts include measures of social validity (Lane, Kalberg, & Edwards, 2008; Lane, Robertson, & Graham-Bailey, 2006). A recent review of schoolwide primary prevention efforts at the elementary level (Lane, Kalberg, Edwards, et al., 2008) revealed that only 6 of 19 studies mentioned and reported social validity (Ervin et al., 2006; Leff et al., 2003; McCurdy et al., 2003; Nelson, 1996; Nelson et al., 2002; Todd et al., 2002). Similarly, a systematic review of primary prevention efforts at the middle and high school levels (Lane, Robertson, Graham-Bailey, et al., 2006) indicated that 8 of 14 studies mentioned social validity from the teacher, student, and/or parent perspective (Cook et al., 1999; Gottfredson et al., 1993; Kartub et al., 2000; Mehas, Boling, Sobieniak, Burke, & Hagan, 1998; Metzler et al., 2001; Skiba & Perterson, 2003; Taylor-Green et al., 1997; Taylor-Greene & Kartub, 2000). Social validity was assessed in a variety of ways (e.g., cost–benefit perceptions, Ervin et al.), but most of the methods were informal, such as ratings scales that were not validated.

We view the absence of social validity information as a possible explanation as to why some interventions fail to be implemented as designed. If the intervention agents (e.g., teachers, staff, and parents) do not view the goal as worthy, the procedures as reasonable, and the desired changes as likely to occur, then it should not be surprising that they lack the motivation to implement the plan as designed (Lane & Beebe-Frankenberger, 2004). Therefore, we suggest assessing social validity prior to and after the intervention for a number of reasons. First, collecting social validity allows people to come to consensus on the target areas for the intervention and to establish a clear picture of the difference between the current and desired level of performance (Bergan & Kratochwill, 1990). Second, social validity data can help identify important feasible target areas for primary prevention efforts. Third, the information can facilitate discussion regarding the procedures and supports necessary to provide natural contingencies and reinforcement for the desired behaviors. Fourth, the information can assist the participants in coming to consensus on goals and procedures to make sure that the intended changes in performance (academic, behavior, and social skills) occur. Fifth, social validity data are an important part of program evaluation as it relates to immediate and maintained intervention outcomes (Lane & Beebe-Frankenberger). When all parties involved participate in choosing intervention goals and procedures, they are more likely to invest effort in paving the path for successful student outcomes (see Box 5.3) that will, in turn, create successful outcomes for faculty, staff, and parents alike. Particularly important to intervention success is attention to the social and cultural values of *all* involved individuals.

Box 5.3. **PBIS Cures the Flu!**

Below is an e-mail we received from a vice principal of a middle school implementing a primary prevention program:

```
Here are numbers of students absent for the past 2 weeks starting
2/14--today, 46, 39, 49, 46, 41, 37, 34, today 18--today just happens
to be reward assembly ... they all happen to get better today,
PBIS a cure for the flu!
```

Note. Reprinted with permission from a school-site vice principal. School name omitted to protect anonymity.

Social Validity: Whom to Ask and How

We recommend assessing social validity from multiple perspectives because each participant plays a different role in the intervention (Lane & Beebe-Frankenberger, 2004). Specifically, we encourage researchers and practitioners to assess social validity from the following perspectives: team members, administrators, teachers and support staff, parents, and students. By assessing the extent to which these parties view the goals as significant, procedures as acceptable, and outcomes as important, we can make important predictions about (1) the extent to which the intervention is apt to be implemented as designed and (2) the likelihood that the new behavioral expectations are likely to generalize and be maintained in other settings. For example, many teachers and staff have certain academic, behavioral, and social expectations for students in their classroom and in the school setting as a whole (e.g., following directions the first time and controlling oneself in conflict situation with peers; Kerr & Zigmond, 1986; Lane, Givner, et al., 2004; Lane, Wehby, Little, & Cooley, 2005a, 2005b; Walker & Rankin, 1983). Yet, teachers also have different teaching styles (Evertson & Weade, 1989) and tolerance levels (Shinn, Tindal, & Spira, 1987). If the schoolwide goals or procedures are in conflict with teachers' instructional styles or tolerance levels, then teachers will be less likely to view the plan as socially valid—which in turn may lead to lower levels of treatment fidelity (Gresham & Kendell, 1987).

Similarly, it is equally important to consider parents' perspectives. (When we say *parent*, we are referring to any significant adult [e.g., guardian, foster parent, grandparent] who assumes primary responsibility for caretaking.) If schoolwide expectations are in conflict with parents' core values for academic and behavioral expectations, it is likely that the student will receive conflicting information as to the importance of meeting the stated schoolwide expectations. It is necessary to enlist parental support in the primary plan because research evidence suggests that students are apt to be more academically successful when their parents are involved in, and supportive of, their education (Brown, Mounts, Lamborn, & Sternberg, 1993). In addition, students are more likely to achieve academic and social success in schools if their parents establish boundaries to support these goals (Alexander, Entwisle, & Dauber, 1994; Walker, Zeller, Close, Webber, & Gresham, 1999). We are not suggesting that teachers and parents must have 100% agreement on the specific behavioral expectations established in the school setting. However, we want to convey that the best-case scenario is to promote behavioral expectations that are acceptable to both parents and teachers so that students are reinforced for meeting these expectations in the home and school setting. If there are differences in expectations in the home and school settings, we encourage that these differences be acknowledged and dealt with respectfully (Lane, Stanton-Chapman, et al., 2007).

We also think it is important to gain student input regarding the plan's social validity. If students view the goals to be important and the procedures reasonable, it is possible that their "buy in" will foster positive intervention outcomes. For example, if students feel it is essential to communicate their opinions, then a behavioral goal of learning how to begin a conversation respectfully when you disagree with someone is likely to be learned and used. The procedures for teaching the targeted behaviors must also be age appropriate. Middle and high school students who perceive that a program is too "babyish" will be unwilling to participate. In addition, student input regarding reinforcement is essential. Preintervention social validity information can be used to determine what is (and is not!) reinforcing to students. It is possible that students' motivation for participating in any intervention is enhanced by including reinforcers (e.g., assemblies that afford time with friends) that are "better" than the types of reinforcement they received for *not* meeting the schoolwide expectations (Horner & Billingsley, 1988). Unfortunately, very few studies have investigated the value of assessing social validity from the student perspective (Elliott, Turco, & Gresham, 1987).

How to Measure Social Validity

As we mentioned previously, only a handful of schoolwide intervention studies have assessed social validity (Cook et al., 1999; Ervin et al., 2006; Gottfredson et al., 1993; Kartub et al., 2000; Leff et al., 2003; McCurdy et al., 2003; Mehas et al., 1998; Metzler et al., 2001; Nelson, 1996; Nelson et al., 2002; Skiba & Perterson, 2003; Taylor-Greene et al., 1997; Taylor-Greene & Kartub, 2000; Todd et al., 2002). For example, Cook and colleagues assessed social validity from three perspectives (teacher, student, and parent). However, many secondary- and tertiary-level prevention programs regularly assess social validity. When conducting schoolwide intervention efforts, it is possible to use several techniques also used by targeted (secondary and tertiary) level supports. These include self-report rating scales and surveys (Finn & Sladeczek, 2001; Kazdin, 1977), interviews (Gresham & Lopez, 1996), and repeated use (i.e., if the intervention is used on an ongoing basis, it is socially valid).

Self-Report Rating Scales and Surveys

In our work we have collected social validity data from teacher, parent, and student perspectives prior to implementing primary prevention programs. To assess different consumer perspectives of social validity, we modified the Intervention Rating Profile-15 (IRP-15; Witt & Elliott, 1985; see Form 4.2 in Chapter 4), which we refer to as the Primary Intervention Rating Scale (PIRS; Lane, Robertson, et al., 2002; see Forms 4.4, 4.5, and 4.6 in Chapter 4 for elementary, middle, and high school versions of the PIRS). The PIRS was used to measure faculty opinion about the social significance of the intervention goals, social acceptability of the intervention procedures, and probability of socially important outcomes (Kazdin, 1997; Wolf, 1978). The IRP-15 is a 15-item, psychometrically sound survey used to measure teacher perceptions of the treatment. Teachers rate each item on a 6-point Likert-type scale ranging from 1 (*strongly disagree*) to 6 (*strongly agree*). Internal consistency reliabilities range from 0.88 to 0.98, suggesting strong psychometric properties. The IRP-15 was adapted for use with primary prevention programs in two ways. First, the wording of some items was changed to reflect a schoolwide, primary prevention program rather than a targeted intervention for a given child. Second, we added two additional items regarding monitoring procedures (Item 15: *The monitoring procedures are manageable*; Item 16: *The monitoring procedures give the necessary information to evaluate the plan*). With the addition of two new items, total scores of the PIRS ranged from 17 to 102. In addition, the PIRS contains four open-ended questions:

1. What do you feel is most beneficial about this primary intervention? What is least beneficial part?
2. Do you think that your and your students' participation in this intervention will cause your students' behavior problems to improve/decrease?
3. What would you change about this intervention (components, design, implementation, etc.) to make it more student-friendly and teacher-friendly?
4. What other information would you like to contribute about this intervention?

A recent validation study of the PIRS data completed by elementary, middle, and high school teachers prior to beginning the schoolwide program suggested strong reliability, with internal consistency estimates ranging from 0.97 to 0.98 (Lane, Kalberg, Bruhn, et al., 2008). However, additional studies of the PIRS are warranted before adopting this measure as a reliable, valid tool for monitoring consumers' opinions over the course of program implementation.

Given that few validated social validity forms have been developed for use with schoolwide, primary prevention programs, another option is to develop and administer social validity surveys to obtain information from administrators, faculty, staff, parents, and students. For example, Form 5.2 is an example of a brief social validity survey, the Primary Prevention Plan: Feedback Form (Lane, 2002), developed to obtain input from faculty and staff. However, it is important to recognize the limitations of using an instrument whose accuracy and consistency of measurement have not been validated.

Interviews

Another option is to conduct interviews with individuals who represent the various parties of interest. Gresham and Lopez (1996) developed a semistructured interview for use with classroom teachers (see Form 5.3). The three sections included in their interview protocol parallel the three components of social validity: the social significance of the goals, the social acceptability of the treatment procedures, and the social importance of the effects. Form 5.4 is a modified version that can be used to obtain information

Primary Prevention Plan: Feedback Form

Your positive behavior interventions and supports team has drafted a primary intervention plan to put in place at your school beginning fall _____. We would like to get your input on this draft. Please read the attached plan and then answer these few questions. Thank you!

1. What are the strengths of the plan?

2. What concerns do you have about the primary intervention plan?

3. What suggestions do you have for modifying the plan?

4. To what extent do you think the plan will achieve the intended goals/objectives?

Please rate each of the following statements.

Statement	Strongly Disagree	Somewhat Disagree	Somewhat Agree	Strongly Agree
1. I think the plan targets important goals and/ or objectives.	1	2	3	4
2. I think the plan is feasible.	1	2	3	4
3. I think the plan is likely to be put in place as planned.	1	2	3	4
4. I will implement the plan.	1	2	3	4
5. I think the plan will produce the desired outcomes.	1	2	3	4

Form 5.3

Semistructured Interview for Social Validation

Consultee's Name _____ Date _____

Consultant's Name _____ School _____

A. Social Significance of Goals

1. What behaviors led you to request consultation?
2. Which behaviors are the most problematic for in your classroom?
3. Describe how these behaviors cause classroom problems.
4. If these problematic behaviors were decreased or eliminated, how would this affect _____ (the client)? Other students in your classroom? Your teaching in your classroom?
5. Do you see these behaviors as skill deficits? Performance deficits? What do you base this on?
6. Define each behavior as specifically as possible.
7. How do these behaviors affect other students in your classroom? Students in other classrooms?
8. How do these behaviors affect other school personnel (e.g., principal, other teachers, staff, etc.)?
9. Which behavior(s) do you think would be the most beneficial for to change now? Why? Which behavior(s) would have the greatest long-term benefits for ? Why?

B. Social Acceptability of Procedures

10. How do you feel about the procedures we discussed to change behavior?
11. Which aspects of the intervention do you like the most? Why? Which do you like the least? Why?
12. Which aspects of this intervention would be the most difficult to implement? Why? Which aspects would be the least difficult to implement? Why?
13. Here are some ways in which we could change the intervention. Do these changes make the intervention more acceptable and easier to implement? Why? What would you recommend for the further changes?
14. What, if any, potential negative effects might this intervention have on ? On other students in your classroom?
15. Do you think this intervention is likely to be effective in solving _____'s problem? Why? Why not? What are some ways we could determine whether or not the intervention had solved _____'s problem?

C. Social Importance of Effects

16. Describe how well you think the intervention worked.
17. What behavior changes did you observe? Did these changes make a difference in _____'s behavior in your classroom? In other school settings (e.g., other classrooms, cafeteria, playground, etc.)?
18. Is 's behavior now similar to that of the average student in your classroom? If not, do you think that continued use of the intervention would accomplish this goal? Why or why not? How long do you think this might take if we continued this intervention?
19. Are you satisfied with the outcomes of this intervention? How satisfied are you? Why?
20. Do you think this intervention would work with similar problems in the future? Why or why not?
21. Would you recommend this intervention to other teachers? Why or why not? What aspects of this intervention would you change before recommending this intervention to other teachers?

Form 5.4

Modified Semistructured Interview for Social Validation

Name _____ Date _____

Role _____ School _____

A. Social Significance of Goals

1. What school-site concerns led your school to develop a three-tiered model of prevention?

2. Which of these concerns are most problematic?

3. How do these concerns influence student and teacher performance?

4. Describe how these concerns cause classroom problems.

5. What are your goals for this program?

6. If this primary prevention program meets the goals, how will that outcome influence your job or experience at the school?

7. Describe the short-term and long-term benefits of participating in the primary prevention plan.

B. Social Acceptability of Procedures

1. How do you feel about the procedures put in place for the primary plan?
   a. Academic responsibilities: procedures for teaching and reinforcing
   b. Behavioral responsibilities: procedures for teaching and reinforcing
   c. Social responsibilities: procedures for teaching and reinforcing

2. Which components of the primary prevention plan do you like the most? Why?

3. Which components of the primary prevention plan do you like the least? Why?

4. Which components of the primary prevention plan would be the most difficult to implement? Why?

5. Which components of the primary prevention plan would be the least difficult to implement? Why?

6. What, if any, potential negative effects might this primary prevention plan have on students? Teachers? Other persons?

7. How do you feel about the procedures put in place for monitoring:
   a. Student performance: Academically? Behaviorally? Socially?
   b. Treatment integrity?
   c. Social validity?

C. Social Importance of Effects

1. Describe how well you think the primary prevention will work (did work).

2. Are/were the costs (time, personnel, resources) required to implement the plan worth the effort? Explain.

3. How satisfied are you with the outcomes of this primary prevention? Why?

4. What aspects of the primary prevention plan would you change?

5. Would you recommend this type of primary prevention plan to other schools? Why or why not?

about your schoolwide plan from administrator, faculty and staff, parent, and student perspectives.

Repeated Use

Yet another method of measuring social validity is to examine the degree to which (1) other consumers use the intervention in the future (e.g., when the vice principal is promoted to a principal position at another school and implements a schoolwide plan); or (2) whether the current consumers sustain the schoolwide intervention in the absence of ongoing university or outside support. In brief, if the intervention is used—and used as designed—then it is acceptable. In short, "use" acts a behavioral marker for "acceptability" (Gresham & Lopez, 1996).

Once you've decided how social validity will be assessed, it is necessary to determine who will actually collect the social validity data. For example, some principals have required an annual social validity survey to be completed both at the beginning of the year (before students attend the first day of classes) and again at the end of the year as part of staff check-in and check-out procedures. In other schools, the PBIS team has asked faculty members and randomly selected groups of parents and their students to complete social validity measures.

Social validity is an important, although often overlooked, component of interventions (Gersten et al., 2005; Horner et al., 2005; Lane et al., 2001). We hope you will consider assessing social validity from a range of perspectives to (1) inform intervention construction, (2) predict treatment integrity, (3) assist in interpreting intervention outcomes, and (4) foster a collaborative partnership between all persons involved (Lane, 1999; Lane & Beebe-Frankenberger, 2004). In order to ensure that consumers answer surveys accurately and honestly, it is essential to establish the program's credibility as well the credibility of those involved with bringing it to the school site. Creating rapport is also essential in fostering a climate in which everyone feels that their suggestions about the design and implementation of the program are valued. Establishing credibility and rapport increases the ability of a school system to accurately measure social validity (Lane & Beebe-Frankenberger).

Monitoring Student Progress:
How Are Students Responding to the Program?

The next big area to monitor is the progress students make in reaching the goals you have set for them. For example, if the school's goal is to decrease office discipline referrals (ODRs), improve attendance, and improve academic performance, then it is necessary to regularly collect and monitor data that directly address these areas. By doing so, you can make judgments about how the plan is influencing student behavior. In essence, the goal is to establish treatment validity (not to be confused with social validity) by linking assessment to the primary prevention plan. More specifically, treatment validity refers to the degree to which assessment information contributes to useful treatment outcomes (Gresham, Lane, & Lambros, 2000).

Once you have identified the types of information that will help you evaluate the effectiveness of your plan, the next step is to collect and analyze these data so that you can monitor all aspects of the plan: behavior measures (e.g., ODRs, in-school suspensions, out-of-school suspensions), academic measures (e.g., standardized measures such as state standardized tests; curriculum-based measures such as the Dynamic Indicators of Basic Early Literacy [DIBELS; Kaminski & Good, 1996] or AIMSweb [Harcourt, 2008]), as well as the treatment integrity and social validity data, as described above. See Tables 5.1, 5.2, and 5.3 for illustrations of sample assessment schedules at the elementary, middle, and high school levels. You will note that the assessment schedules for the

Table 5.1. **Orange Elementary School Assessment Schedule**

Measure	Aug.	Sept.	Oct.	Nov.	Dec.	Jan.	Feb.	Mar.	Apr.	May
Report cards and progress reports		X			X	X			X	
Writing assessment		X			X				X	
Curriculum-based measures	X	X	X	X	X	X	X	X	X	X
Statewide assessment										X
Office discipline referrals	X	X	X	X	X	X	X	X	X	X
SRSS (Drummond, 1994)		X			X				X	
SSBD (Walker & Severson, 1992)		X			X				X	
Attendance	X	X	X	X	X	X	X	X	X	X
Counseling referrals	X	X	X	X	X	X	X	X	X	X
Bullying referrals	X	X	X	X	X	X	X	X	X	X
Social validity survey: PIRS (Lane, Robertson, & Wehby, 2002)		X							X	
SET 2.1 (Sugai, Lewis-Palmer, et al., 2005)		X							X	
Treatment integrity: self-report and direct observations by an outside observer	X	X	X	X	X	X	X	X	X	X
Rate of access to reinforcement (PBIS tickets)		X							X	
EBS 2 (Sugai, Horner, & Todd, 2003)		X					X			

Table 5.2. **Sample Middle School Assessment Schedule**

Measure	Aug.	Sept.	Oct.	Nov.	Dec.	Jan.	Feb.	Mar.	Apr.	May
GPA		×			×	×			×	
Course failures	×	×	×	×	×	×	×	×	×	×
Writing assessment									×	
Curriculum-based measurement	×	×	×	×	×	×	×	×	×	×
Statewide assessment										×
Office discipline referrals	×	×	×	×	×	×	×	×	×	×
SRSS (Drummond, 1994)		×			×				×	
SDQ (Goodman, 1997)		×			×				×	
Attendance	×	×	×	×	×	×	×	×	×	×
Students Taking a Right Stand (STARS) counseling referrals	×	×	×	×	×	×	×	×	×	×
Bullying referrals	×	×	×	×	×	×	×	×	×	×
Social validity survey: PIRS (Lane, Robertson, & Wehby, 2002)		×							×	
SET 2.1 (Sugai, Lewis-Palmer, et al., 2005)		×							×	
Treatment integrity: self-report and direct observations by an outside observer	×	×	×	×	×	×	×	×	×	×
Rate of access to reinforcement (PBIS tickets)		×							×	
EBS 2 (Sugai, Horner, & Todd, 2003)		×							×	

Table 5.3. **Contra Costa High School's Assessment Schedule**

Measure	Aug.	Sept.	Oct.	Nov.	Dec.	Jan.	Feb.	Mar.	Apr.	May
GPA (quarterly)		×			×		×		×	
Course failures (quarterly)	×	×	×	×						
Writing assessment									×	
ACT scores	×	×	×	×	×	×	×	×	×	×
Statewide assessment										×
Office discipline referrals	×	×	×	×	×	×	×	×	×	×
SRSS (Drummond, 1994)		×			×				×	
SDQ (Goodman, 1997)		×			×				×	
Attendance	×	×	×	×	×	×	×	×	×	×
Students Taking a Right Stand (STARS) counseling referrals	×	×	×	×	×	×	×	×	×	×
Social validity survey: PIRS (Lane, Robertson, & Wehby, 2002)		×							×	
SET 2.1 (Sugai, Lewis-Palmer, et al., 2005)		×							×	
Treatment integrity: self-report and direct observations by an outside observer	×	×	×	×	×	×	×	×	×	×
Rate of access to reinforcement (PBIS tickets)		×							×	
EBS 2 (Sugai, Horner, & Todd, 2003)		×							×	

elementary and high school levels align with the primary prevention plans introduced in Chapter 4 in Boxes 4.2 and 4.3, respectively. Box 5.4 contains a list of suggestions for how to accurately measure the variables (outcome measures) presented in these three assessment plans. For example, when monitoring variables such as ODRs and attendance, it is important to compute the rate for each month because not all months have the same number of instructional days.

Central to each assessment schedule is to (1) collect data as part of regular school practices (provided that the data [e.g., ODRs] are collected using a reliable system to

Box 5.4. **Assessment Schedule Information**

Measure	Frequency of data collection	Suggestions on how to analyze data
Report cards and progress reports	Per grading period	• Determine which content or behavior areas of the report card to monitor (e.g., language arts, math, listening skills). • Decide which grades or proficiency levels signal at-risk status on the report and progress reports. • Aggregate number of at-risk-level grades each grading period. Track and compare aggregated numbers over time.
GPA	Per grading period	• Identify when GPA signals unacceptably low level of academic achievement (e.g., below 2.0). • Compute schoolwide average GPA. Track and compare over time (e.g., compare annual GPAs; see Figure 6.4 in Chapter 6).
Course failures	Per grading period	• Grade of D or F in one or more courses indicates at-risk status and warrants further investigation. • Aggregate number of failed courses each grading period. Track and compare aggregated course failures over time.
Writing assessment	3 times per year	• Establish proficiency levels. Those below acceptable performance signal at-risk status. • Aggregate number of scores below proficient. Track and compare aggregated scores over time.
Curriculum-based measures	Monthly	• Establish proficiency levels. Those below acceptable performance signal at-risk status. • Aggregate number of scores below proficient. Track and compare aggregated scores over time.
ACT scores	Annually	• Identify the minimum acceptable score. • Aggregate number of scores in the unacceptable range. Track and compare aggregated scores over time.
Statewide assessment	Annually	• Scores in the bottom quartile indicate at-risk performance. • Aggregate number of scores in the bottom quartile. Track and compare aggregated scores over time.
Office discipline referrals	Monthly	• When collecting ODR data, use a reliable system such as the School-Wide Information System (SWIS; May et al., 2000) for monitoring major and minor infractions. When analyzing data, be sure to compute a variety of comparisons with minor and major offenses (e.g., quarter 1 fall 2010 to quarter 1 fall 2011; see Figure 6.1 in Chapter 6). This method provides for a more sensitive analysis and allows you to observe differences in the number of minor versus major referrals (e.g., the number of major referrals may have decreased whereas minor referrals increased). Also look at context (e.g., settings, time of day). • Compute rate across months, quarters, and/or years.

Box 5.4 (*cont.*)

Measure	Frequency of data collection	Suggestions on how to analyze data
SRSS (Drummond, 1994)	3 times per year	• Compute percentages across risk categories (low, moderate, and high). • Examine comparisons (e.g., fall scores over time; see Figures 6.2 and 6.11 in Chapter 6) or compare fall to winter data to identify students for additional supports. • If you are interested in students who have obtained a 3 (often) on any of the specific items, you can locate these students and perhaps refer them to an appropriate intervention (see the secondary and tertiary grids in this chapter for examples).
SSBD (Walker & Severson, 1992)	3 times per year	• Compute percentage of students in the school who exceed normative criteria on the internalizing and externalizing dimensions, according to the rating scales completed in Stage 2. • Compare percentages and number across time (e.g., fall 2010 to fall 2011; see Figure 6.7 in Chapter 6).
SDQ (Goodman, 1997)	3 times per year	• Compute total score and subscale scores for each student. Aggregate data and compute percentage of students in each level of risk category. • Compare percentage of students in borderline and clinical categories over time (see Figures 6.8, 6.9, and 6.10 in Chapter 6).
Attendance	Monthly	• Compute rate across months and/or years to examine tardiness and absenteeism (see Figure 6.3 in Chapter 6).
Counseling referrals (e.g., STARS)	Monthly	• Compute rate across months and/or years.
Bullying referrals	Monthly	• Compute rate across months and/or years.
PBIS tickets	Monthly	• Compute rate across months and/or years.
Social validity survey (e.g., PIRS [Lane, Robertson, & Wehby, 2002])	2 times per year	• Compute averages both at the item level and total score for each time point. • Compare averages across time (e.g., preimplementation fall 2010 to post-implementation spring 2011).

(cont.)

Box 5.4 (*cont.*)

Measure	Frequency of data collection	Suggestions on how to analyze data
EBS 2 (Sugai, Horner, & Todd, 2003) Survey	2 times per year	• Compute percentage of systems (e.g., schoolwide, nonclassroom, classroom, and individual) in place, partially in place, and not in place. • Compute percentage of respondents who viewed each system (e.g., schoolwide, nonclassroom, classroom, and individual systems) to be high, medium, and low priority for improvement. • Compare averages across time (e.g., preimplementation fall 2010 to postimplementation spring 2011).
Treatment integrity: SET 2.1 (Sugai, Lewis-Palmer, et al., 2005)	Onset and end of the academic year.	• Compute subscale scores (percentage of the possible points for each of the seven features of PBIS) as well as the overall total summary score (average of the seven subscale scores). • Compare subscale and total summary scores over time.
Treatment integrity	Monthly	• Use behavioral checklists and compute percentages across months and/or years

Note. The frequency of data collection may vary among schools. Rate is computed by taking the total number of occurrences (e.g., ODRs, referrals, absences) and dividing it by the number of instructional days (per month or year). Average is computed by summing all components and dividing it by the total number of components (e.g., sum all individual students' GPA scores and divide by total number of students). Percentage is computed by taking the number earned/present and dividing it by the total possible and multiplying by 100 (e.g., number of students who fall into high-risk category divided by the total number of students and multiplied by 100).

ensure that accurate information is obtained); (2) decide who will monitor each type of data (e.g., attendance secretary responsible for monitoring attendance data; vice principal monitoring ODR data); (3) allot time for the primary intervention team to analyze and interpret data; (4) make sure that data collection procedures are reasonable (if it is too time consuming or difficult, it won't get done); and (5) ensure that findings are shared with all parties involved (e.g., teachers, parents, and students) on a regular basis so that they see the value of collecting the information.

An assessment schedule is essentially a detailed calendar that reminds everyone when the agreed-upon measures are to be collected and by whom. This process provides the intervention team with timely information to assist them in making objective decisions about how the plan is working and whether any changes or adjustments need to be made during the following academic year. The most effective plan is one that responds quickly to the school's needs. Establishing an assessment schedule ensures a systematic approach to efficiently evaluating your schoolwide plan.

In the next section of the chapter, we discuss a variety of assessment measures that can be used for systematic screening of students for behavioral and academic concerns. These assessments will help the team identify students who would benefit from more intensive intervention than the primary plan provides. The chapter concludes with guidelines for putting a screening system into place.

Screening to Identify Nonresponsive Students: Who Needs More Support?

The Importance of Systematic Screening

In addition to collecting extant schoolwide data to monitor student performance, we also strongly encourage schools to incorporate systematic screening tools and procedures to identify students who are not responding to the primary prevention efforts. By using validated screening tools and procedures, students can be identified for possible participation in more focused interventions efforts (e.g., secondary- and tertiary-level prevention efforts).

Ideally, effective screening tools and procedures should possess certain core features (Gresham et al., 2000). First, to reduce the potential for false positives and false negatives, systematic screeners need to be psychometrically sound. This means that the measures should have reliable and valid *cut scores* (i.e., the score that identifies a student as belonging to a particular category). A measure's *validity* refers to the extent to which theory and evidence support the interpretations of the test scores as the test was intended for use (American Educational Research Association, 1999). For a measure to be valid it must also be reliable. *Reliability* refers to the extent to which a particular test, when administered repeatedly over time, produces the same (or similar) results (Hatcher & Stepanski, 1994).

Ideally, systematic screeners should have evidence of the following characteristics (Lane, Kalberg, Parks, et al., 2008; Lane, Parks, et al., 2007). First, they should have high internal consistency (Cronbach alpha of 0.70 or higher) to make sure that the measure is actually assessing the defined construct of interest (e.g., behavior disorders). Second, a screener should have high test–retest stability (correlation between two sets of scores) to make sure that the screening tool affords consistency over time. Third, a screener should evidence convergent validity with other established instruments that measure the same construct of interest (when both measures are completed at the same time). Fourth, a systematic screening tool should have both positive predictive value (the probability that a student above a selected cut score is actually a member of the target group) and negative predictive value (the probability that a student below a selected cut score is a member of the control or nonclinical group; Lanyon, 2006). Fifth, a systematic screener should have specificity (proportion of the comparison or typical group that is not identified, given the same cut score) and sensitivity (proportion of the target population correctly identified Lanyon; Lane, Parks, et al., 2007).

In addition to having strong psychometric properties, systematic screeners also need to be reasonable to administer and process for teachers and administrators with respect to available resources (e.g., personnel, time, and money; Lane, Parks, et al., 2007). Ideally, a feasible screener is a reliable screening tool that also (1) costs little to no money and (2) takes limited time to administer, score, and analyze (Walker et al., 2004). No matter how wonderful the instrument, if it is too cumbersome to administer, score, and analyze, then school sites will be less likely to put such a screener in place.

The next section reviews existing tools and procedures for monitoring students' behavioral and academic performance. The examples offered are all psychometrically sound but have a range in terms of feasibility.

Existing Tools and Procedures for Monitoring Students' Behavior

During the past 15 years, researchers have developed several user-friendly, empirically validated instruments to detect students at risk for emotional and behavioral disorders (EBD), with most of the screeners developed for use at the elementary level. Three such instruments are the Strengths and Difficulties Questionnaire (SDQ; Goodman, 1997), Student Risk Screening Scale (SRSS; Drummond, 1994), and Systematic Screening for Behavior Disorders (SSBD; Walker & Severson, 1992; see Box 5.5 for ordering information).

Strengths and Difficulties Questionnaire

The SDQ (Goodman, 1997) is a systematic screener designed to examine students' (ages 4–17) strengths and deficits in sociobehavioral domains (Goodman, 2001; Goodman, Meltzer, & Bailey, 1998). The SDQ includes a number of forms available at no cost online. Specifically, there are teacher-completed (ages 4–10; 11–17), parent-completed (ages 4–10; 11–17), and self-report forms (ages 11–17). The teacher version requires teachers to fill out one page for *each* student in his or her class. The 25 items on the SDQ are equally distributed across five factors: emotional symptoms, conduct problems, hyperactivity, peer problems, and prosocial behavior. Teachers evaluate each item, some of which are positively phrased and others that are negatively phrased, on the following 3-point, Likert-type scale: *not true* = 0, *somewhat true* = 1, *certainly true* = 2. The authors estimate that it takes teachers approximately 60 minutes to rate an entire class.

Subscale scores range from 0 to 10, with high scores indicating higher degrees of risk for emotional symptoms, conduct problems, hyperactivity, and peer problems as well as higher degrees of prosocial behavior. The total score ranges from 0 to 40 and reflects the values of the first four factors. Each student is placed into one of three categories (normal, borderline, or abnormal) for each subscale as well as the total score. Cutoff scores vary for each subscale.

The teacher-completed version has strong psychometric properties with alpha coefficients at or above 0.70 on each subscale and total score (Hatcher & Stepanski, 1994). The SDQ scores also have high concurrent validity with the Child Behavior Checklist (CBCL; Achenbach, 1991a, 1991b) and the Rutter Questionnaires (Goodman & Scott, 1999; Rutter, 1967). Also, the SDQ identifies individuals with a psychiatric diagnosis as abnormal with a specificity of 94.6% (95% CI: 94.1–95.1%) and a sensitivity of 63.3%

Box 5.5. Systematic Screening Tools for Behavior and Academic Performance

Tool	Description	Ordering information
Strengths and Difficulties Questionnaire (Goodman, 1997)	The SDQ is a behavioral screening questionnaire for students ages 4–17 years old. There are several versions of the SDQ, including the self-report form (ages 11–17), parent form (ages 4–10 and 11–17), and teacher form (ages 4–10 and 11–17). The SDQ contains 25 items regarding positive and negative attributes of the student. These items are equally divided between five scales: emotional symptoms, conduct problems, hyperactivity, peer problems, and prosocial behavior. In addition, there is a total difficulty score.	The SDQ is available on the internet to download: *www.sdqinfo.com*
Student Risk Screening Scale (Drummond, 1994)	The SRSS is a seven-item behavioral screening scale used to detect antisocial behavior. Teachers rate each student in their class on seven items using a 4-point Likert-type scale. Total scores range from 0 to 21, placing students into three levels of risk: low (0–3), moderate (4–8), and high (9–21).	Can be created based on the description given; not copyrighted.
Systematic Screening for Behavior Disorders (Walker & Severson, 1992)	The SSBD is a three-stage multiple-gating screener designed to identify students with externalizing or internalizing behaviors. The process begins with teacher ranking, followed by teacher ratings on two measures (the Critical Events Index and the Combined Frequency Index). Students passing through the first two gates are then observed in structured and nonstructured settings.	Order from publishing company; Sopris West: *store.cambiumlearning.com*. The cost is approximately $120 per kit, with only one kit required per school. E-mail: *customerservice@soprisvest.com* Phone: 800-547-6747 Address: 4185 Salazar Way Frederick, CO 80504
Dynamic Indicators of Basic Early Literacy Skills (Kaminski & Good, 1996)	DIBELS, a series of CBMs for early reading, was developed by the University of Oregon's Center on Teaching and Learning. It includes fluency probes for initial sounds, letter naming, phoneme segmentation, nonsense words, oral reading, retell, and word use. DIBELS is considered to have good reliability and validity and is predictive of later reading success.	The DIBELS Data System is a service allowing schools to enter students and DIBELS scores online and generate automated reports and analyses, for $1 per student per year. All DIBELS Data System fees are used exclusively to support further research and education. *dibels.uoregon.edu*

(cont.)

Box 5.5 (*cont.*)

Tool	Description	Ordering information
AIMSweb (Harcourt, 2008)	AIMSweb is a commercially available assessment system for grades K–8 that provides CBMs in early numeracy and literacy, spelling, written expression, mathematics, and reading. It is organized to be utilized with three-tier intervention models and generates progress monitoring data that can be used to identify at-risk students.	Phone: 866-313-6194 Address: Harcourt Assessment, Inc. AIMSweb Customer Service P.O. Box 599700 San Antonio, TX 78259 Order online: *www.aimsweb.com* Fax: 866-313-6197 Faxed orders *must* include Visa/MC information or signed purchase.

(CI: 59.7–66.9%; Goodman, 1997). In short, this is a reliable, valid measure that can be used to screen students for behavioral concerns and strengths across the K–12 continuum. Furthermore, according to our studies, the SDQ also has convergent validity with the SRSS at both the middle school level ($r = .66$; Lane, Parks, et al., 2007) and the high school level ($r = .47$; Lane, Kalberg, Parks, et al., 2008).

Student Risk Screening Scale

The SRSS (Drummond, 1994) is a no-cost, brief, mass screening tool originally designed to identify K–6 students at risk for antisocial behavior. This is a one-page instrument that includes a listing of all students in the first column, with seven items listed across the top row. Homeroom teachers rate each student in their class on the following items: steals; lies, cheats, sneaks; behavior problems; peer rejection; low academic achievement; negative attitude; and aggressive behavior. Teachers rate each item on a 4-point Likert-type scale as follows: *never* = 0, *occasionally* = 1, *sometimes* = 2, or *frequently* = 3. Total scores are used to classify students into three levels of risk: low (0–3), moderate (4–8), and high (9–21). Administration time is only 10–15 minutes for an entire class. The SRSS is a practical, psychometrically sound tool for distinguishing among students who do and do not exhibit behaviors indicative of antisocial behavior (Drummond, Eddy, & Reid, 1998a, 1998b). In our work we have placed this information into an Excel file and included formulas to compute total scores for each students (see Figure 5.2 for an illustration). The PBIS team members can send this information to teachers to complete electronically, or hard copies can be printed and then completed by team members.

    Validity studies at the elementary level indicate that the SRSS has strong internal

TEACHER NAME

0 = Never
1 = Occasionally
2 = Sometimes
3 = Frequently

Use the above scale to rate each item for each student

		Student Risk Screening Scale (SRSS)							
Student ID	Student Name	Steal	Lie, Cheat, Sneak	Behavior Problem	Peer Rejection	Low Academic Achievement	Negative Attitude	Aggressive Behavior	Total
1111	Smith, Sally	0	0	3	1	3	3	3	13

Figure 5.2. **Illustration of the Student Risk Screening Scale (SRSS; Drummond, 1994)**. From Walker, Ramsey, and Gresham (2004). Copyright 2004 by Wadsworth, a part of Cengage Learning, Inc. Reproduced by permission. www.cengage.com/permissions.

consistency, with an alpha coefficient of 0.83 (Lane, Little, et al., 2008). Analysis of receiver operating characteristics curves indicated that the SRSS is more accurate at detecting externalizing (area under the curve [AUC] = .952) than internalizing behaviors (AUC = .802; Lane, Little, et al., 2008), as measured by the Systematic Screening for Behavior Disorders (SSBD; Walker & Severson, 1992). SRSS total score and the aggressive behavior subscale of the CBCL (Achenbach, 1991a, 1991b) are significantly correlated (*r* = .79; Walker et al., 2004). Longitudinal studies of the SRSS at the elementary level indicate that SRSS total scores are predictive of negative academic and behavioral outcomes from 18 months to 10 years later (Drummond et al., 1994).

Initial studies of score reliability and validity at the middle school level (Lane, Parks, et al., 2007) demonstrate high internal consistency, test–retest stability, and convergent validity with the SDQ (Goodman, 1997). In addition, short-term predictive validity is established at the middle school level, with students with low (*n* = 422), moderate (*n* = 51), or high (*n* = 12) risk status best differentiated by behavioral variables (e.g., ODRs and in-school suspensions). Although academic variables differentiated between those with (moderate or high) and without (low) risk, these variables did not differentiate between students in the moderate- and high-risk groups, as did the behavioral variables.

Initial studies of score reliability and validity at the high school level (Lane, Kalberg, Parks, et al., 2008) also demonstrate high internal consistency, test–retest stability, interrater reliability, and convergent validity with the SDQ (Goodman, 1997). Predictive validity was established over 2 academic years, with students at low risk for antisocial behavior differentiated on behavioral (ODRs) and academic variables (GPAs) from students with moderate and high levels of risk, according to the SRSS. However, neither ODR nor GPA variables could differentiate between students with moderate- or high-risk status. In short, there is initial evidence to support the use of this brief, no-cost, systematic screening scale across the K–12 continuum.

Systematic Screening for Behavior Disorders

The SSBD (Walker & Severson, 1992) is a relatively inexpensive, empirically validated, three-stage multiple-gating procedure used to screen elementary-age students for externalizing and internalizing behavior disorders (see Figure 5.3). The screening process begins with teacher nominations and rankings, then becomes more focused in successive stages. In Stage 1 each teacher reads descriptions of internalizing and externalizing behaviors, including examples and nonexamples of each behavior pattern. Then the teacher categorizes his or her students in either the internalizing or externalizing domain, ranking them in each group from "*most like*" (1) to "*least like*" (10) the given definitions. Typically, the three highest-ranked students on the internalizing and externalizing dimensions pass into Stage 2.

In Stage 2 teachers complete two nationally normed rating scales, the critical events index (CEI) and the combined frequency index (CFI) for the six students. The goal is to gain more specific information regarding the students' behavior patterns. The CEI is a 33-item checklist of high-intensity, low-frequency behaviors (e.g., sets fires, steals,

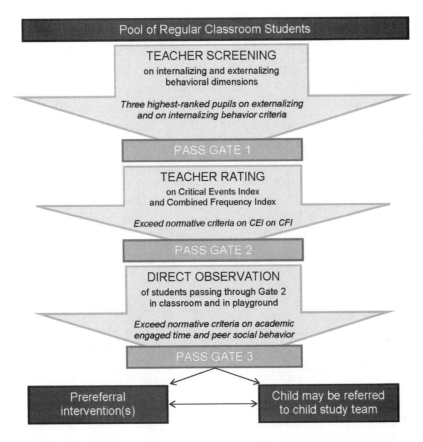

Figure 5.3. **Illustration of the Systematic Screening for Behavior Disorders (SSBD; Walker & Severson, 1992).** Adapted from Walker and Severson (1992) with permission from Sopris West Educational Services.

vomits after eating). Teachers record the presence or absence of each behavior, with total scores ranging from 0 to 33. The CFI assesses low-intensity, high-frequency behaviors on adaptive (e.g., does seat work as directed) and maladaptive (e.g., pouts or sulks) domains. Students exceeding normative criteria move to Stage 3, which involves direct observations of their behavior in structured (academic engagement) and nonstructured (social interactions) settings. Field trials of the SSBD indicate that it is highly useful in distinguishing between students with externalizing, internalizing, and typical behavior patterns as well as between students receiving special education services under the category of emotionally disturbed (e.g., Walker et al., 1994; Walker et al., 1990).

These three validated screeners can be used to detect students who are at risk for various behavior concerns. In Chapter 6 we explore the possibility of using these systematic screening tools, implemented as part of K–12 primary prevention programs, to (1) assess the overall index of risk as well as (2) identify how different types of students respond to the primary plan over time (Lane, Kalberg, Bruhn, et al., in press). In the section that follows, we illustrate how to monitor students' academic progress.

Existing Tools and Procedures for Monitoring Students' Academic Progress

Just as for behavioral measures, academic screeners need be technically sound, and easy to administer, score, and interpret. It is also essential that they are a valid measure of the curriculum that your school site implements. Both curriculum-based assessments (CBAs) and norm-referenced assessments can be utilized as screeners, but CBAs provide the most accurate information about educational growth because they deliver specific information about what students learn in their classes. CBAs also offer a more sensitive measure of growth than norm-referenced tests, meaning that they detect smaller increases in student progress. However, group norm-referenced tests, such as those used to assess a school's yearly academic progress, also can be used initially to identify students who need further monitoring. This next section discusses the use of norm-referenced tests, CBAs, and curriculum-based measurement (CBM) as systematic screeners to identify students who are not making adequate academic progress.

Norm-Referenced Assessments

Wide-scale norm-referenced assessments are intended to compare an individual student's performance to a statistically constructed "average" student. This measure provides a benchmark for a teacher, parent, or other school personnel to use when evaluating student achievement. However, norm-referenced tests do not necessarily measure what a student learns at his or her school (Popham, 1999) and, because they are constructed to create a distribution of scores, they are not intended to monitor individual student progress but to furnish an approximate estimate of how an entire school is doing overall. Yet, when used carefully, it is possible to employ these assessments as a very rough guide in identifying students who may be at risk for school failure. For example, if a student scores in the bottom quartile on a state-administered reading achievement test, this performance may be a cause for concern.

The intervention team will want to use norm-referenced tests in conjunction with other CBAs. For example, the team may decide to establish an at-risk category of all students who score below the 25th percentile on the districtwide norm-referenced assessment. Once these students have been identified, the team can examine additional measures such as GPA or grades in language arts or mathematics. If students are doing poorly on all the measures that are thought to be important indicators of student progress, then this group is established as at risk and will require additional monitoring and/ or intervention.

Curriculum-Based Assessments and Curriculum-Based Measurement

CBAs directly measure a student's progress in the school's formal curriculum. They include assessments as various as chapter tests from textbooks, teacher-made quizzes, portfolios, and anecdotal notes. They may also include assessments such as capstone projects or final exams. An advantage of using CBAs as part of your systematic screening plan is that they are often already in place, are feasible, and provide a relatively easy-to-interpret measure of a student's academic skills. When choosing which assessments to use as screeners, several issues need to be considered. The school-site team will have to make decisions about reliability and validity, as well as ease of administration, scoring, and aggregation of data.

For example, the team must identify assessments that are common across grade levels so that all students in a grade are measured using the same criterion. This uniformity makes it possible to establish "local norms"—that is, what a school's typical student performance looks like at a particular grade level. If each teacher uses a different CBA, a school is likely to either over- or underidentify students. Teacher A may use an advanced reading passage whereas Teacher B uses a connect-the-dots worksheet. In this case, Teacher A will probably have more students who appear to be at risk than does Teacher B. This issue is also related to concerns about validity. Teachers must agree that the measure accurately represents the key academic demands in a particular grade level. The assessment should be appropriately difficult and in the appropriate domain (e.g., reading and not physical education). The assessment must also be administered frequently enough so that it is possible to monitor student progress throughout and across the years.

Many school districts now employ curriculum-based "multiple measures" that are administered at all their school sites in order to track progress across the district (see Lane & Menzies, 2003, 2005). These measures are most often given in reading and mathematics, are leveled by grade, and provide cut scores that establish above-average, average, and below-average performance. In addition, they are typically administered several times a year. Multiple measures are a good choice as an academic screener because they establish local norms and address many of the issues related to reliability and validity. Teachers are already familiar with administering them and collecting and analyzing the data that they produce. Parents, too, are often familiar with these assessments and, because they are curriculum based, it is easy to discuss what performance means in terms of student achievement.

CBM was originally designed as a formative evaluation tool to assist teachers in adjusting instruction to better meet students' needs. Increasingly, it is used to screen students who may be at risk academically (Deno, 2003). While CBM does reflect a school's general curriculum, it differs from CBA in that it is a standardized set of procedures that has established technical adequacy, uses stimulus materials that are representative and equivalent, is efficient in terms of time, and consists of short probes that are easy to administer. Because of their design, CBMs are ideal for use as academic screeners. School sites can create their own CBMs, but some are commercially available and others are accessible for free on websites. For example, the DIBELS (Kaminski & Good, 1996), developed by the University of Oregon's Center on Teaching and Learning, is a series of CBMs for early reading that includes fluency probes for initial sounds, letter naming, phoneme segmentation, nonsense words, oral reading, retelling, and word use. DIBELS measures are considered to have good reliability and validity and are predictive of later reading success. A full report of their technical adequacy is available at *dibels.uoregon. edu/techreports/dibels_5th_ed.pdf*.

Similarly, AIMSweb is a commercially available assessment system for grades K–8 that provides CBMs in early numeracy and literacy, spelling, written expression, mathematics, and reading. It is organized to be utilized with three-tiered intervention models and generates progress monitoring data that can be used to identify at-risk students. More information about these measures can be accessed at *aimsweb.com* (see Box 5.5 for ordering information).

When using CBMs, be sure to note the cut scores that indicate risk. Cut scores are different for each of the subtests *within* a program as well as *between* them (e.g., DIBELS and AIMSweb). For example, a score of < 10 on the DIBELS midyear *initial sound fluency* probe indicates at-risk performance; however, for the *letter naming fluency probe* a midyear score of < 15 is at-risk performance.

A variety of assessments can be used as academic screeners. Intervention teams must choose those that are a good fit with the school's curriculum, as well as consider their validity and reliability. Equally important is that teachers, parents, and students find the assessments meaningful and a significant indicator of student academic progress.

Recommendations for Conducting Screenings

When conducting systematic screenings in behavioral and academic domains, we encourage you to consider logistical issues such as (1) when to do them, (2) who should prepare them, (3) who should administer them, (4) who completes them, (5) who should score them, and (6) when and how to share results with the faculty. We have put together some suggestions based on our work in K–12 schools (see Boxes 5.6 and 5.7; however, we encourage you to recognize that these are just suggestions and there are many "right ways" to conduct screenings).

Summary

In this chapter, we provide information for monitoring treatment integrity and assessing social validity. In addition, we provided procedures for monitoring student progress and systematically screening all students for possible behavior and academic concerns. In the next chapter we will provide a series of illustrations across the K–12 grade span to show you how to use schoolwide data to (1) monitor how the school as a whole is responding the schoolwide plan, (2) determine how different types of students responded to the primary plan, and (3) identify students who require additional supports in the form of secondary and tertiary interventions.

Box 5.6. **Suggestions for Conducting Systematic Behavioral Screeners**

Questions	Suggestions
When to do them?	• When conducting behavioral screenings, consider administering them three times per year: 6 weeks into the school year, prior to winter break, and 6 weeks prior to year end. • Once you have chosen dates to complete the screeners, include these on your assessment schedule. This may avoid scheduling several assessments during the same time period. • It is important to provide teachers time to complete the screeners. Consider allocating time during regularly scheduled faculty meetings or during department/grade-level meetings.
Who should prepare them?	• The PBIS team should determine a representative to coordinate the behavioral screeners (e.g., attendance secretary, counselor, administrator). This person should have access to school attendance and teacher rosters because he or she will need to prepare forms that include all student names.
Who should administer them?	• The behavioral screeners should be administered by PBIS team members after they have received training in administration, scoring, and interpretation.
Who completes them?	• All classroom teachers. • In an elementary school, classroom teachers should rate all students in their class. Support teachers (i.e., art, music, P.E.) do not complete the screeners because their students will be rated by their homeroom teacher. • In a middle school consider having homeroom teachers complete the screeners on their groups of students (see Lane, Parks, et al., 2007). • In a high school consider choosing a teacher in a content area that students are required to take for 4 years (e.g., English teacher). Or perhaps choose a period (e.g., second period, fifth period; see Lane, Kalberg, Parks, et al., 2008) during which everyone teaching will administer the screening to all students on their roster. • Note that whatever method you choose, it is necessary to rate every student at least once. Some schools have chosen to have two different teachers complete screeners on students to offer multiple perspectives (Lane, Kalberg, Bruhn, et al., in press).
Who should score them?	• The behavioral screeners should be scored by the PBIS team after they have received training in administration, scoring, and interpretation. • We also encourage the PBIS team to do reliability checks on the scoring to make sure that systematic screeners were scored accurately.
When and how should results be shared?	• Once the scorer has aggregated the information, it should first be shared with an administrator and/or the PBIS team to determine how to share the results with the full faculty. • Consider spending some time during a regularly scheduled faculty meeting to share this information.

Box 5.7. **Suggestions for Conducting Systematic Academic Screeners**

Questions	Suggestions
When to do them?	• Identify state- and districtwide assessments that can be used as screeners. As these are administered at predetermined times, they should be scheduled into your assessment calendar first. • Create or designate CBAs or CBMs to administer weekly or monthly. If they are aligned with the curriculum, administering the measures will not be an extra task but an integral part of a teacher's instruction. • Be sure to consider your assessment schedule for behavior screeners to avoid the collection of too many items at the same time.
Who should prepare them?	• State- and districtwide assessments are prepared in accordance with state and district guidelines. • CBAs that are an integral part of teachers' instruction are prepared by each teacher. • If schoolwide CBMs have been purchased, they may be web based and therefore can be downloaded by teachers or a designated PBIS team member.
Who should administer them?	• Teachers • Make certain that teachers and PBIS team members receive necessary training in administration, scoring, and interpretation.
Who completes them?	• Students
Who should score them?	• State and districtwide assessments are scored in accordance with state and district guidelines. State assessments are sent to the testing company to be scored. Teachers typically score district assessments and report the results to administrators or test coordinators. • Make certain that teachers and PBIS team members receive the necessary training in scoring.
When and how should results be shared?	• Administrators should develop systems for aggregating and sharing schoolwide academic assessments. Graphs or charts can be developed to clearly display how the school is performing. • The administrator may want to report results to the PBIS team and then to the full faculty. Consider dedicating time during a regularly scheduled faculty meeting to share this information.

Chapter Six

Determining How Well the Program Is Working

Monitoring Outcomes and Identifying Nonresponsive Students

As we mentioned in Chapter 5, it is important to collect and analyze schoolwide data as a means of (1) monitoring how the school as a whole is responding to the schoolwide plan, (2) determining how different types of students responded, and (3) identifying students who require additional supports in the form of secondary and tertiary interventions. In this chapter we provide additional information on how to accomplish these objectives and provide several detailed illustrations of how to use schoolwide data to identify elementary, middle, and high school students in need of secondary supports. We also discuss a range of supports in each of the domains (academic, social, and behavioral) that includes options that are typically available at schools as well as other research-based programs.

Examining the Schoolwide Data

As we discussed in Chapter 5, collecting data that address the purpose statement or main goals of the primary prevention program is essential if you want to know whether your schoolwide plan is working. If the goals are to decrease ODRs, improve attendance, and improve grades, then the team must monitor student progress on each of these variables. For example, Contra Costa High School's assessment schedule (see Table 5.3 in Chapter 5) shows us the types of information the team is monitoring. During the planning process (see Chapter 4), the school-site team identified three main objectives to operationalize the school's purpose statement:

1. Decrease problem behaviors, as measured by ODRs and the SRSS (Drummond, 1994).
2. Improve attendance, as measured by unexcused absences and unexcused tardies.
3. Improve academic performance, as measured by GPAs.

Collecting and monitoring this information for each student in the school offers the team a clear picture of how the school as a whole is responding. Many schools already collect large amounts of information, such as daily attendance, ODRs, CBMs of academic performance (e.g., reading, writing, and math skills), standardized state and district assessments, and, in some cases, behavioral screeners. Yet, questions arise as to how well (or if) these data are used to inform decision making and to subsequently support students who need assistance. In our work, teachers have expressed concern that they are asked to conduct a plethora of assessments, but the information is rarely used and the results are not shared. When information is collected but not analyzed and used, it can be a source of frustration to teachers as well as those who are asked to complete the assessments. Therefore, we urge practitioners and researchers alike to *use* the information they collect and *share it* in a meaningful way with the parties involved. This can be done with brief reports that include clear graphics displaying trends in the collected data.

Consider Contra Costa High School's first goal to decrease problem behaviors as measured by ODRs and the SRSS (Drummond, 1994). Figure 6.1 presents one method of sharing data with faculty that shows the rate of ODRs per instructional day during the beginning of the first year of implementation (quarter 1 of 2010) as compared to the beginning of the second year of implementation (quarter 1 of 2011). In this graph

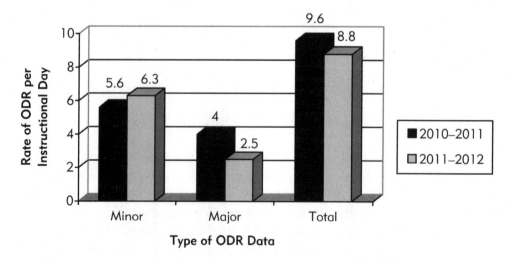

Figure 6.1. **ODR data across school years for Contra Costa High School: Quarter 1 of 2010 to quarter 1 of 2011.**

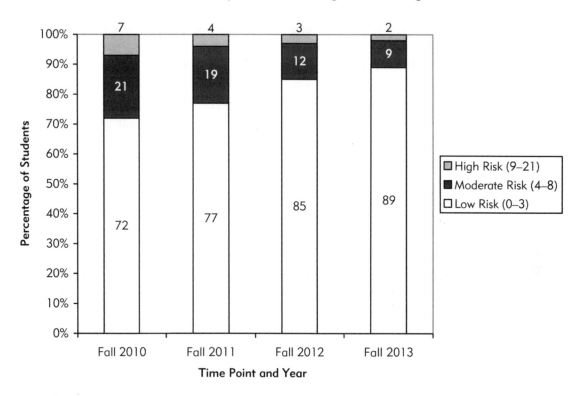

Figure 6.2. **SRSS data over time for Contra Costa High School: Fall 2010 to fall 2013.**

you can see that when looking at combined ODRs (for both minor and major infractions; the two bars on the right-hand side of the graph), the rate of ODRs during quarter 1 has declined over this time frame. However, closer inspection of the data shows
that although the rate of major offenses has decreased, the rate of minor offenses has
increased. This information could be shared to help inform practices. For example, the
PBIS team might recommend that teachers adjust the rate of reinforcement (in terms
of PBIS tickets paired with verbal praise) by acknowledging more frequently students
who are meeting the schoolwide expectations. Had the school-site team not looked at
both major and minors infractions, they would not have become aware of this increasing trend in minor infractions.

Figure 6.2 presents a graphic of SRSS fall results over the first 4 years of implementation. The lower portion of each bar contains the percentage of students scoring in
the low-risk category (0–3), the middle portion of each bar contains the percentage of
students scoring in the moderate-risk category (4–8), and the upper portion of each bar
contains the percentage of students scoring in the high-risk category (9–21). In looking
at the low-risk category over time, the percentage of students in the low-risk category
has increased steadily over the past 4 years. For example, in the fall of 2010, 72% of
students placed in the low-risk category, 77% in the fall of 2011, 85% in the fall of 2012,
and 89% in the fall of 2013. The percentage of students in the moderate-risk category
has declined from 21% in the fall of 2010 to 9% in the fall of 2013. Furthermore, the

percentage of students in the high-risk category has also declined, from 7% in the fall of 2010 to 2% in the fall of 2013. Overall, SRSS data suggest that risk has declined over the past 4 years at Contra Costa High School. However, be certain *not* to draw causal conclusions that the primary prevention plan caused these changes because an experimental design was not used. However, you *can* say that results of the descriptive analyses suggest a decline in the percentage of students at risk for antisocial behavior since the program was introduced.

Contra Costa High School's second goal was to improve attendance, as measured by unexcused tardies and unexcused absences. Figure 6.3 presents one method of sharing this information with faculty, staff, parents, and students. This figure illustrates that the rate of unexcused tardies decreased from a rate of 67 per day in November 2010 to a rate of 43 per day in November 2011. Also, unexcused absences declined from a rate of 40 per day to a rate of 30 per day during this same period of time.

Contra Costa High School's third goal was to improve academic performance, as measured by GPAs. Figure 6.4 is a bar graph of the student body's GPA over the course of the first 4 years of implementation. In this illustration, the school's GPAs remained relatively stable during the first 2 academic years. However, the school's average GPAs showed an increasing trend during the 2012–2013 and 2013–2014 academic years.

These illustrations are but a few methods of summarizing data. There are numerous other comparisons that could be made to examine how your school as a whole is responding to the plan. For example, you could examine ODR data in different settings, compare SRSS data from fall and winter time points, and compare quarter 1 and quarter 2 GPAs. Just remember to stay focused on the objectives, collect the necessary data, and then share the findings with all consumers in a meaningful, easy-to-understand way that does not overstate or understate the case.

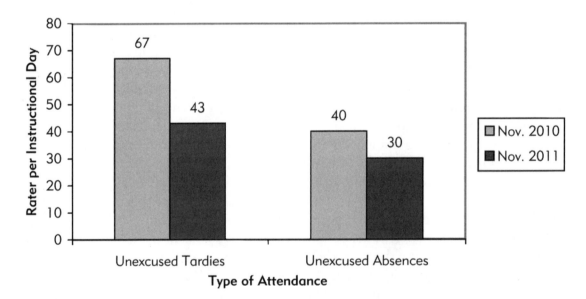

Figure 6.3. **Unexcused tardies and absences data across school years for Contra Costa High School Graph: November 2010 to November 2011.**

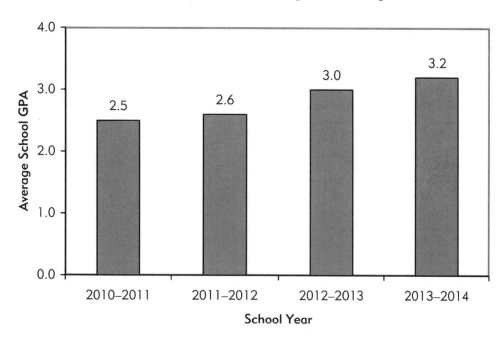

Figure 6.4. **GPA data for Contra Costa High School.**

Interpreting your data so that you know how well your schoolwide plan is working provides very useful information, but another important objective is to understand how different types of students are responding to your primary prevention program (e.g., Lane & Menzies, 2005; Lane, Wehby, et al., 2007). For example, it is highly likely that not all students will respond the same way to the schoolwide plan; it may be that students with externalizing (e.g., aggression, noncompliance), internalizing (e.g., anxiety, depression), or comorbid behavior patterns respond differently to primary prevention efforts (Lane, Kalberg, Bruhn, et al., in press; Lane, Wehby, et al.). Therefore, looking closely at how different groups of students respond will offer information about how to work more effectively with them.

Determining How Different Types of Students Respond

To date, only a handful of studies has examined how different types of students, such as those at risk for behavior difficulties, students with typical behavior patterns, and those with high-incidence disabilities, have responded to schoolwide, primary prevention programs. Furthermore, most of these investigations have been conducted at the elementary level (e.g., Cheney, Blum, & Walker, 2004; Lane & Menzies, 2005; Walker, Cheney, Stage, & Blum, 2005), leaving us with limited information about middle and high school settings. In this section we briefly review two studies we have conducted to illustrate how different types of students at the elementary and high school settings respond to primary prevention efforts.

How Students Respond at the Elementary Level

Lane and Menzies (2005) examined the degree to which elementary-age students with and without academic and behavioral problems ($n = 86$) responded to a multilevel intervention program. Teachers nominated up to three students from their classrooms in each of four categories: academic concerns only, behavioral concerns only, academic and behavioral concerns, and typical performance. Nomination procedures followed a modified version of Walker and Severson's (1992) Systematic Screening for Behavior Disorders (SSBD), with a goal of identifying students with early literacy and/or behavioral concerns.

Analysis of student outcome data suggested that the program was not equally effective for all types of students; there were differences in how students responded. For example, in terms of reading, students in the academic and behavioral concerns group made significantly more progress on the reading measures than did students in the typical performance group. So at-risk students benefited more from the academic reading intervention than did those who were not at risk. In terms of behavioral performance, student risk scores (as measured by the SRSS) showed improvement for the combined concerns group. The combined group showed significant decreases in risk and improvement in written expression, despite the lack of a significant improvement in reading skills. In addition, students in the combined concerns and those in the academic concerns groups showed significant improvement in attendance as compared to the typical performance and behavioral concerns groups. Perhaps the combination of the literacy and behavioral components provided enough reinforcement and individualized focus to make school a less aversive place for students with academic concerns, with and without behavioral concerns, thereby promoting attendance (Lane & Menzies, 2005).

How Students Respond at the High School Level

Lane, Wehby, and colleagues (2007) conducted a similar study at the high school level to determine how high school students ($n = 178$) with externalizing, internalizing, comorbid, and typical behavior patterns, as well as students receiving special education services for high-incidence disabilities, responded to a PBIS intervention program. In this study English teachers from two high schools with SWPBS programs nominated one student from each class period for each of the following categories: externalizing, internalizing, comorbid (externalizing and internalizing), and typical using a modified version of the SSBD (Walker & Severson, 1992).

Results suggest that while students in the externalizing, internalizing, and typical groups all showed improved GPA, decreases in unexcused tardies, and decreases in suspension, students with internalizing behaviors appeared to be the most responsive group. Findings also suggest that students in the comorbid group (with both externalizing and internalizing behaviors) were perhaps the least responsive. This is not surprising, given that students with comorbid concerns are often highly resistant to intervention efforts (Gresham, Lane, & Lambros, 2000; Lynam, 1996).

Summary

These are just two studies that examine how different types of students respond to primary prevention efforts. While replication is needed to see if the differences noted above are consistent in other geographic areas and in programs implemented without university support, these initial findings suggest that not all students respond in the same way. Therefore, be sure to collect and analyze data to determine whether particular groups of students are responding differently to primary prevention efforts (e.g., Lane, Kalberg, Bruhn, et al., 2008). These same types of data can also be used to determine which students will require additional support in the form of targeted prevention efforts.

Identifying Students Who Need Targeted Supports

As we discussed in Chapter 2, three-tiered models include secondary- and tertiary-level prevention efforts for students who are not responsive to primary prevention efforts. Due to its intensive nature, tertiary prevention efforts are reserved for students with multiple risk factors as well as those who did not respond to secondary prevention programs (Sugai & Horner, 2006; Lane, 2007). Central to this model is the use of data-based decision making (Sugai & Horner). Namely, rather than relying solely on teacher judgment, data collected to monitor the schoolwide plan are also used to determine which students require secondary and tertiary prevention efforts (Lane).

Before the data can be used to place students in programs, we encourage teams to develop two intervention grids: one containing all of the secondary prevention programs currently available at the school or in the community (see Boxes 6.1 and 6.2 for examples at the elementary [Box 6.1], middle, and high [Box 6.2] school levels) and one containing all of the tertiary prevention programs currently available at the school or in the community (see Boxes 6.3 and 6.4 for examples at the elementary, middle, and high school level). As you'll see in Boxes 6.1–6.4, each intervention grid contains five pieces of information. The first column identifies the type and name of the support (e.g., Homework Club [see Box 6.2]). The second column contains a brief description of each intervention. The description includes information such as (1) the content of the intervention; (2) treatment dosage (e.g., the number of days per week, the length of each intervention session) and context (e.g., in the cafeteria after school, in the conference room during Friday flex time); and (3) the person responsible for conducting the intervention (e.g., guidance counselors, paraprofessionals, teachers). For example, in Box 6.2 the behavior education plan (BEP; Crone, Horner, & Hawkins, 2004) is a secondary intervention that includes both teacher and parent support. Each day a student's teacher completes a daily progress report to provide immediate feedback about the student's work habits that day. The report is then taken home to be shared with parents.

The third column contains the entry criteria: the specific cutoff scores on school-wide data used to place students in the targeted support groups. These data specify how students qualify for the intervention. For example, middle or high school students par-

Box 6.1. **Secondary Intervention Grid: Elementary Level**

Support	Description	Schoolwide data: Entry criteria	Data to monitor progress	Exit criteria
Study Skills Group	Identified students meet 3 days a week during the enrichment block in which 30-minute lessons are taught focusing on study skill strategies. This group can be run by teachers, trained parent volunteers, or paraprofessionals in a designated classroom, an office, or in the school library or cafeteria.	• Report cards: Earned a "needs improvement" score on study skills or a C– or lower in any academic content area, or • Below proficient on curriculum-based measures, or • Scored in the bottom quartile on standardized state assessments.	• Weekly grades collected by the teacher (accuracy percentage). • Weekly completion collected by the teacher (percentage of assignments completed).	Complete the program when they (a) demonstrate mastery of study skills taught on a criterion-referenced assessment, and (2) weekly teacher records reflect a minimum of 80% accuracy and 90% work completion over a 3-week period.
Behavior Education Program (BEP; Crone, Horner, & Hawken, 2004)	The BEP is designed for students with persistent behavior concerns who are not dangerous. The BEP provides a daily check-in/check-out system that helps teachers give students (a) immediate feedback on their behavior by completing a daily progress report (DPR) and (2) additional opportunities for positive adult interactions. Parents participate by signing off on daily sheets.	Academic and behavioral concerns: *Academic* • Report cards: Earned a "needs improvement" score on study skills or a C– or lower in any academic content area, or • Below proficient on curriculum-based measures, or *Behavioral* • SRSS score in the moderate-risk range, or • SSBD score exceeding normative criteria on externalizing or internalizing behavior on Stage 2 rating scales	Daily progress monitoring forms collected by teacher and viewed by parent	Move into the maintenance self-monitoring phase when students meet their goals for 3 consecutive weeks. Self-monitoring phase ends when the next academic reporting period and behavior rating results indicate the absence of risk following the same criteria stated in the inclusion criteria.

Box 6.1 (*cont.*)

Support	Description	Schoolwide data: Entry criteria	Data to monitor progress	Exit criteria
Incredible Years Training for Children	This curriculum builds skills in anger management, school success, and interpersonal problem solving. It is delivered as a "pullout" for small groups in a designated classroom or office. (See Blueprints for Violence Prevention [www.colorado.edu/cspv/index.html] for further details.)	• Scored in the moderate-risk range on the SRSS, with a 2 or higher on item 4 (peer rejection) or 5 (low academic achievement), or • Two or more bullying referrals turned in, or • Three or more major ODRs.	• Information pertinent to elements of the intervention are established, then collected and analyzed (e.g., results of social skills training, academic tutoring) by teacher.	• Students complete the curriculum components and are then assessed and compared to initial inclusionary criteria. • Students are exited if they score in the low-risk range on the SRSS during the next systematic screening period and do not receive bullying referrals or ODRs for 3 consecutive weeks during the same rating period.
Social Skills Group	Identified students meet 3 days each week during the enrichment block for 30-minute lessons focused on improving specific social skills. Students meet with school psychologist or interns 2 days a week for 30-minute lessons for 10 weeks in their specific areas of concerns (see Lane et al., 2003; Miller, Lane, & Wehby, 2005). This group would be held in a designated classroom or office.	Behavioral concern *Internalizing group* • SSBD score exceeding normative criteria on internalizing behavior on Stage 2 rating scales, or • One or more unexcused absences or three or more unexcused tardies during the first 6 weeks of school. *Externalizing group* • SSBD score exceeding normative criteria on externalizing behavior on Stage 2 rating scales, or • One or more ODRs for major offenses during the 6 weeks of school.	School psychologist monitors: *Internalizing group* • Daily attendance patterns • Daily social interactions on the playground *Externalizing group* • Daily discipline records • Daily social interactions on the playground	Concludes the social skills group when (1) teacher-completed SSRS (Gresham & Elliott, 1990) scores indicate average performance on the social skills and problem behavior subscale scores, and (2) the SSBD scores collected during the next behavior rating period indicate the absence of risk.

Note. See Blueprints for Violence Prevention (*www.colorado.edu/cspv/index.html*) and What Works Clearing House (*ies. ed.gov/ncee/wwc* for overviews of additional model and promising programs.

Box 6.2. **Secondary Intervention Grid: Middle and High School Level**

Support	Description	Schoolwide data: Entry criteria	Data to monitor progress	Exit criteria
Homework Club	Assists students while they complete homework and other missing school assignments. Meets four times a week for 30 minutes after school. This group can be run by teachers, trained parent volunteers, or paraprofessionals in a designated classroom, an office, or in the school library or cafeteria.	• Low GPA (e.g., < 2.5), or • Failing grade, or • Miss, on average, more than 1 day a month	• Daily progress monitoring forms completed by teachers and viewed by parents. • Individual class grades collected by the teacher during the given reporting period. • Weekly makeup work list collected by the teacher. • Percentage of assignments completed each week for each period. • Weekly attendance collected by attendance secretary.	Completes all missing assignments and passes all academic classes during the next grading period, with a cumulative GPA ≥ 2.5.
Remedial Reading or Writing Program	Improves reading and/or writing skills. Thirty minutes a day after school or offered as an elective class. This program could be staffed by a certified teacher, trained tutors, or paraprofessionals in a designated classroom.	Reading difficulties • Scored below the 25th percentile on schoolwide reading measure, or Writing difficulties • Writing assessment score < 25	• Weekly reading probes collected by the reading teacher. • Weekly writing probes collected by the writing teacher.	Reading score improves to above 25th percentile and/ or meets story element criteria of 5+.

Box 6.2 (*cont.*)

Support	Description	Schoolwide data: Entry criteria	Data to monitor progress	Exit criteria
Social Skills Group	Focuses on improving students' social skills. Two days a week, 45 minutes, to address students' specific acquisition deficits. Sessions conducted by school psychology intern or practicum student (see Lane et al., 2003; Miller et al., 2005) or as part of an elective course (Robertson & Lane, 2007)	Behavior problems • Three or more ODRs that reflect peer-related problems, or • Moderate-risk status on SRSS, with a score of 2 or 3 on the problem behavior item. • SDQ score in the abnormal range on peer problems or prosocial behavior subscale scores.	• Number of ODRs (during given period). • Daily social skills checklist completed by social skills instructor. • Daily class participation collected by the social skills teacher. • Direct observations of social interaction.	Student scores in the low-risk status during the next SRSS screening; normal score on the SDQ peer problems and prosocial behavior subscale score; and there are no ODRs related to peer problems during the same reporting cycle.
Behavior Education Program (BEP; Crone, Horner, & Hawken, 2004)	The BEP is designed for students with persistent behavior concerns who are not dangerous. The BEP provides a daily check-in/check-out system that help teachers give students (1) immediate feedback on their behavior by completing a daily progress report (DPR) and (2) additional opportunities for positive adult interactions. Parents participate by signing off on daily sheets.	Academic and behavioral concerns: *Academic* • Report cards: Earned a "needs improvement" score on study skills or a C– or lower in any academic content class, or *Behavioral* • SRSS score in the moderate-risk range, or • Three or more ODRs during a grading period.	• Daily progress monitoring forms completed by teachers and viewed by parents. • Number of ODRs (during given period).	Move into the maintenance self-monitoring phase when students meet their goals for 3 consecutive weeks. Self-monitoring phase ends when the next academic reporting period and behavior rating results indicate the absence of risk following the same criteria stated in the inclusion criteria.

Note See Blueprints for Violence Prevention (*www.colorado.edu/cspv/index.html*) and What Works Clearing House (*ies.ed.gov/ncee/wwc*) for overviews of additional model and promising programs.

Box 6.3. **Tertiary Intervention Grid: Elementary Level**

Support	Description	Schoolwide data: Entry criteria	Data to monitor progress	Exit criteria
Functional Assessment-Based Intervention	Individualized interventions developed by the behavior specialist and PBIS team.	Students who: *Behavior* • Scored in the high-risk category on the SRSS, or • Exceeded Stage 3 scores on the SSBD, or • Earned more than five ODRs for major events during a grading period. *Academic* • Identified at highest risk for school failure: Recommended for retention, or scored far below basic on statewide or districtwide assessments.	• Data collected on both the (1) target (problem) behavior and (2) replacement (desirable) behavior identified by the team on an ongoing basis. • Weekly teacher report on academic status. • ODR data collected weekly.	The function-based intervention will be faded once a functional relation is demonstrated, using a validated single-case methodology design (e.g., withdrawal design), and the behavioral objectives specified in the plan are met.
Meeting with School Psychologist and Community Mental Health Professionals	School psychologist facilitates services with local mental health services representative and parents/guardians.	Students who: • Received counseling referrals for serious mental health or behavior issues, or • Exceeded Stage 3 scores on the SSBD	• Bullying referral data collected daily. • Number of ODRs collected weekly. • Parent input collected daily. • School psychologist and mental-health-identified measures. • Weekly teacher report on academic status.	Services are maintained until parents, school personnel, and mental health providers agree on appropriate course of action.

<table>
<tr><td colspan="5" align="center">Box 6.3 (cont.)</td></tr>
<tr>
<th>Support</th>
<th>Description</th>
<th>Schoolwide data: Entry criteria</th>
<th>Data to monitor progress</th>
<th>Exit criteria</th>
</tr>
<tr>
<td>Fast Track</td>
<td>This program is designed for the prevention of chronic and severe conduct problems. It is comprised of several components, including parent training, social skills training, academic tutoring, and classroom intervention.</td>
<td>Students who:

Behavior

• Scored in the high-risk category on the SRSS, or
• Exceeded Stage 3 scores on the SSBD, or
• Earned more than five ODRs for major events during a grading period.

Academic

• Identified at highest risk for school failure: Recommended for retention, or scored far below basic on statewide or districtwide assessments.</td>
<td>• ODRs collected weekly.
• Data pertinent to elements of intervention are established, then collected and analyzed on an ongoing basis (e.g., results of social skills training, academic tutoring).
• Weekly teacher report on academic status.</td>
<td>Intervention team agrees tertiary support is not longer required.</td>
</tr>
</table>

Note. See Blueprints for Violence Prevention (*www.colorado.edu/cspv/index.html*) and What Works Clearing House (*ies. ed.gov/ncee/wwc*) for overviews of additional model and promising programs.

ticipate in the BEP intervention when they demonstrate either academic problems (e.g., a report card grade lower than a C– in any academic content class; a "needs improvement" score on study skills) or behavior problems (e.g., moderate-risk score on the SRSS; three or more ODRs during a given grading period).

The fourth column contains data monitoring procedures such as the information that will be collected, by whom, and how often to determine if the student is responding. For example, the student's daily progress report and ODRs are the monitoring procedures used to indicate whether the student's performance is improving.

The fifth column contains information regarding exit criteria—that is, the criteria and performance levels that must be met before the intervention is concluded. In other words, how will you determine when a student no longer needs the intervention? Once students participating in the BEP have met their designated goals for 3 consecutive weeks during the maintenance phase, and the next academic reporting period and

Box 6.4. Tertiary Intervention Grid: Middle and High School Level

Support	Description	Schoolwide data: Entry criteria	Data to monitor progress	Exit criteria
Functional Assessment-Based Intervention	Individualized interventions developed by the behavior specialist and PBIS team	Students who: *Behavior* • Scored in the high-risk category on the SRSS, or • Scored in the clinical range on one of the following SDQ subscales: Emotional Symptoms, Conduct Problems, Hyperactivity, or Prosocial Behavior, or • Earned more than five ODRs for major events during a grading period and may have the following: *Academic* • Identified at highest risk for school failure: Recommended for retention, or scored far below basic on statewide or districtwide assessments.	• Data collected on both the (1) target (problem) behavior and (2) replacement (desirable) behavior identified by the team on an ongoing basis. • Weekly teacher report on academic status. • ODR data collected weekly.	The function-based intervention will be faded once a functional relation is demonstrated using a validated single-case methodology design (e.g., withdrawal design), and the behavioral objectives specified in the plan are met.
Meeting with School Psychologist and Mental Health Professionals	School psychologist facilitates services with local mental health services representative and parents/guardians.	Students who: • Scored in the clinical range on either of the following SDQ subtests: Emotional Symptoms or Conduct Problems, or • Received counseling referrals for serious mental health or behavior issues.	• Weekly parent input • School psychologist and mental-health-identified measures.	Services are maintained until parents, school personnel, and mental health providers agree on appropriate course of action.

Support	Description	Schoolwide data: Entry criteria	Data to monitor progress	Exit criteria
Students Taking a Right Stand (STARS) Individual Counseling	Individualized counseling program designed to support students with issues including substance abuse, violence, bullying, harassment, family conflicts and divorce, loss, and grief.	Students who: *Behavior* • Identified as high risk per above, or • Scored a 3 on item 7 (aggressive behavior) of the SRSS, or • Exhibited other risk factors addressed by program and may also have the following: *Academic* • Identified at highest risk for school failure: Recommended for retention, at risk for dropping out, or scored far below basic on statewide or districtwide assessments.	• STARS counseling surveys completed weekly. • Data pertinent to elements of intervention are established, then collected and analyzed (e.g., results of social skills training, academic tutoring).	• Completion of counseling sessions as determined by individual counselor. • Intervention team agrees tertiary support is no longer required.

Note. See Blueprints for Violence Prevention (www.colorado.edu/cspv/index.html) and What Works Clearing House (ies.ed.gov/ncee/wwc) for overviews of additional model and promising programs.

behavior ratings indicate the absence of risk following the same criteria stated in the inclusion criteria, they are exited from the program.

When you are ready to design these secondary and tertiary intervention support grids, we encourage you to begin by making a master list of the secondary and tertiary prevention programs you already have available at your school (again, see Boxes 6.1–6.4) as well as those you would like to employ. We strongly encourage you to select interventions that are evidenced-based practices, or at least those that are promising practices (e.g., function-based interventions for students with EBD; Lane, Kalberg, & Shepcaro, 2008), meaning that scientifically rigorous evaluations support the use of such practices (Gersten et al., 2005; Horner et al., 2005). We also suggest that you see the Blueprints for Violence Prevention, available online at *www.colorado.edu/cspv/index.html*, and What Works Clearing House, online at *ies.ed.gov/ncee/wwc*, for overviews of additional model and promising programs.

If the practices in which you are interested have not been validated yet, then consider testing these practices using either single-case or group-design methodologies. In short, incorporate practices that are supported by scientific testing and are feasible in relation to the multiple task demands placed on teachers (Lane, 2007).

In the sections that follow we offer illustrations of how to identify and support students across the K–12 continuum who require secondary and tertiary levels of prevention. Specifically, we describe different approaches to analyzing (1) academic data in isolation, (2) behavioral data in isolation, and (3) academic and behavioral data together. The goal in each of these approaches is to identify students who require additional support by using data-based decision making. In addition, we recommend that you rely on scientifically rigorous, defensible designs to determine the extent to which these extra supports meet the intended goals.

Analyzing Academic Data

A vast amount of academic data is collected on a regular basis: CBMs, work samples, standardized tests, and grades. In this section we provide two illustrations, one traditional and one nontraditional, for using existing schoolwide data to identify and support elementary and high school students who require additional academic supports.

Identifying and Supporting Elementary-Age Students with Varying Reading Skills

Curriculum-based data can be used across the K–12 continuum as a practical, cost-effective, accurate method of identifying students who require additional supports. In this section we illustrate practices from an elementary school that used curriculum-based reading data as part of their schoolwide primary prevention program to monitor student progress and then identify students who required either remediation or enrichment (Lane, Robertson, Parks, & Edwards, 2006).

At this particular school, three CBM probes were administered to each student at three time points: at the onset of the school year (Time 1), prior to winter break (Time 2), and at year end (Time 3), taking the median probe as the score to be compared. In addition, teachers administered one probe per student each week to use when making instructional decisions in the classroom (Lane, Robertson, Parks, et al., 2006).

Figures 6.5 and 6.6 present graphs with four quadrants showing results of Time 1 and Time 2 administrations (Lane, Robertson, Parks, et al., 2006). Specifically, data were analyzed to determine how students responded to instruction between Time 1 and Time 2 CBM administrations to help determine how instruction needed to be shaped. The vertical and horizontal lines that divide the graph into four quadrants represent the benchmarks for performance. Students whose benchmark scores placed them in Quadrant I were identified as needing enrichment activities beyond the scope of the current reading program, as evidenced by above benchmark scores at Time 1 and Time 2 (Responders: High—Grow). Students placing in Quadrant II showed improvement by moving from below benchmark at Time 1 to at or above benchmark at Time 2 (Responders: Low—Grow), indicating that the present curriculum and instruction were sufficient. Students placing in Quadrant III were identified as needing remediation

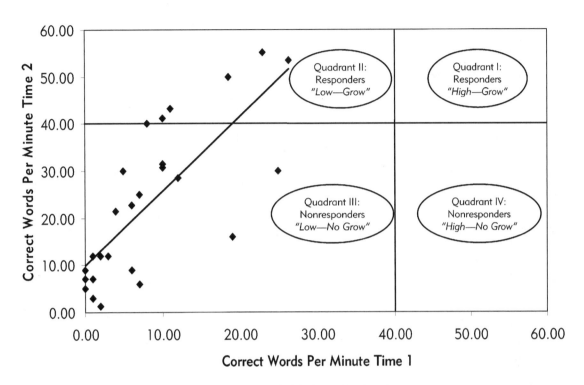

Figure 6.5. **Analyzing CBM data for kindergarten.**

in the form of either secondary or tertiary intervention efforts, as evidenced by below benchmark scores at Time 1 and Time 2 (Nonresponders: Low—No Grow). Finally, students placing in Quadrant IV were also identified as needing remediation in the form of either secondary or tertiary intervention efforts, given that although they initially scored above benchmark at Time 1, they now scored below benchmark at Time 2, indicating that they were not making the necessary gains in reading fluency (Nonresponders: High—No Grow).

In the kindergarten illustration (Figure 6.5), you'll see that although some students responded to the program (Quadrant II Responders: Low—Grow), the majority of the class was still below benchmark at Time 2 (Quadrant III Nonresponders: Low—No Grow). Given this profile, one suggestion is to supplement the kindergarten reading curriculum with a program aimed at improving early literacy skills, such as Phonological Awareness Training for Reading (PATR; Torgesen & Bryant, 1994) or Ladders to Literacy: A Kindergarten Activity Book (O'Connor, Notari-Syverson, & Vadasy, 2005). Either intervention could be implemented immediately following winter break.

In the fourth-grade illustration (Figure 6.6), all but a few students met or exceeded the benchmark requirements (Quadrant I Responders: High—Grow; Lane, Robert-

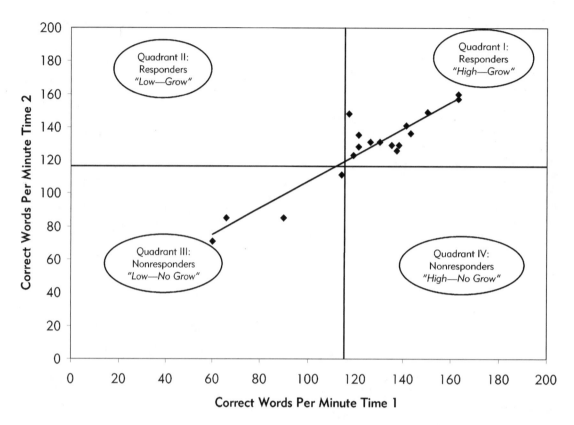

Figure 6.6. **Analyzing CBM data for fourth grade.**

son, Parks, et al., 2006). Only four students required additional supports (Quadrant III Nonresponders: Low—No Grow). In this case, you might consider a one-to-one reading intervention to provide intensive support for students in Quadrant III. A multiple baseline across-participants design could be used to evaluate how these students respond to the tertiary level support (a great thesis option!).

Supporting High School Students as They Prepare for the ACT

Several of us (Lane, Robertson, Mofield, Wehby, & Parks, in press) took a less traditional approach to secondary interventions by supporting an entire subgroup of students—11th-grade students taking the ACT test—who historically had been less than successful on college entrance exams. In this study we conducted a targeted, secondary intervention implemented within the context of a three-tiered model to prepare 11th-grade students for the ACT college entrance exam. Rather than waiting for some students to perform poorly on the ACT and then providing support, this intervention was conducted with the entire 11th-grade class. Although it is not typical to offer a secondary intervention to a group that includes students who respond to the primary plan, this was a proactive measure based on data that indicated the previous years' 11th-grade students had not performed as desired on the ACT test and that participation would likely benefit *all* students as they prepared for the test.

The principal and the PBIS team at a rural high school elected to implement an ACT preparation program, Preparing for the ACT, as part of the PBIS plan (see Lane, Robertson, Mofield, et al., 2008, for a detailed description of the curriculum). Homeroom teachers taught an ACT preparation program to all 11th-grade students 1 day per week. As part of this program, students ($N = 126$) completed practice probes with sample ACT test items and took a practice test before and after completing the curriculum. One aspect of this intervention was a quasi-experimental study that compared actual ACT performance of students who did and did not participate in the intervention (current academic year versus previous academic year). Results suggested improved performance on the ACT for students who did participate in the program. Also, there was an increase in the percentage of students who met or exceeded the district target scores, and school mean ACT scores exceeded state mean scores following intervention participation.

Summary

These are just two illustrations of how to use schoolwide academic data to determine which groups of students are in need of additional supports. There are a multitude of options for how to develop more focused intervention efforts to support students who need more than what is offered in the primary prevention program. The same is true when analyzing behavioral data, which we consider next.

Analyzing Behavior Data

As mentioned in Chapter 4, empirically validated screening tools are available for use across the K–12 continuum. In this section we provide three illustrations of how to analyze screening data at the elementary, middle, and high school levels to identify nonresponders. Then we review a secondary intervention conducted as part of a three-tiered model of prevention at the elementary level.

Identifying Elementary Students Using the SSBD

Figure 6.7 offers an illustration of how to analyze data from the SSBD to determine which students require additional supports (Lane, Kalberg, Menzies, et al., 2008). One of the schools reported in this study implemented the SSBD at three times as part of regular school practices: 6 weeks after school started (fall), prior to winter break (winter), and again at year end (spring). Figure 6.7 contains the data for the first two time points: fall 2007 and winter 2007.

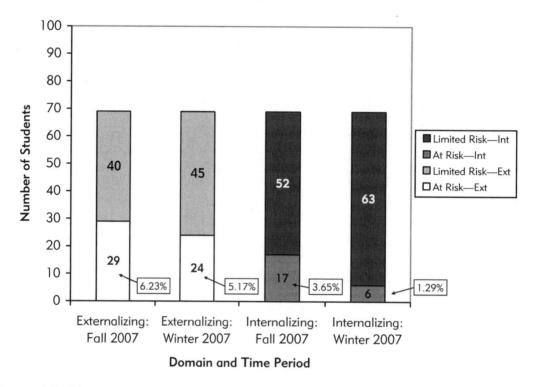

Figure 6.7. SSBD data fall 2007 to winter 2007 for Payton Povey Elementary School: Comparing limited-risk to at-risk students for both externalizing and internalizing domains.

The first two bars contain information about students who were nominated in the externalizing category. During the fall of 2007 a total of 69 students received a ranking of 1, 2, or 3 for externalizing behaviors on the SSBD. Of these 69 students, 29 students (6.23% of the school) exceeded normative criteria for externalizing behavior during Stage 2 as determined by scores on the critical events index and combined frequency index rating scales (see Chapter 5 for a detailed description of the SSBD screening tool). A few months later, another 69 students were ranked 1, 2, or 3 on the externalizing dimension of the SSBD. Of these 69 students, 24 (5.17% of the school) exceeded normative criteria for externalizing behavior during Stage 2. Thus, there was a small reduction in the percentage of students exceeding normative criteria with regard to externalizing behaviors.

The next two bars contain information about students nominated in the internalizing category. During the fall of 2007 a total of 69 students received a ranking of 1, 2, or 3 for internalizing behaviors on the SSBD. Of these 69 students, 17 students (3.65% of the school) exceeded normative criteria for internalizing behavior during Stage 2, as measured by scores on the critical events index and combined frequency index rating scales. A few months later, another 69 students were ranked 1, 2, or 3 on the internalizing dimension of the SSBD. Of these 69 students, only 6 (1.29% of the school) exceeded normative criteria for internalizing behavior during Stage 2. This suggests that the primary prevention program was particularly effective for students with internalizing behavior patterns.

In terms of secondary prevention efforts, the 24 students exceeding normative criteria for externalizing behavior and the 6 students exceeding normative criteria for internalizing behavior at the winter 2007 time point could be placed into either secondary or tertiary levels of prevention. The information examined by grade level indicated that the majority of students with externalizing concerns are in first grade, and the majority of students with internalizing concerns are in third grade. In looking at the secondary intervention grid (see Box 6.1), these students may be eligible for participation in the social skills group or the BEP available at this school, depending on the extent to which the other inclusionary criteria are met for the secondary prevention efforts.

Identifying Middle School Students Using the SDQ

Figures 6.8 (total difficulties scores), 6.9 (peer problems subscale scores) and 6.10 (prosocial behavior subscale scores) are examples of how to analyze data from the SDQ to see how the middle school as a whole is responding and determine which students require additional supports (Lane, Kalberg, Menzies, et al., 2008). At this particular

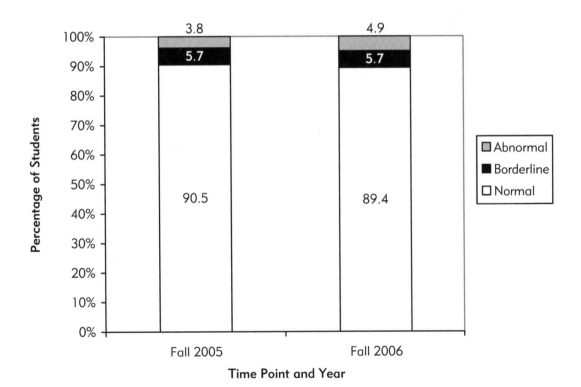

Figure 6.8. **SDQ total difficulties data over time for Foster Middle School: Fall 2005 to fall 2006.**

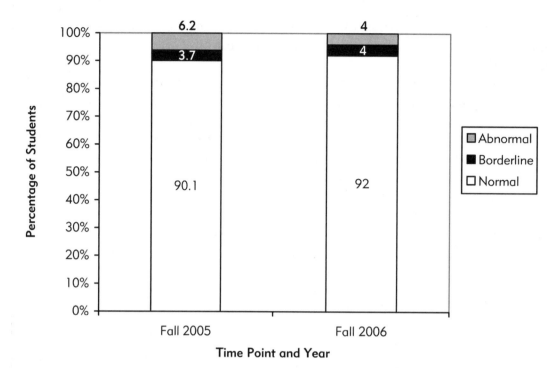

Figure 6.9. **SDQ peer problems data over time for Foster Middle School: Fall 2005 to fall 2006.**

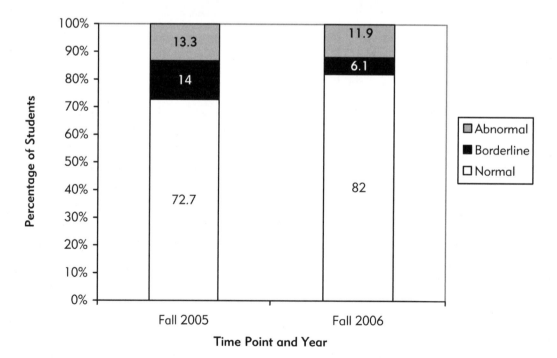

Figure 6.10. **SDQ prosocial behavior data over time for Foster Middle School: Fall 2005 to fall 2006.**

school, the SDQ and the SRSS were implemented at three times as part of regular school practices: 6 weeks after school started (fall), prior to winter break (winter), and again at year end (spring).

Figure 6.8 reflects the total difficulties scores (a composite score reflecting the first four subscales), with normal, borderline, and abnormal ranges for fall 2005 and fall 2006 (Lane, Kalberg, Menzies, et al., 2008). Figures 6.9 and 6.10 present the same results for peer problems (Figure 6.9) and prosocial behavior subscales (Figure 6.10). You can complete similar figures for all five subscales: Emotional Symptoms, Conduct Problems, Hyperactivity, Peer Problems, and Prosocial Behavior. One of the outcomes you'll notice is that the percentage of students in the school in the normal category for prosocial behavior scores increased from 73% in the fall of 2005 to 82% in the fall of 2006, with the percentage of students in the borderline category decreasing from 14 to 6%. Furthermore, the percentage of students in the abnormal category decreased from 13 to 12%. Thus, prosocial behavior is increasing for the school as a whole.

Additionally, these data can be used to identify students with emotional symptoms, conduct problems, hyperactivity, and peer problems who fall into the abnormal category and could benefit from secondary (see Box 6.2, social skills groups) or tertiary interventions (see Box 6.4). For example, students scoring in the abnormal range for conduct problems or emotional symptoms may be eligible to meet with the school psychologist or receive mental health services as a tertiary level of prevention (Box 6.4).

Identifying High School Students Using the SRSS

Figure 6.11 is an example of how to analyze data from the SRSS at the high school level to see how the school as a whole is responding and determine which students require additional supports (Lane, Kalberg, Menzies, et al., 2008). At this particular school, the SRSS was implemented three times as part of regular school practices: 6 weeks after school started (fall), prior to winter break (winter), and again at year end (spring). Figure 6.11 contains the data for two time points: fall of 2004 (first year of implementing a primary prevention program) and fall of 2005 (second year of implementation).

As you may recall from earlier in this chapter, the lower portion of each bar contains the percentage of students scoring in the low-risk category (0–3), the middle portion of each bar contains the percentage of students scoring in the moderate-risk category (4–8), and the upper portion of each bar contains the percentage of students scoring in the high-risk category (9–21). One of the outcomes you'll notice is that the percentage of students in the low-risk category increased from 81.88% in the fall of 2004 to 90.72% in the fall of 2005, after just 1 year of implementation. The percentage of students in the moderate-risk category decreased (suggesting a lowering of risk) from 13.01 to 7.86%. The percentage of students in the high-risk category decreased from 5.11 to 1.42%, with just 9 students (compared to 31 in the previous fall) at high risk (Lane, Kalberg, Menzies, et al., 2008).

These data can be used to identify students with high-risk status for placement in tertiary-level prevention efforts and those in the moderate-risk category into secondary-level prevention programs. For example, you might place students into a secondary-

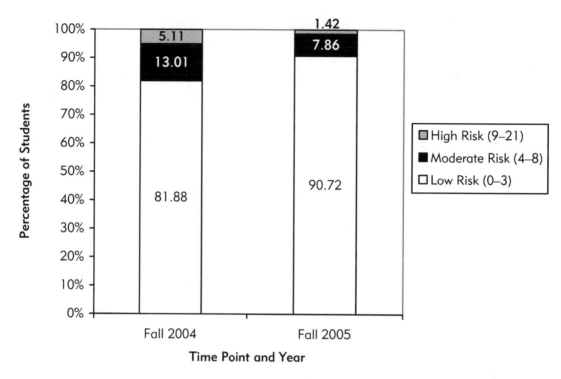

Figure 6.11. **SRSS data over time for Finlay High School: Fall 2004 to fall 2005.**

level prevention program such as the BEP, as discussed above. Or, you might place them in a social skills group if they (1) score in the moderate-risk range on the SRSS with a score of 2 or 3 on the peer problem item, (2) earn three or more ODRs for peer-related problems, or (3) score in the abnormal range on the Peer Problems or Proso-cial Behavior subscale scores on the SDQ (Goodman, 1997; see Box 6.2). You might also consider more intensive supports such as tertiary-level function-based intervention if the students meet those inclusion criteria. For example, to receive a function-based intervention, students would need to meet the following inclusion criteria on the behavior dimensions: (1) high risk on the SRSS or scoring in the clinical range on Emotional Symptoms, Conduct Problems, Hyperactivity, or Prosocial subscales of the SDQ or (2) earn 5 or more ODRs during a grading period (see Box 6.4).

Identifying and Supporting Elementary Students with Behavioral Concerns

A more formal study developed a targeted social skills training program to support elementary-age students identified by their teachers as at risk for antisocial behavior (Lane et al., 2003). Specifically, they designed a secondary-level social skills program to determine the degree to which (1) participation in the program improved behavior in the classroom and playground setting and (2) improved social competence influenced the amount of time students were engaged academically.

Students in grades 2–4 were selected for this study based on how they responded to a schoolwide primary prevention program that contained literacy and behavioral components as determined by the SRSS data. Students who maintained or moved into high-risk status (scores of 9–21) after the first 4 months of the school year, in addition to a problem behavior rating of 2 (*sometimes*) or 3 (*frequently*), were invited to participate in this social skills prevention effort. Eight students met these criteria; however, one was expelled, so seven at-risk students along with seven peers who were not at risk were placed in one of three social skills groups. These groups were conducted 2 days per week (for 30 minutes) for a total of 10 weeks (10 hours) by doctoral students in a school psychology program. Non-at-risk peers served as models for their at-risk peers during the intervention sessions to help the students at risk learn the new skills and to provide prompts for them in other settings (e.g., playground) to encourage generalization of the skills learned in the intervention sessions. Each intervention group focused on students' specific social skills deficits, as determined by the SSRS (Gresham & Elliott, 1990; see Lane et al., 2003, for a detailed discussion of the curriculum). The lessons to address the specific acquisition deficits, which came from Elliott and Gresham's (1991) *Social Skills Intervention Guide: Practical Strategies for Social Skills Training*, were taught during 17 of the 20 sessions, with the additional three sessions used for review and to plan for generalization.

Results of this multiple baseline across-intervention group design study indicated that students in the three groups experienced lasting decreases in disruptive classroom behavior and negative social interactions on the playground. In addition, there were increases in academic engaged time in the classroom. Social validity results revealed that students rated the intervention procedures favorably and used their new skills in several settings.

Summary

The above illustrations are practical examples of how to analyze behavioral data to identify students who require additional behavior supports. These examples range from more global (e.g., social skills) to more specific (e.g., emotional problems) supports. It is also possible to analyze academic and behavioral data to identify and support students with multiple needs.

Analyzing Academic and Behavior Data Together

In the material that follow, we provide examples from our work of how to analyze academic and behavioral data together to identify and assist students in elementary and secondary schools who have deficits in both areas. However, please keep in mind that there are also a number of other studies offering other illustrations of how to examine academic and behavioral data together (e.g., Cheney et al., 2004; Frick et al., 1991; Kamps et al., 2003; Lane, Barton-Arwood, et al., 2006; Lane & Menzies, 2005; Walker et al., 2005).

Identifying and Supporting First-Grade Students with Literacy and Behavioral Concerns

Several of us (Lane et al., 2003) conducted a supplemental early literacy program for first-grade students identified by their teachers as at risk for antisocial behavior and who were not responding to a schoolwide program that contained both behavioral and academic components. Specifically, students were invited to receive this extra literacy instruction if they met two criteria. First, students had to be rated by their teachers as at high risk (scores 9–21) on the SRSS (which was completed by all teachers as part of the schoolwide assessment plan) at the midpoint assessment. Second, students had to be identified by their teachers as being in the bottom third of their class in terms of early literacy skills.

In this study the intervention was conducted in a general education classroom during the course of the regular school day. The seven participants were assigned randomly to one of two intervention groups (Group 1: $n = 4$; Group 2: $n = 3$) and evaluated using a multiple baseline design. The school literacy leader, a doctoral candidate, conducted both intervention groups in a general education classroom. Thirty lessons 30 minutes in length were held 3–4 days per week over a 9-week period. Although students showed initial variability in their decoding skills and behavior in the classroom, all students showed improved word attack skills and decreased levels of disruptive behavior in the classroom following the completion of the intervention. Improved early literacy skills were associated with lasting decreases in disruptive classroom behavior, which has also been observed in other academic interventions in relation to students with EBD (Falk & Wehby, 2001; Wehby, Falk, Barton-Arwood, Lane, & Cooley, 2003).

Identifying and Supporting Elementary-Grade Students with Reading and Behavioral Concerns

We also investigated the effects of a schoolwide program on the academic and behavioral skills of all students in an urban elementary school (Menzies, Lane, & Kalberg, 2008). The primary-level behavior intervention included the teaching and reinforcement of 10 social skills the teachers identified as necessary for school success. In addition, a common discipline plan was used by all teachers. The plan was created by the teaching staff and used elements from both the Lee Canter (1990) and Harry Wong (Wong & Wong, 1998) approaches to student discipline. The schoolwide academic plan relied on the use of small-group instruction in language arts to target the particular needs and strengths of students (see Menzies, Mahdavi, & Lewis, 2008, for a complete description of the small-group program used in first grade). Small-group instruction supplemented and supported the school's regular whole-group language arts instruction.

Students were administered the SRSS at three time points to examine changes in risk status. Academic risk status was assessed using district multiple measures as well as standardized CBMs. These were administered at the same time as the behavioral measures. Results indicated that the program may have positively influenced students' behavior and academic growth by promoting academic gains and maintaining stability in prosocial behaviors.

Students who were nonresponsive to the primary intervention efforts and who were still identified as at high risk for antisocial behavior at the midpoint were invited to participate in secondary interventions. Paraprofessionals were trained to use a social skills curriculum (Elliott & Gresham, 1991) to provide 20 lessons that were focused on students' areas of deficit as identified by their teachers. Students attended the lessons two times a week for 30 minutes each session. These were conducted in small groups that included two to three target children as well as two model students. The results indicated that students were responsive to the secondary intervention. At the study's end they displayed higher rates of academic engaged time, lower rates of disruptive behavior during instructional times, and lower rates of negative social interactions on the playground.

Identifying and Supporting First-Grade Students with Writing and Behavioral Concerns

We examined the effects of a secondary academic intervention focused on improving the writing skills of second-grade students with poor writing skills who were also at risk for emotional and behavioral disorders (Lane, Harris, et al., 2008). This study was conducted in a large rural elementary school that had a three-tiered model of positive behavior interventions and supports.

Second-grade students were selected for possible participation by analyzing both the behavior screening data and the standardized writing measures, each of which was collected as part of regular school practices. Specifically, students who (1) scored at high or moderate risk on the SRSS or who exceeded normative criteria on Stage 2 of the SSBD and (2) scored at or below the 25th percentile on a standardized measures of writing (the Test of Written Language–3; Hammil & Larsen, 1996) were invited to receive this extra support. Of the 11 second-grade students who had both writing and behavior concerns, parental consent and student assent were received for 8 students. Six students completed the program (one student moved and one did not finish before year end).

Once students were identified and the necessary permissions obtained, research assistants (RAs) worked individually with students to teach them how to plan and write a story using the self-regulated strategy development (SRSD) model. RAs worked with the students three to four times per week for 30 minutes each session. Students needed between 13 and 15 lessons to learn the strategies, knowledge, and skills necessary to write stories.

Results of this multiple-probe design suggested that the six students improved in story completeness, length, and quality. Moreover the improvements were sustained into the maintenance phase. Social validity data indicated that the students and teachers found the intervention acceptable, with some raters indicating that the intervention actually exceeded their expectations.

*Identifying and Supporting Middle School Students with Academic
and Behavioral Concerns*

In another study students nonresponsive to the primary PBIS plan were identified using existing schoolwide data (Robertson & Lane, 2007). Sixty-five students were selected as having both academic and behavior concerns. A behavior concern was operationally defined as scoring moderate or high on the midpoint administration of the SRSS or obtaining one or more ODRs within the first 4 months of school. Further, an academic concern was defined as obtaining one or more failing grades or a low GPA (< 2.7) during the second quarter. Upon selection, any student with poor reading skills (defined by enrollment in a remedial reading program) was excluded because the curriculum required independent reading skills. Selected students were assigned randomly into one of two intervention groups: (1) a study skills program or a (2) study skills plus conflict resolution skills program. Students remained in the intervention group led by teachers with the support of counselors for 21 weeks or 56 lessons. Results suggested that students in both intervention groups showed similar patterns of responding in terms of their knowledge of study skills, but they did not display significant gains in study habits. According to behavioral outcome measures, students who received the conflict resolution skills curriculum demonstrated improvements in their knowledge of these skills. However, changes in their *knowledge* of skills did not generalize to changes in conflict resolution *styles*. This study illustrates one way to identify nonresponsive students using existing schoolwide data.

*Identifying and Supporting Elementary and Middle School Students with Tertiary
Levels of Prevention*

In another study we used schoolwide data to identify students who were nonresponsive to both primary and secondary prevention efforts (Lane, Rogers, et al., 2007). Two students, one at the elementary level and one at the middle school level, received function-based interventions using a systematic approach to (1) identify the function of the target behavior, (2) select an appropriate intervention focus, and (3) design an intervention with the components necessary to accurately interpret intervention outcomes (e.g., treatment integrity, social validity, and generalization and maintenance; Umbreit et al., 2007).

The elementary student, Claire, was identified for a secondary intervention due to high levels of internalizing behaviors, as measured by the SSBD. She went on to receive a behavior intervention that did produce some decreases in internalizing behavior (e.g., isolating herself from others), but she still showed very high levels of internalizing behaviors as measured by the Internalizing subscale of the SSRS (Gresham & Elliott, 1990). In addition, Claire continued to perform below average in reading skills, as evidenced by earning a broad reading score below the 25th percentile (Woodcock–Johnson III Tests of Achievement [WJ III]; Woodcock, McGrew, & Mather, 2001).

To increase her participation in class, Claire next received a function-based intervention that was measured using event recording. Functional assessment data were analyzed by placing the data into a function matrix (see Umbreit et al., 2007) to determine if the target behavior occurred to either seek (positive reinforcement) or avoid (negative reinforcement) attention from others, activities or tasks, or tangibles. Based on results of the function matrix, Claire's nonparticipation served to help her avoid attention from her teacher and peers. Her intervention was designed using the function-based intervention decision model (Umbreit et al.). This model guides the intervention design process using two key questions: (1) Is the student able to perform the replacement behavior? (2) Does the classroom environment represent effective practices? It was determined that Claire was able to participate in class (the replacement behavior) and that the classroom environment did represent effective practices. Claire's intervention focused on *adjusting the contingencies*. In accordance with this intervention method, "Adjust the Contingencies," as defined within the intervention decision model, conditions within the environment were structured to increase the likelihood that Claire would participate in class. Further, when she did participate, the consequences that previously reinforced the target behavior (nonparticipation) were provided. Finally, the same consequences were withheld when Claire did not participate.

Results of a changing criterion design demonstrated a functional relation between the introduction of the intervention and increases in Claire's participation. In short—it worked! Further, both Claire and her teacher rated the intervention procedures favorably.

Aaron, a middle school student receiving special education services, was identified for a secondary intervention because he was initially nonresponsive to the primary prevention program. Nonresponsiveness to the primary plan was defined as having concerns in both academic (low GPA [$\leq$ 2.7] or one or more failing grades, according to the second quarter) and behavioral (one or more ODRs within the first 4 months of the school year or scoring in the moderate- or high-risk status on the SRSS) domains. As a result, Aaron was placed into a secondary intervention, as described above (see "Identifying and Supporting Middle School Students with Academic and Behavioral Concerns"). Aaron met the academic inclusion criteria by earning one failing grade, and he met the behavior inclusion criteria by earning a score of 9 (high risk) on the SRSS as well as earning four ODRs. Aaron's secondary intervention consisted of 21 weeks of instruction (28 hours) in study skills and conflict resolution skills, which were conducted by credentialed teachers as part of an elective class during the second semester (see Robertson & Lane, 2005). However, although Aaron showed changes in his knowledge of study skills, he was considered nonresponsive to the secondary plan because he continued to demonstrate concerns in academic (GPA 2.17 and one failing grade) and behavioral (year-end SRSS score of 14 and nine ODRs) domains. According to school-wide data, Aaron was *the* least responsive of all students who were in the secondary prevention plan, which is why he was selected to receive a function-based intervention.

To increase his compliance during his science class, Aaron received a function-based intervention that was measured using whole-interval recording. Based on the results of the functional assessment data, which were analyzed using the function matrix, noncompliance was maintained by teacher attention. When applying the function-based intervention decision model (Umbreit et al., 2007) to Aaron's case, the team decided that he was capable of performing the replacement behavior, but that the classroom environment and methods could be improved to support Aaron better. Therefore, the intervention focused on *improving the environment*. In accordance with the "Improve the Environment" method of the intervention decision model, antecedents were adjusted to increase the likelihood that Aaron would comply during class while decreasing the likelihood of his noncompliant behavior. Additionally, positive reinforcement was given when Aaron complied, whereas noncompliance was placed on extinction (no reinforcement).

Results of a withdrawal design also revealed a functional relation between the introduction of the intervention and increases in compliance, with dramatic increases in compliance during the intervention phases as compared to baseline. Furthermore, Aaron's teachers reported that Aaron's overall science grade increased from a 55% during the first 9-week session to an 82% during the third 9-week session. His cumulative GPA also increased.

Summary

As you can see from the illustrations above, there are a number of methods for using academic and behavioral data to identify and support students with secondary and tertiary interventions (see Boxes 6.1–6.4 for additional suggestions). When getting started with the identification process, we encourage you to consider the following suggestions for managing data.

Guidelines for Establishing Secondary Supports

The first step for intervention team members is to identify the secondary and tertiary levels of prevention that may already be in place at the school site. Also, they will need to decide the criteria for determining which students are placed in the more intensive programs. Criteria for entry and exit need to be established as well as procedures for monitoring student progress. In addition, the team will decide who should be assigned to teach the interventions. Another consideration is when and where the intervention will be offered. As team members begin this process, they should create secondary and tertiary intervention grids to serve as a graphic reminder of the resources available and the specific criteria for providing them to students.

The second step for the school-site team is to decide on additional secondary and tertiary levels of prevention that they might like to consider. There may be resources available in the community in addition to published programs or research-based recommendations, ideally those that are established as an evidenced-based practice (Gersten et al., 2005; Horner et al., 2005). A team member might take on the task of vetting programs to determine which are validated, feasible, and fit well with school goals and philosophies. These can then be brought to the team for further discussion and a final decision. Finally, it is critical to make sure that procedures are manageable—don't attempt to start all secondary and tertiary interventions at the same time. Begin by putting in just one or two secondary supports. Teams are often tempted to put all elements in place rapidly. However, if primary and secondary prevention efforts are not firmly established, then the percentage of students requiring tertiary prevention will be larger. In the end, this preemptive approach makes it more difficult to provide the most at-risk students the supports they need to be successful.

Guidelines for Managing Data

We offer the following guidelines for managing data within the school day, based on recommendations from Sugai and Horner (2002, 2006) as well as our own work. First, schools have access to a plethora of data; use the data collected as part of regular school practice (taking steps to ensure that the data are collected in a reliable manner) and focus on adopting validated behavior and academic screening tools (see Assessment Grids in Tables 5.1–5.3).

Second, as a general rule of thumb, handle the data as few times as possible. In other words, instead of "pushing papers," refine your system so that data are entered immediately. For example, many schools have systems in which teachers enter ODRs or attendance records online (e.g., School-Wide Information Systems [SWIS©]; May et al., 2000). This is an efficient and effective way of entering data. Instead of the teacher filling out a piece of paper in which a copy goes to the office and into a filing system and is entered only later, do it all just one time (whenever possible).

Third, devote no more than 1% of the school day to collecting and analyzing data (Sugai & Horner, 2002). Similar to handing data as few times as possible, be efficient with time and personnel resources when collecting data. Feasible, effective data collection systems are much more likely to be adopted and maintained over time. If you find yourself devoting a significant amount of the school day to data management, consider ways to monitor student outcomes more efficiently.

Fourth, build data collection into daily routines. In other words, make it a part of the job or the school day for certain personnel (e.g., attendance secretaries and vice principals) so that it is not considered one more *extra* thing. So, if a teacher assesses his or her students on reading probes, allow him or her to build the assessment and data entry into his or her routine.

Fifth, establish data collection procedures. When designing your primary prevention plan (which is a working document, remember) include data collection procedures so that if the person in charge of entering the data is absent, another person can still carry on the job. This will also give others a chance to read over procedures and perhaps develop more efficient methods.

Finally, regularly share findings with faculty. Updates on schoolwide data should be reviewed at each faculty meeting (or at a minimum, distributed via e-mail, being careful not to include individual student names to maintain confidentiality). This sharing of data does not need to take up a lot of time, but presenting the information often will make

Box 6.5. **Examples of Disseminating Findings**

Handout in Faculty Meeting	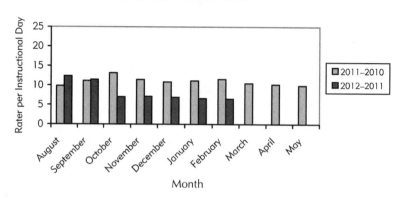 Comparing Rates of Unexcused Tardy Data across School Years: 2010–2011 to 2011–2012

Check out our current schoolwide unexcused tardy data as compared to last year.

Note that the first bars represent the rate of tardies per instructional day each month during last school year, and the second bars represent this year! We've heard many students say that they love the new morning announcement drawings! Keep up the good work!

Mr. Nathan
Principal, Finlay High School

E-mail to faculty and staff	Dear Staff,

- Thought I'd send this along before we go home 'till 2011!

- Through 11/30, 877 students (94%) have NO OFFICE REFERRALS!

- Behavior Screeners: Student Risk Screening Scale—Remember our goal of 80% + scoring in the low-risk category? Well, we exceeded that goal! 92% of our students scored in the low-risk category this December!

- Thank you for all of your efforts this fall. Have a wonderful and relaxing break.

See you in 2011!

Katie Scarlett,
Principal, Fanning Elementary School

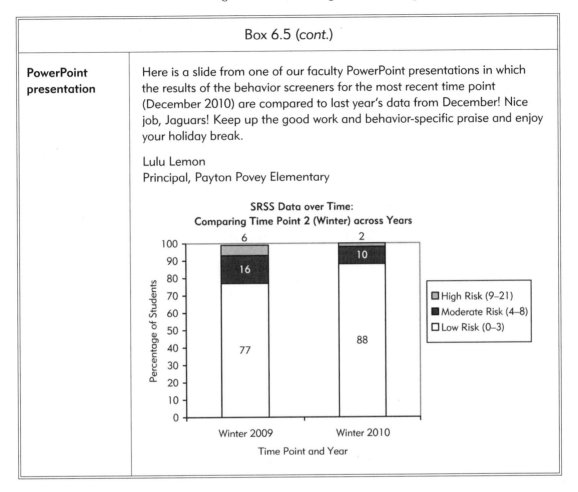

Box 6.5 (cont.)

PowerPoint presentation

Here is a slide from one of our faculty PowerPoint presentations in which the results of the behavior screeners for the most recent time point (December 2010) are compared to last year's data from December! Nice job, Jaguars! Keep up the good work and behavior-specific praise and enjoy your holiday break.

Lulu Lemon
Principal, Payton Povey Elementary

faculty and staff alike aware of the changes that are occurring. Box 6.5 provides some other ways in which the PBIS team may want to disseminate findings, either through e-mail or PowerPoint presentations. Consider these guidelines when creating and refining procedures in which your school collects, analyzes, and shares schoolwide data.

Summary

In this chapter we have discussed the importance of collecting and analyzing schoolwide data to (1) monitor how the school as a whole is responding to the schoolwide plan; (2) determine how different types of students responded; and (3) identify students who require additional supports in the form of secondary and tertiary interventions. To accomplish these objectives, we provided several illustrations on how to use schoolwide data to identify elementary, middle, and high school students in need of secondary supports, inclusive of academic, social, and behavioral domains. We do not presume to think that these are a comprehensive list of illustrations, but rather a starting point to shape your thinking.

In the final chapter we pose and answer commonly asked questions with a goal of giving you the practical information to get a primary prevention program started in your school. We also feature quotes from administrators and teachers who have not only survived, but thrived, through the planning, implementation, and evaluation processes!

Chapter Seven

Getting Started in Your School

Frequently Asked Questions

After reading this book, we hope that you recognize the wide range of challenges that administrators and educators face as they work to meet the academic, behavioral, and social needs of an increasingly diverse group of students. This range includes students with, and at risk for, EBD. While many general education teachers did not enter their teaching careers expecting to address issues such as violence and antisocial behavior, these are the unfortunate realities associated with the growing incivility of today's society (Kauffman, 2005; Lane, 2007; Quinn & Poirier, 2004; Walker, 2003). Due to the emphasis on inclusive programming and the fact that not all students with EBD will necessarily qualify for special education services (Individuals with Disabilities Education Improvement Act, 2004), schools must know how to assist these students in ways that support their educational success.

Fortunately, data-driven three-tiered models of prevention are now embraced by many schools to prevent the development of problem behavior and to use as a structure for responding to students with identified concerns (Lane, 2007). The model introduced in this book incorporates many elements of the traditional PBIS model developed by Sugai and Horner (2002, 2006) to address the social and behavioral domain. In addition, this book introduces elements of the RTI model (Gresham, 2002a; Sugai et al., 2002) that addresses the academic domain. One benefit of the comprehensive, primary prevention plan posed here is that it recognizes the multiple needs of students with EBD, as well as the fact that academic, behavioral, and social concerns co-occur and tend to interact with one another (Lane & Wehby, 2002; Walker et al., 2004). Learning and behavior are rarely mutually exclusive.

In Chapter 1, "Preventing and Managing Problem Behavior in Our Schools: A Formidable Task," we provided an overview of antisocial behavior in schools and offered a three-tiered model as one possible solution for preventing and responding to it. In Chapter 2, "Primary Prevention across the K–12 Grade Span: Developing a Solid Foundation," we reviewed the literature on primary prevention models at the elementary, middle, and high school levels, emphasizing (1) the challenges of conducting schoolwide primary prevention programs in secondary schools, and (2) the importance of considering core quality indicators when designing, implementing, and evaluating primary plans

(Gersten et al., 2005; Horner et al., 2005). In Chapter 3, "A Closer Look at the Positive Behavior Interventions and Supports Model," we defined and explained in detail the PBIS model as conceptualized by Sugai and Horner (2006).

In Chapter 4, "Designing and Implementing Primary Prevention Models," we presented a step-by-step approach to creating a comprehensive primary prevention model containing academic, behavioral, and social components, illustrating one method of constructing primary plans that has been used across the K–12 continuum (Lane, Kalberg, Bruhn, et al., in press; Lane & Menzies, 2003, 2005; Lane, Wehby, et al., 2007; Robertson & Lane, 2007). In Chapter 5, "Assessment and Screening at the Primary Level," we discussed the importance of conducting a sound evaluation (i.e., one that is characterized by treatment integrity, social validity, and systematic screenings) to determine the extent to which the primary program influences student outcomes in terms of academic, behavioral, and social performance. Finally, in Chapter 6, "Determining How Well the Program is Working: Monitoring Outcomes and Identifying Nonresponsive Students," we offered a rationale for collecting data to make decisions about students and provided illustrations of how to (1) monitor how the school as a whole is responding to the schoolwide plan; (2) determine how different types of students respond; and (3) identify students who require additional supports in the form of secondary and tertiary interventions.

In this final chapter we provide a comprehensive list of frequently asked questions and their answers to assist you when designing, implementing, and evaluating your primary prevention plan. The intent of this chapter is to offer concrete information to address logistical issues. The questions are organized by topic and reflect the ideas introduced in Chapters 4–6.

Determining Faculty Interest

How Should We Present This Idea to the School?

Before broaching the idea of a primary prevention plan with the entire faculty, talk to your site administrators. They will help provide the leadership and resources you will require. If you know someone who has been involved in a PBIS program, ask him or her to present it. If not, perhaps someone at your site knows something about PBIS because

---

"The most important part before bringing PBIS to our school was figuring out how to sell it to the faculty. . . . It took time to get buy-in, but we knew it was better than saying here's what we are going to do. Some teachers were against it in the beginning . . . and, funny enough, those teachers became some of our biggest supporters and have really bought into it!"—*Middle School*

"It is a basic schoolwide plan that is easily implemented by all teachers and staff and easily crossed over grade levels. It was a schoolwide experience to involve teachers/staff with 'all' students."—*Elementary School*

---

he or she is interested in it or has read this book or has gone to a training. If not, don't worry. If you are enthusiastic about what PBIS can do for your site, then go ahead and introduce it to the staff. Your enthusiasm will communicate itself, and it may be more meaningful to have a teacher present his or her ideas about PBIS instead of the principal. Think back to the basic reasons why PBIS appeals to you … perhaps because it is a *proactive* rather than a *reactive* approach. Be creative. We've had faculty leaders start the faculty meeting by passing out "good" notes to teachers paired with verbal praise.

How Do We Get Teacher Buy-In?

Assure your faculty that this is not a preset plan, nor is it just one more thing to do; rather, PBIS is a structured way to provide support to your entire student body by coordinating what is already in place at your school and filling in any missing pieces. Perhaps your school already has small-group programs for students with similar concerns (e.g., study groups, reading groups, social skills groups), but the only way students get into those groups is through teacher referral. PBIS offers better communication mechanisms to make sure that all students who need assistance get into the appropriate club by using existing schoolwide data (e.g., GPAs, failure list) or additional screeners (e.g., SDQ [Goodman, 1997]; SSBD [Walker & Severson, 1992]; and SRSS [Drummond, 1994]). During the faculty presentation and introduction of PBIS, encourage questions from the faculty to ensure that all concerns are heard.

What Can We Do If Some Teachers Don't Buy In?

Typically, some teachers will be hesitant to add what they think is another "to do" to their days. It is critical to listen and address these kinds of concerns. Rather than discounting naysayers, pay careful attention to their reasons for not wanting to implement PBIS. Perhaps the plan can be tailored to address their concerns. In schools with which we have worked, we ask staff to sign a *no sabotage* agreement, as mentioned earlier in this book, which states that while they may be reluctant to support the program, they will not interfere with its integrity or make negative comments to students about it. In addition, reluctant staff members are encouraged to continue bringing new concerns to administrators and/or PBIS representatives. Also, consider telling potential new faculty about the PBIS program during interviews so that they are aware of what is expected of them if they are hired.

"When we interview and look for new a teacher, which is a big part of my job, we talk about our PBIS program to ensure that they are a good fit with our school culture."—*Middle School*

Establishing a School-Site Team

Who Should Be a Part of My PBIS Team?

When we began training schools, we required that each PBIS team contain the following key players: one administrator or designee, two general education teachers, one special education teacher, a parent, and a student. In time we learned that it was also important to include teachers from different grade levels and/or different departments to be sure that all major groups were represented. We also learned that it was important to have *students* from various grade levels because different age groups are motivated by different reinforcers (e.g., parking permits). In addition, cohorts often have different characteristics (e.g., some more social than others) and tend to participate in the program in unexpectedly different ways.

When Should We Meet?

During the initial training and planning year, PBIS teams ideally should meet frequently for longer blocks of time to adequately develop the plan. Then the team members must go back to the groups they represent (e.g., second-grade team, fellow peers) and discuss the plan. Additionally, the entire faculty should discuss the progress of the plan during regularly scheduled faculty meetings to address any schoolwide concerns and provide a structured place for feedback. After adopting the primary prevention plan, the PBIS team can expand to include additional members to help with implementation. This step typically occurs toward the end of a school year and in the summer before the first year of implementation. We suggest that the PBIS team create a calendar (to be discussed further in this section) and a "to do" list prior to implementation. Each meeting should include an update on the progress team members are making with their respective duties. Once the PBIS plan is in place, the team should meet monthly to troubleshoot any difficulties and to monitor schoolwide data, as well as to organize screenings and social validity assessments and to monitor program fidelity.

Developing a Data-Based Action Plan

What Should Your Team Be Able to Answer at the Onset of Plan Development?

Your team should be able to clarify the answers to three questions before developing a primary plan: What are the main concerns? What are the main objectives for participating in the training series? What do the faculty and staff value in terms of student behavior? Answering these questions will allow your team to tailor a plan that meets the specific needs of your school, staff, and students.

How Do We Identify My School's Main Concerns?

Schools have access to a large amount of data that can help you determine the primary concerns at your school. Consider using scores on standardized academic measures, ODRs, academic performance on CBMs, frequency of suspensions and expulsions, and absenteeism or tardiness. In addition, if your school currently conducts systematic screeners, this data can also help identify primary concerns. Finally, we often have schools complete a survey to determine the extent to which processes are "in place" or are in need of improvement (e.g., EBS; Sugai, Todd, & Horner, 2003). Consider each of these methods when determining your school's main concerns.

How Do We Identify the Plan's Main Objectives?

Once concerns are identified, the next step is to determine your main objectives. Your school should develop (1) a mission statement, (2) a purpose statement, (3) clearly defined schoolwide expectations, (4) procedures for teaching and reinforcing, (5) targeted supports (secondary and tertiary), (6) procedures for monitoring the plan, and (7) procedures for monitoring student progress.

How Do We Determine What Our School Values in Terms of Student Behavior?

The process of determining the shared values of the entire faculty should be done formally. Rather than discussing desired behaviors, you may want to conduct a formal survey in which all faculty (or adults) rate the importance of various skills. This information can then be analyzed to determine common expectations.

Constructing the Primary Plan

What Should Be Included in Our School's Mission Statement?

Creating a school mission statement is a great opportunity for school staff to discuss the values they believe are important in guiding their work. A mission statement is a comprehensive statement that communicates to the public the types of values and environment the school is striving to create and sustain. For example, Roosevelt High School's mission—to *"cultivate the unique potential and ability of each student by providing an enriched, supportive environment that addresses the needs of all learners"*—signals to parents, staff, and the wider community that the school believes it is valuable to focus on each and every student.

What Should Be Included in Our School's Purpose Statement?

A purpose statement is more concrete than a mission statement and spells out exactly what the staff will do to achieve the mission. So, for example, Roosevelt High School's staff should detail how they plan to provide an enriched supportive environment. They might say, *"We will address the needs of each student by providing an enriched curriculum in conjunction with a schoolwide plan that supports any students who may be at risk."*

How Do We Identify Schoolwide Expectations?

School staff members must reach consensus on the most important "rules" or expectations for the behavior that they want students to know and use. Because every school is different, the expectations are customized to meet the needs at your particular site. They must be positively stated, defined, and then illustrated for each setting. This approach produces a common set of expectations and language for all teachers, students, and parents. One way to reach agreement is to first brainstorm all the possibilities, type them up, and then have staff rank-order them. You can then discuss the top 10, narrow your choices, and, if necessary, rank-order the items again until you reach the three to five on which you can all concur. Another option, which we have used in our work, is to take a data-based approached by using the SSRS (Gresham & Elliott, 1990) to identify the specific skills rated by faculty and staff as critical for school success. These skills then become the content of the expectation matrix (see Chapter 4 for details).

What Is an Expectation Matrix?

Once your school has identified its schoolwide expectations, typically three to five, you can create an expectation matrix to clearly define them in specific school settings. For example, if your school identifies *respect, responsibility,* and *good effort* as the three schoolwide expectations, create a grid vertically listing these expectations on the left. Across the top of the grid you would list the specific school settings in which they are expected to be displayed (e.g., cafeteria, classroom, bathroom, hallway). In the box ("cell") where an expectation meets a setting, include a description of what the expectation looks like in that setting. For example, *responsibility in the hallway* may mean that students pick up trash, but in the classroom it might be that students are expected to bring necessary materials. The grid is a great visual cue for students (and teachers)! Grids can be posted around the school with specific settings highlighted or set in larger font. See procedures in Chapter 4 for identifying the content to be included in the expectation matrix.

Implementing the Primary Plan: Student, Faculty, Parent, and Administrator Responsibilities and Activities for Teaching the Plan

How Do We Introduce the Plan to the Students?

The new PBIS plan should be introduced to all students on the first day of school. Typically you would hold a schoolwide assembly where students are introduced to the different aspects of the PBIS plan (e.g., schoolwide expectations, PBIS tickets, drawings). To get the students excited, you can organize a drawing on this first day. For example, at one elementary school parents, volunteers, and teachers passed out PBIS tickets to students displaying the schoolwide expectations as they arrived at school in the morning. Students were flooded with tickets and had many questions. Instead of explaining in detail to each student, teachers and parents asked students to write their name on the ticket and hold on to it for now. Later in the day classes were invited to an assembly where students placed their PBIS tickets into a large box as they entered the auditorium.

> "It's a super plan, I LOVED IT!"
> —*Elementary School*

During the assembly the plan was explained to all students and then a drawing for a prize was held. This was a very immediate way to get students excited about having a PBIS plan at their school.

How Can We Teach the Students the Schoolwide Expectations in Each Setting?

One option is to have teachers take their classes on a tour of the school and explain what the schoolwide expectations look like in each setting. Some of our schools have put on skits (performed by staff) about the expectations and others used video clips. In addition, posters can be hung in each setting displaying the schoolwide expectations. Some schools also elect to display the expectation matrix, highlighting the specific setting.

How Can We Remind the Students of the Schoolwide Expectations?

Posting visual cues around the schools and in classrooms is a great way to remind students of the schoolwide expectations. Some schools have developed a school pledge that includes all their expectations and is read aloud each morning following announcements.

What Is the Stop, Drop, and Teach Plan?

Stop–drop–teach lesson plans are one option for introducing and teaching schoolwide expectations. These direct-instruction types of lessons can be developed to teach students how to display a certain social skill. The idea is that all teachers in the school literally stop any other instruction to teach a schoolwide expectation lesson at a designated time. Then the school staff follows up by reinforcing the skill for the remainder of the week/month.

> "I think one thing that helped was that we tied together what the teachers were doing and made a connection between their discipline and the kids' behavior. This made it clear as to how the rules affect the kids."—*Middle School*

How Often Should We Teach Social Skills?

Depending on how many social skills your school selects, you may want to teach one skill per month. Reserve 30 minutes to an hour for teaching each skill.

How Can We Use Morning Announcements to Support Teaching the Primary Plan?

As mentioned above, some schools have students recite a school pledge that includes the schoolwide expectations each morning before announcements. Many schools also made morning announcements regarding upcoming prizes and/or PBIS events. They even held "live" surprise drawings over the public announcement system. In addition to starting the day out with a motivating drawing, it also encouraged students to arrive to school on time because you could only win a prize if they were present. Some schools have used their networked TV system to show "PBIS videos," which were student-made videos clarifying and teaching the schoolwide expectations.

What Is a PBIS Video and How Do We Make One?

PBIS videos are student-made videos that teach schoolwide expectations and are broadcast over a school-networked TV. One school's PBIS video team became so popular that one of the monthly drawing prizes was a star role in a PBIS video! These videos not only teach specific social skills, but they can also be used as "booster." For example, at

"We were aware that we did not want to put one more thing on the teacher's plate. ... That's why we choose to teach the schoolwide expectations through the PBIS videos."—*Middle School*

one middle school the boys' bathroom became a site that generated many ODRs. In response, the PBIS video team developed an entertaining video addressing the problems in the boys' bathroom. All staff and students submitted ideas for videos.

How Can We Teach Substitutes and Volunteers about Our Schoolwide Plan upon Arrival?

When substitutes and other new volunteers check in at the front office, they should receive a PBIS packet containing an implementation manual (or at least a quick reference sheet of the plan) along with PBIS tickets. Several of our schools have developed bookmarks that contain a brief overview of their PBIS plan—what it is, how to use the tickets, and the expectation matrix. When adults sign in to volunteer or substitute, they simply pick up a bookmark with this information along with a pack of PBIS tickets.

Procedures for Reinforcing: Using PBIS Tickets

What Is a PBIS Ticket?

PBIS tickets look different at every school. The PBIS ticket does not have to be called a PBIS ticket; it can be given a catchy name related to your school site, such as *Panther Buck* or *Dolphin Dollar*. The ticket should include basic information such as the school's name (or name of the ticket), a place for the student to write in his or her name, and a list of the schoolwide expectations. Some schools choose to include the teacher's name, grade level, location where ticket was given (hallway, classroom, office, cafeteria), month, and date. Although not necessary, the additional information can be very useful. For example, some administrators are interested in knowing which grade level is using the most tickets or which month had the highest number of tickets distributed. Several of our schools have developed "picture" versions of PBIS tickets for use with younger students.

How Do We "Catch a Student" Performing the Schoolwide Expectations?

In the hallways, during class, in the lunch line, at recess, during an assembly … these are all great times to catch a student displaying schoolwide expectations. Whenever any staff member sees a student exhibiting one of the schoolwide expectations, he or she should praise the student verbally, using behavior-specific praise, and then give him or her a PBIS ticket. PBIS tickets can also be used to prompt the correct/desired behavior in other students. For example, if you notice students straggling to class, pass out tickets to the first five students who are at their desks before the bell rings. This will give encourage the stragglers to try to earn tickets. It is critical to "catch" them right away to support the new behavior.

What Do We Say to the Teacher Who Thinks That Tickets Are Bribery?

Whereas bribery is using strategies to increase the likelihood of people doing things that are *not* in their best interest, positive reinforcement is a behavioral principle that involves the contingent introduction of any stimuli to increase the probability of the desired behavior occurring in the future. *All* human behavior is shaped by consequences. It is important to be prepared to respond to teachers who have concerns regarding issues of reinforcement.

"Philosophically, I can't be supportive of PBIS. I feel that teaching young people good behavior is effected by changing them from within, not by giving physical material rewards.—*High School*

Why Should the Color of the PBIS Tickets Change?

Changing the color of PBIS tickets each month allows you to easily monitor when students received their tickets. For example, some schools have events that can be paid for with PBIS tickets. If the cover charge is five PBIS tickets, and you do not want to allow students to turn in tickets from months ago, then only green tickets from that month will be accepted. Other schools give away big prizes that change each month, and students can keep their tickets until there is a prize they are really interested in winning. If your PBIS tickets change color each month, then you will know which prizes are the most motivating when students are willing to part with many months' worth of tickets. Again, it is not necessary to change colors, but doing so nets an additional source of data.

Who Is Responsible for Preparing the PBIS Tickets?

This is up to the PBIS team and should be decided in the training and planning year. We've seen schools handle this logistical piece in different ways. Some schools had their

Parent Teacher Student Organization (PTSO) prepare tickets, whereas others relied on student council members, and still others, on office workers.

How Are PBIS Tickets Distributed to Teachers?

Several of the schools with which we work pass out between 100 and 250 tickets to each teacher and staff member at the beginning of each month (some had tickets with teachers' names preprinted). They also made sure to have a location, such as the office, where extra tickets could be gotten, if needed.

How Can We Track How Many PBIS Tickets Are Passed Out Each Month in Our School?

If you plan to keep track of how many tickets are passed out each month, there are several ways to so this. One easy way, as we've mentioned, is to change the color of your tickets or perhaps print the month on the ticket. At the end of each month you can count (or just estimate) how many tickets are turned in; however, this number does not include those tickets that are saved up or never turned in. Another option is to hand out a set number of tickets each month to each teacher. If you want teachers to still have the option to get more tickets, then they can be instructed to record how many they are taking (have the tickets available in packets of 50 or 100). In addition, teachers need to turn in unused tickets so that they can be deducted from the total taken by teachers.

How Can We Determine If Students Are Getting Comparable Amounts of Tickets?

In our work, several schools collect "ticket samples" to see if students are getting access to the same rate of reinforcement. They collect all tickets turned in during a given week, count the number of tickets each student received, and divide that number by the number of instructional days in the sample. Then they can make comparisons to see the range of reinforcement rates in the building. Some schools also check to see if certain types of students (e.g., students in the high-risk category on the SRSS [Drummond, 1994] or students receiving special education services) are getting the same rate of access to reinforcement.

What Should I Do with the Tickets That My Students Receive?

If you choose to use tickets as part of a classroom system, then they should be returned to the box so that they are included in the end-of-the-week/school/quarter drawing for big prizes. The PBIS team determines where all the tickets go in preparation for the assembly. Some schools require students to keep track of their tickets until the assembly.

How Can We Modify PBIS Tickets to Make Them Work for Young Elementary-Age Students?

Tickets can be altered to be child-friendly by using images that represent each of the expectations and using fewer words. In addition, a larger space to write the student's name may be necessary. Remember, the point is to make the tickets useful to students and teachers, so you should design them specifically to meet the needs at your site.

What Do We Say When We Give a Student a PBIS Ticket?

Tell the student the behavior you observed that earned him or her the ticket and use specific praise. For example, if you saw Johnny walking appropriately in the hallway, you might say: "Johnny, I noticed that you walked in a straight line with your classmates, keeping your hands to yourself and not talking. That shows me that you are being responsible! Here's a Tiger Ticket for your good work." However, you may not always know the student's name, especially in the upper schools. So, to a high school student you might say something along these lines: "Hey, I noticed that you threw away all of your lunch trash and recycled what could be recycled. Nice work showing responsibility in the school cafeteria. Here's a PBIS ticket for your good work!"

Who Fills Out the PBIS Ticket?

Generally adults check off or circle the expectation displayed when they hand out a ticket and students fill out the rest. However, that can depend on the age of the child. In kindergarten classes teachers may fill out the name of the child. Sometimes kindergarten students write their name on the back of the ticket where there is more space.

Where Does the PBIS Ticket Go?

The ticket usually ends up in some sort of box or tub in the classroom for classroom drawings or in a larger container (e.g., plastic trash can with a lock) for the schoolwide drawing.

Where Should We Put Ticket Boxes?

High schools often put their boxes in common areas (e.g., hallways, library, front office, guidance counselor's office); however, some middle schools have chosen to keep the sixth-, seventh-, and eighth-grade tickets separate because they have three separate awards assemblies at the end of each month. In this case, boxes designated for each grade level are placed in grade-level hallways (i.e., the sixth-, seventh-, and eighth-grade hallways). In many elementary schools teachers elect to collect tickets in their individual classroom so that they are able to use the box of PBIS tickets to draw student names for various jobs (e.g., line leader, office runner).

How Can I Use My PBIS Tickets as Part of My Classroom System?

Some schools collect all PBIS tickets inside the classroom so that teachers can use them as part of their classroom system. The tickets are kept in a designated container. When a student receives a ticket he or she writes his or her name on the ticket and puts it into the container. The teacher has a place where he/she can pull names for various class jobs and/or prizes. For example, if the teacher needed someone to bring something to the front office, he or she could pull a PBIS ticket and identify the selected student. Other times the teacher may pull a ticket to select who will be first in line to go out to recess or receive a fancy pencil. These tickets are then returned to the container to be brought to the PBIS assembly to be eligible for bigger prizes.

What Happens to the PBIS Ticket?

Upon receiving tickets, students put their names on them, and turn them into the designated location (e.g., grade-level box, classroom box), unless the school requires a "cover charge" for entering awards assemblies. In this case students will need to keep their tickets until the assembly (this method is recommended only for older students). Prior to the assembly, boxes are collected and put in one central location for the drawing. Some schools decide to keep each grade separate so that a representative from each grade will be drawn (or because assemblies/drawings are be held at different times). After the drawing or assembly most schools choose to throw away (i.e., recycle) tickets or store them elsewhere. At one high school the auto shop class bought and fixed up an old car that was raffled at the end of the school year. In this case the school elected to keep all of the tickets from the entire school year so that they could be included in the end-of-the-school-year drawing. Remember to hold on to tickets if you are interested in answering questions about which prize was most desirable, determining which month were the most tickets turned in, how many tickets were turned in all year, etc.

How Often Are Ticket Bins Emptied?

As mentioned above, tickets are typically cleared away following big drawings, which may occur monthly or weekly. Clearing out old tickets before the next assembly reinforces students who recently received or entered a ticket because it increases their chances of winning.

How Can We Tie PBIS Tickets into an Assembly?

As mentioned, some schools hold monthly "awards assemblies," in which students who meet certain requirements are invited to attend, and where drawings occur, games are played, and other activities are organized to keep them busy for about 45 minutes. At one middle school the PBIS team looked at their schoolwide data, specifically the monthly D/F list (list of students who had earned a D or F on a progress note) and their ODRs. Any student who had earned Saturday school for an ODR or appeared on the D/F list during the grading period was restricted from attending the awards assembly. All other students were eligible if they had obtained a certain number of PBIS tickets (cover charge). The cover charge was determined by the PBIS team, and its cost increased during the school year (e.g., one ticket for the August assembly, two tickets for the September assembly, and so on). Students who were not eligible to attend the assembly were required to attend a study hall period. Teachers took turns running the study hall and helped students with missing work and/or other assignments.

Reinforcers

What Kind of Prizes Can We Give Away?

The prizes should be attractive to your students. You have to find out what motivates students to earn the tickets. Many students simply enjoy earning the tickets and verbal praise. Many schools have set up motivating systems whereby students can place PBIS tickets into designated boxes to make sure that they have a chance at winning the specific prizes they want. Still other schools have set up a system in which PBIS tickets can be used to "purchase" desired items (e.g., 25 PBIS tickets for a free movie pass, 5 PBIS tickets for a cool pencil) to appeal to students who do not want to take a chance of not "winning."

How Can We Fundraise?

Many schools use their parent and student organizations to fundraise. As stated earlier, one middle school we worked with chose to have an optional "lock-in" one Friday night. Tickets were sold for $20, and parents could drop their students off from 5 P.M. until 10 P.M. Upon entry students were supervised by both parent and teacher volunteers. Activities were set up to keep students busy (dancing, music, movies, video games, basketball games, ping pong, etc.) and pizza was ordered. The school raised enough money to purchase prizes such as bicycles, CD players, sports equipment, and food coupons from local restaurants. In addition to buying prizes, the team wrote letters soliciting donations of money and prizes. Many schools are also able to get prizes at a discount.

What If We Don't Want to Give Away Big Expensive Prizes?

At one elementary school the PBIS team felt strongly about not using material prizes, both for financial reasons and because they did not want to reinforce students with

"After surveying our students, we found that the number one thing that they want is time with their friends."—*Middle School*

material goods. Rather, they wanted to provide students with activities, so they came up with ideas such as reading time with the principal, sitting with a friend and teacher at a special table for lunch, being an office assistant for an afternoon, and 5 minutes extra of recess. The PBIS team created coupons with the activity printed and laminated on colorful paper and then wrapped it so it looked like a present.

How Often Should We Have a Prize Drawing?

Frequency can vary from school to school. Many schools hold monthly drawings in which there are larger/more desirable prizes. In addition, many schools choose to hold random drawings weekly for smaller prizes (as a reminder and incentive to turn in tickets).

What Might an Elementary Student Want?

Very modest items often appeal to elementary students. One of the most reinforcing items is time with the teacher or another adult in the building or time with a peer. These types of reinforces don't cost anything. Many students also want a little time on their own, maybe escaping from part of the classroom activity (5 or 10 minutes on the computer or reading). Students often appreciate items such as a book, a stuffed animal, or a (very) special pencil.

What Might a Middle or High School Student Want?

Students are involved in many activities during their junior and senior years, such as dances and yearbook projects. You could hold a drawing for a free pass to a school dance or a sports event. You might even offer a prom package that could include a donated dinner from a local restaurant or a discount on tuxedo rentals or dress or even a limousine. Some high schools raffle a parking space close to the school entrance for those who drive. Many of these options do not have to cost your school money and will still be desirable to many students.

> "One time a girl came into my office crying, saying that her purse had been stolen. When I asked her if she had money in her purse, she replied by telling me that she had no money . . . just her PBIS tickets!"—*Middle School*

How Can We as PBIS Team Members Support the Teachers Who Are Giving Out Tickets?

Don't forget that anyone who is caught in the act of doing what is expected should be reinforced. That includes teachers who pass out tickets appropriately and support the PBIS program! Consider holding teacher drawings during faculty meetings using the PBIS tickets that have been turned in to date. Pull a ticket and instead of the student receiving a prize, the teacher whose name is on the ticket gets one (be sure to return the ticket to the bucket so that the student still has a chance to be drawn for a student drawing). Prizes such as an hour of class coverage by an administrator (so that teacher can take a little bit of a break or prep period), free tickets to a school event (e.g., play, sporting event), or discount at a local restaurant will be greatly appreciated by staff members. One school had a spa package donated that they offered as a prize in the teacher drawing.

Dissemination: Sharing the Plan and Discussing How Things Are Going

How Can We Get Full Faculty Feedback?

The important point to remember is that not all staff members will want to offer feedback in the same way. Some may feel comfortable talking in a large group; others may prefer the smaller group of their grade-level team. In order to elicit all types of feedback, you must choose your PBIS team carefully. The most essential part of a PBIS team member's responsibilities is to gather informal feedback from other staff members. As a result, team members must be people with whom the staff feels comfortable. Trusting PBIS team members makes it more likely that staff members will voice their concerns. In addition, faculty meetings (particularly when updates are given) can include regularly scheduled discussions about any concerns. Your school should also collect written feedback (some of it may be anonymous). You may also want to tie in this feedback with assessing social validity (see Chapter 5).

What Is an Implementation Manual?

Think of an implementation manual as the "go to" place for any questions. It will include your schoolwide expectations, procedures for teaching these expectations, and the procedures for reinforcing them. It will also include the answers to questions such as "Where do I get more PBIS tickets?" The implementation manual should be considered a *working* document in that typically, people will ask questions that you may not have thought of, and you should add these questions (and answers) to the manual at the end of the academic year. Again, just a reminder that revisions should not occur *during* the academic year, but instead should occur *between* academic years. If revisions are made during the academic year, then the school-site PBIS team cannot accurately examine the impact of the primary prevention program.

Who Receives an Implementation Manual?

A manual should be passed out to every adult in the building (e.g., administrators, teachers, staff, substitutes). It is important that all staff members have their own copies so that they know all the details. For new staff, you may want to consider adding a one-page "cheat sheet" at the front of the implementation manual that provides the basics. This sheet will be a lifesaver for substitutes who come to your school for the first time and don't know what in the world a PBIS ticket is ... consistency is key!

How Do We Introduce This Program to Parents?

To involve parents in what is happening at school, some schools elect to send parents a copy of the PBIS plan along with an implementation manual. One school created a refrigerator magnet containing all of the schoolwide expectations as a visual prompt for families. Others have scheduled a "coffee talk" before school begins or during the first few weeks to introduce the plan so that parents can ask questions and join discussions. An administrator or the PBIS team can host the coffee talks. Further, the PBIS plan can be part of the back-to-school packet for parents to read and sign that they have received it. Some schools even invite parents to take part in the introduction assembly on the first day of school.

Treatment Integrity and Social Validity

How Can We Be Sure That the Adults in the Building Are Doing Their Part?

This question can be answered by monitoring treatment integrity. In Chapter 5 you learned about a number of ways to monitor treatment integrity. One approach is to ask people to complete behavior checklists containing the core components of the plan. For example, teachers could use these checklists to evaluate their performance each quarter. Or an outside observer such as an administrator or a member of the PBIS team could use these same behavior checklists to evaluate a teacher (or all teachers) each semester. Another approach is to administer the School-wide Evaluation Tool Version 2.1 (SET; Sugai et al., 2005). In our work, we use a variety of tools to monitor treatment integrity over the course of the school year, including behavior component checklists completed by teachers and outside observers, monthly or quarterly teacher ratings, and the SET.

We encourage PBIS staff to share the results of these different treatment integrity measures in a respectful manner with faculty and staff. Instead of talking to those who don't participate, recognize those who do (which is the mission of any PBIS plan: Be proactive rather than reactive). PBIS team members should be aware of those teachers and staff who are supportive and those who may have some resistance. Continue to share schoolwide outcomes and changes, and reinforce participating teachers through verbal praise and recognition. Be sure you are providing opportunities for feedback, so that if there is a reason why they aren't doing their part, there is also an available avenue for communication.

How Can We Get Honest Feedback from Students and Teachers?

As discussed earlier, be sure to solicit feedback from those involved with the plan: team members, administrators, teachers and support staff, parents, and students. The intent of monitoring social validity is to gain participants' perspectives on the social importance of the goals, the social acceptability of the procedures, and the social significance of the outcomes—both before beginning a program and again at year end. Whether via faculty meetings, student

> "I have learned how important collaboration is: Two heads are better than one. It is important to involve as many people as possible, especially if you want buy-in. If you aren't able to involve everyone, it is critical to get ongoing feedback from everyone and have them a part of the decision-making process to obtain buy-in and allow everyone to feel heard."—*Middle School*

council meetings, written anonymous feedback, structured interviews, or more formal surveys such as the Primary Intervention Rating Scale (PIRS; Lane, Robertson, et al., 2002), *ask for feedback*. People will feel comfortable giving feedback in different ways, so be sure to provide a variety of opportunities to discuss how the program is going.

Screening to Identify Nonresponsive Students

What Are the Characteristics of a Good Screening Tool?

An effective screening tool should be psychometrically sound. Therefore, it should have (1) high internal consistency, (2) high test–retest stability, (3) convergent validity with similar established measures, (4) positive and negative predictive value, and (5) specificity and sensitivity. It should also be efficient for teachers and administrators to use, meaning that it is reasonably priced or free and takes limited time to administer, score, and analyze (Lane, Parks, et al., 2007).

What Are Some Examples of Behavioral Screeners?

Some empirically validated instruments developed to identify students at risk for emotional and behavioral disorders or antisocial behavior, in general, include Strengths and Difficulties Questionnaire (Goodman, 1997), Student Risk Screening Scale (Drummond, 1994), and Systematic Screening for Behavior Disorders (Walker & Severson, 1992).

What Are Some Examples of Academic Screeners?

Many schools use both curriculum-based assessments (CBAs) and norm-referenced assessments for screeners; however, CBAs offer more sensitive measures of growth and can detect smaller increases in student progress.

How Often Should Screeners Be Completed?

One approach is to complete behavioral and academic screeners three times per year: 6 weeks into the school year, midway, and toward the end of the school year. Some academic screeners require ongoing assessments and may be completed weekly or even monthly.

How Should We Share the Information with the Faculty?

Like other data, schoolwide screening data should be shared with faculty on a regular basis and as soon as the data are available. Updates and findings can be presented at faculty meetings or at individual grade-level meetings as a way to (1) monitor how the school as a whole is progressing in terms of academic, behavioral, and social progress, and (2) discuss supports for students who are not responding to the primary prevention plan (Lane, Kalberg, Bruhn, et al., in press).

What Do We Do with the Information from the Screeners?

The information from the screeners can be used to monitor schoolwide change over time as well as to identify students who may need additional supports. The screening information can also be used as part of the entry and/or exit criteria for targeted supports.

Targeted Interventions

What Is the First Step to Establishing Targeted Interventions?

The first step in establishing additional supports for students in need of targeted interventions is to identify the secondary and tertiary levels of prevention that may already be in place in your schools. The team should determine the criteria (both entry and exit) used to place students in such targeted interventions as well as ongoing monitoring procedures. Additionally, the team should determine various logistics, including who will teach the intervention, where the class will meet, and other similar details. It may be helpful for the team to develop a grid to keep track of this information.

How Do We Begin Designing Intervention Grids?

Once you have identified targeted supports at your school, an intervention grid will help you to organize important information. Select programs that are evidenced-based practices or at least promising practices that have been evaluated.

What Should Be Included in an Intervention Grid?

An intervention grid should be developed for secondary interventions as well as a separate grid for tertiary interventions. Both grids should contain, at a minimum, the following information: (1) the name of the support, (2) a description (e.g., content of the intervention, treatment dosage, where the intervention will take place, and who will conduct the intervention), (3) entry criteria according to schoolwide data, (4) data to monitor progress, and (5) exit criteria. You may have additional information that you will also want to include in your grid.

What If Our PBIS Team Finds That We Don't Have the Supports That We Want?

If your school finds that there are areas for which you don't have supports in place, you may want to discuss potential programs that could be used at your school—particularly for students who require targeted support. There are many resources in the community as well as published programs that may be of interest. Be sure to select a program that is an evidenced-based practice. We encourage you to see Blueprints for Violence Prevention (*www.colorado.edu/cspv/index.html*) and What Works Clearing House (*ies.ed.gov/ncee/wwc*) for overviews of model and promising programs. Also, when selecting a program, be sure the procedures are manageable for you and your school. Begin by adding just one or two supports at a time to avoid burnout and to increase sustainability.

Managing Data

What Data Should We Use?

As a school you have access to a plethora of data at your fingertips! Data collection should be part of regular school practices and is likely a part of your school routine already. However, it is very important that data (e.g., ODRs) be collected using reliable procedures to ensure accurate measurement. Only then can you be certain that changes in the data are due to changes in student performance rather than measurement error. Also, we encourage you to adopt validated behavioral and academic screening measures if you don't already have them.

How Do We Set Up Systems to Make Data Entry Efficient?

Keep in mind that you should limit the number of times that you handle data. So, when deciding who will enter data, consider procedures that will allow data to go directly into a system (whenever possible) and avoid unnecessary paper pushing. For example, perhaps your teachers can enter ODR data online from their classroom rather than sending a paper referral to the office.

How Much Time Should We Spend on Collecting and Analyzing Data?

Data collection and analyzing should take up no more than 1% of your school day. Think carefully about the procedures that are put into place to achieve this efficiency.

Who Should Be Responsible for Collecting the Data?

Data should be an integral part of the school day; you've heard that one before! Build data collection and entry into everyday routines so that it is not just one more thing on top of everything else.

When Should We Start Collecting Data?

When you design your primary plan, data collection procedures should be built in from the start. The success of your plan will be based upon many things, including the efficiency of data collection. Take time to plan these procedures carefully.

When Should We Share Data with Faculty?

Data should be shared consistently and regularly. Updates can be presented at weekly/monthly faculty meetings. E-mailing can also be an effective means of sharing this information. However, if you e-mail information, make sure that confidentiality is protected and that students' names are not included in your document. Instead, use e-mail to share aggregated data (information presented in group format).

Future Questions

As you read through these questions, we're sure you'll think of many more questions and even more answers. We encourage you to foster questions and look for creative, data-based answers as you move through this process of designing, implementing, and evaluating three-tiered models of prevention to (1) prevent the development of behavior concerns and (2) respond more effectively to existing cases, using the secondary and tertiary prevention efforts.

A Few Final Thoughts

We firmly believe that a comprehensive schoolwide primary intervention plan can improve student outcomes; however, we also know that creating and implementing a plan for your school site requires hard work and commitment. Our experience with schools has provided us with insight into some of the obstacles and challenges you may encounter as you put your plan into place. We offer the following final suggestions:

- Reach consensus in terms of goals and procedures.
- Establish an active leadership team to promote long-term continuity.
- Make decisions based on data.
- Share ongoing findings with the entire school community.
- Don't change horses midstream: Commit to a full year of implementation before revising the plan.
- Implement the entire plan (proactive and reactive components) with fidelity.
- Consider available resources to make the best use of existing programs.

When you design a comprehensive primary plan based on the values held by faculty, staff, parents, and students, you have the potential to effect powerful change at your school academically, behaviorally, and socially, provided that the plan is implemented with fidelity. We hope that this book will be a useful tool as you move through the process. Although the process may seem overwhelming at points, we would like to encourage you to focus your resources and energy on this proactive approach. Rather than losing valuable instructional time by having to respond to behavior problems, primary prevention refocuses your efforts so that you spend more time noticing and reinforcing students who adhere to the academic, behavioral, and social expectations established in your plan. A primary intervention plan helps level the playing field because it explicitly teaches all students the schoolwide

> "I have noticed students being much more polite and thoughtful since the plan was implemented."—*High School*

expectations. In this way it motivates many students who, in the past, may not have had the ability or opportunity to earn positive recognition. We've had numerous teachers tell us that they feel less frustrated, more productive, and pleased with the changes at their school sites. In short, instead of trying to survive the school day, we encourage you to design, implement, and evaluate a plan that makes it possible for all parties involved to thrive. We wish you the best as you move forward with this process.

Below are comments from elementary students written at the end of the first year of program implementation.

"Thacke you for all the thigs you did to prtec this scool and all of us."—*Kindergarten Student*

"Dear Dr. Lane, Thank you for makeing tiger tickets! Tahnk you for makeing [our school] a better place to go."—*First-Grade Student*

"We have nicer kids cose we have PBIS."—*First-Grade Student*

"Thank you for PBIS! If we didn't have PBIS I would be a nervous wreak! PBIS gets us excited for Friday. Evry body in the school loves PBIS, and evry body LOVES the PARTY BUS!"—*First-Grade Student*

"Thank you for PBIS tickets. They made our school a much better plase. WE do not have bul-lys."—*Second-Grade Student*

"If it wasn't for you and PBIS I think school wouldn't be as fun. Pluss I think without the rules the school would be: TOTALLY OUT OF CONTROLL!"—*Second-Grade Student*

"I like PBIS becouse no bullys any more!!"—*Second-Grade Student*

"I like PBIS because it makes me fele responibl."—*Second-Grade Student*

"Dear Dr. Lane, We are thankful that we have PBIS it is the best. We are good people now." —*Second-Grade Student*

"Dear Dr. Lane, Thank you for PBIS at [school]. Recently my best friend Alex and I got picked from the tiger ticket box and we got to go to the party bus. A lot of my friends and I got tiger tickets and got stuff but the most important thing is to do well in school."—*Second-Grade Student*

"To get a PBIS ticket you need to respect others and their properties. And you need to partici-pate with your best effort."—*Third-Grade Student*

"Dear Dr. Lane and the PBIS team, I have really enjoyed PBIS tickets. It gives kids a chance to be proud of their good behavior. I was totally overjoyed when I got drawn out of the huge bucket. I hope you continue to teach people about PBIS."—*Fourth-Grade Student*

"Dear Dr. Lane and the PBIS team, Thank you for bringing PBIS to our school. I have enjoyed getting rewards for just doing the right thing: being respectful, being responsible, and participating and showing best effort. PBIS had made things better at school."—*Fourth-Grade Student*

"Thank you for the PBIS tickets. I love them. They make us feel very happy. I hope you keeping doing them. But, please make them a little smaller so we can save trees."—*Fourth-Grade Student*

"Dear Dr. Lane and PBIS team, I am glad you came up with PBIS. It is a great way to motivate kids to be good. If I become a teacher then I will use it. I especially [like] the prizes. I also like how you would get noticed and rewarded for your good actions."—*Fourth-Grade Student*

References

Achenbach, T. M. (1991a). *Integrative guide for the 1991 CBCL/4-18, YRS, & TRF profiles*. Burlington: University of Vermont, Department of Psychiatry.

Achenbach, T. M. (1991b). *Manual for the child behavior checklist/4–18 and 1991 profile*. Burlington: University of Vermont, Department of Psychiatry.

Alberto, P. A., & Troutman, A. C. (2003). *Applied behavior analysis for teachers* (6th ed.). Englewood Cliffs, NJ: Merrill/Prentice Hall.

Alexander, K., Entwisle, D., & Dauber, S. (1994). *On the success of failure: A measurement of the effects of primary grade retention*. New York: Cambridge University Press.

Alspaugh, J. W. (1998). Achievement loss associated with the transition to middle school and high school. *Journal of Educational Research*, *92*, 20–25.

American Educational Research Association. (1999). *Standards for educational and psychological testing*. Washington, DC: Author.

American Psychiatric Association. (2000). *Diagnostic and statistical manual of mental disorders* (4th ed., text rev.). Washington, DC: Author.

Baer, D. M., Wolf, M. M., & Risley, T. R. (1968). Some current dimensions of applied behavior analysis. *Journal of Applied Behavior Analysis*, *1*, 91–97.

Baer, D. M., Wolf, M. M., & Risley, T. R. (1987). Some still-current dimensions of applied behavior analysis. *Journal of Applied Behavior Analysis, 20*, 313–327.

Battistich, V., Schaps, E., Watson, M., & Solomon, D. (2000). Effects of the child development project on students' drug use and other problem behaviors. *Journal of Primary Prevention*, *21*(1), 75–99.

Bell, S. K., Coleman, J. K., Anderson, A., & Whelan, J. P. (2000). The effectiveness of peer mediation in a low-SES rural elementary school. *Psychology in the Schools*, *37*, 505–516.

Bergan, J., & Kratochwill, T. (1990). *Behavioral consultation and therapy*. New York: Plenum Press.

Black, S. A., & Jackson, E. (2007). Using bullying incident density to evaluate the Olweus Bullying Prevention Programme. *School Psychology International*, *28*, 623–638.

Botvin, G. J., Mihalic, S. F., & Grotpeter, J. K. (1998). *Life skills training: Blueprints for violence prevention* (Book 5). Blueprints for Violence Prevention Series (D. S. Elliott, Series Editor). Boulder, CO: Center for the Study and Prevention of Violence, Institute of Behavioral Science, University of Colorado.

Brown, B. B., Mounts, N., Lamborn, S. D., & Steinberg, L. (1993). Parenting practices and peer group affiliation in adolescence. *Child Development*, *64*, 467–482.

Business Resource Software. (2007). *www.businessplans.org*. Retrieved September 25, 2007.

Canter, L. (1990). *Lee Canter's back to school with assertive discipline.* Santa Monica, CA: Canter & Associates.

Center for the Prevention and Study of Violence. (2004). Blueprints for violence prevention. Retrieved February 13, 2008, from *www.colorado.edu/cspv/blueprints.*

Cheney, D., Blum, C., & Walker, B. (2004). An analysis of leadership teams' perceptions of positive behavior support and the outcomes of typically developing and at-risk students in their schools. *Assessment for Effective Intervention, 30,* 7–24.

Colvin, G. (2002). Designing classroom organization and structure. In K. L. Lane, F. M. Gresham, & T. E. O'Shaughnessy (Eds.), *Interventions for children with or at risk for emotional and behavioral disorders* (pp. 159–174). Boston: Allyn & Bacon.

Colvin, G., Kame'enui, E. J., & Sugai, G. (1993). Reconceptualizing behavior management and school-wide discipline in general education. *Education and Treatment of Children, 16,* 361–381.

Colvin, G., Sugai, G., Good, R. H., III, & Lee, Y. Y. (1997). Using active supervision and precorrection to improve transition behaviors in an elementary school. *School Psychology Quarterly, 12,* 344–363.

Committee for Children. (2007). *Second steps violence prevention.* Seattle: Author.

Cook, T. D., Habib, F. N., Phillips, M., Settersten, R. A., Shagle, S. C., & Degimencioglu, S. M. (1999). Comer's school development program in Prince George's County, Maryland: A theory-based evaluation. *American Educational Research Journal, 36,* 543–597.

Cooper, J. O., Heron, T. E., & Heward, W. L. (2007). *Applied behavior analysis.* Upper Saddle River, NJ: Pearson Education.

Coutinho, M. J. (1986). Reading achievement of students identified as behaviorally disordered at the secondary level. *Behavioral Disorders, 11,* 200–207.

Crick, N., Grotpeter, J., & Bigbee, M. (2002). Relationally and physically aggressive children's intent attributions and feelings of distress for relational and instrumental peer provocations. *Child Development, 73,* 1134–1142.

Crockett, J. J., Gerber, M. M., & Landrum, T. J. (2007). *Achieving the radical reform of special education: Essays in honor of James M. Kauffman.* Mahwah, NJ: Erlbaum.

Crone, D. A., Horner, R. H., & Hawkins, L. S. (2004). *Responding to problem behavior in schools: The behavior education program.* New York: Guilford Press.

Deno, S. L. (2003). Developments in curriculum-based measurement. *Journal of Special Education, 37,* 184–192.

Developmental Studies Center. (n.d.). *Caring school community.* Oakland, CA: Author. Unpublished manuscript.

DeVoe, J. F., Peter, K., Kaufman, P., Ruddy, S. A., Miller, A. K., Plany, M., et al. (2003). *Indicators of school crime and safety: 2003.* Washington, DC: National Center for Educational Statistics, U.S. Departments of Education and Justice.

Drummond, T. (1994). *The Student Risk Screening Scale (SRSS).* Grants Pass, OR: Josephine County Mental Health Program.

Drummond, T., Eddy, J. M., & Reid, J. B. (1998a). *Follow-up study #3: Risk screening scale: Prediction of negative outcomes by 10th grade from 2nd grade screening.* Unpublished technical report. Eugene, OR: Oregon Social Learning Center.

Drummond, T., Eddy, J. M., & Reid, J. B. (1998b). *Follow-up study #4: Risk screening scale: Prediction of negative outcomes in two longitudinal samples.* Unpublished technical report. Eugene, OR: Oregon Social Learning Center.

Drummond, T., Eddy, J. M., Reid, J. B., & Bank, L. (1994, November). *The Student Risk Screening*

Scale: A brief teacher screening instrument for conduct disorder. Paper presented at the fourth annual Prevention Conference, Washington, DC.

Dunlap, G. (1993). Promoting generalization: Current status and functional considerations. In R. V. Houten & S. Axelrod (Eds.), *Behavior analysis and treatment* (pp. 269–296). New York: Plenum Press.

DuPaul, G. J., & Hoff, K. E. (1998). Reducing disruptive behavior in general education classrooms: The use of self-management strategies. *School Psychology Review, 27,* 290–303.

Dwyer, K. P., Osher, D., & Warger, W. (1998). *Early warning, timely response: A guide to safe schools.* Washington, DC: U.S. Department of Education.

Elliott, S. N., & Gresham, F. M. (1991). *Social skills intervention guide: Practical strategies for social skills training.* Circle Pines, MN: American Guidance.

Elliott, S. N., Turco, T. L., & Gresham, F. M. (1987). Consumers' and clients' pretreatment acceptability ratings of classroom-based group contingencies. *Journal of School Psychology, 25,* 145–154.

Epstein, L., Plog, A., & Porter, W. (2002). Bully proofing your school: Results of a four-year intervention. *Emotional and Behavioral Disorders in Youth, 2,* 53–80.

Ervin, R. A., Schaughency, E., Goodman, S. D., McGlinchey, M. T., & Matthews, A. (2006). Merging research and practice agendas to address reading and behavior school-wide. *School Psychology Review, 35,* 198–223.

Evertson, C. M., & Weade, R. (1989). Classroom management and teaching style: Instructional stability and variability in two junior high English classrooms. *Elementary School Journal, 89,* 379–393.

Falk, K. B., & Wehby, J. H. (2001). The effects of peer-assisted learning strategies on the beginning reading skills of young children with emotional and behavioral disorders. *Behavioral Disorders, 26,* 344–359.

Farrell, A. D., Meyer, A. L., Sullivan, T. N., & Kung, E. M. (2003). Evaluation of the responding in peaceful and positive ways (RIPP) seventh grade violence prevention curriculum. *Journal of Child and Family Studies, 12,* 101–120.

Farrell, A. D., Valois, R. F., Meyer, A. L., & Tidwell, R. P. (2003). Impact of the RIPP violence prevention program on rural middle school students. *Journal of Primary Prevention, 24*(2), 143–167.

Fawcett, S. (1991). Social validity: A note on methodology. *Journal of Applied Behavior Analysis, 24,* 235–239.

Finn, C. A., & Sladeczek, I. E. (2001). Assessing the social validity of behavior interventions: A review of treatment acceptability measures. *School Psychology Quarterly, 16,* 176–206.

Fishbein, J. E., & Wasik, B. H. (1981). Effect of the good behavior game on disruptive library behavior. *Journal of Applied Behavior Analysis, 14,* 89–93.

Flannery, D. J., Vazsonyi, A. T., Liau, A. K., Guo, S., Powell, K. E., Atha, H., et al. (2003). Initial behavior outcomes for the PeaceBuilders universal school-based violence prevention program. *Developmental Psychology, 39,* 292–308.

Frick, P., Kamphaus, R., Lahey, B., Loebert, R., Christ, M., Hart, E., et al. (1991). Academic underachievement and the disruptive behavior disorders. *Journal of Consulting and Clinical Psychology, 59,* 289–294.

Garrity, C., Jens, K., Porter, W., Sager, N., & Short-Camilli, C. (1994). *Bully-proofing Your School: A comprehensive approach for elementary schools.* Longmont, CO: Sopris West.

Gay, L. R., & Airasian, P. (2000). *Educational research: Competencies for analysis and application* (6th ed.). Columbus, OH: Merrill.

George, M. P., White, G. P., & Schlaffer, J. J. (2007). Implementing school-wide behavior change: Lessons from the field. *Psychology in the Schools, 44,* 41–51.

Gersten, R., Fuchs, L. S., Compton, D., Coyne, M., Greenwood, C., & Innocenti, M. S. (2005). Quality indicators for group experimental and quasi-experimental research in special education. *Exceptional Children, 71,* 149–164.

Goodman, R. (1997). The Strengths and Difficulties Questionnaire: A research note. *Journal of Child Psychology and Psychiatry, 38,* 581–586.

Goodman, R. (2001). Psychometric properties of the Strengths and Difficulties Questionnaire (SDQ). *Journal of the American Academy of Child and Adolescent Psychiatry, 40,* 1337–1345.

Goodman, R., Meltzer, H., & Bailey, V. (1998). The Strengths and Difficulties Questionnaire: A pilot study on the validity of the self-report version. *European Child and Adolescent Psychiatry, 7,* 125–130.

Goodman, R., & Scott, S. (1999). Comparing the Strengths and Difficulties Questionnaire and the Child Behavior Checklist: Is small beautiful? *Journal of Abnormal Child Psychology, 27,* 17–24.

Gottfredson, D. C., Gottfredson, G. D., & Hybl, L. G. (1993). Managing adolescent behavior: A multiyear, multischool study. *American Educational Research Journal, 30,* 179–215.

Greenbaum, P. E., Dedrick, R. F., Friedman, R. M., Kutash, K., Borwn, E. C., Lardierh, S. P., et al. (1996). National Adolescent and Child Treatment Study (NACTS): Outcomes for children with serious emotional and behavioral disturbance. *Journal of Emotional and Behavioral Disorders, 4,* 130–146.

Greenberg, M. T., Kusché, C., & Mihalic, S. F. (1998). *Promoting alternative thinking strategies (PATHS): Blueprints for violence prevention* (Book 10). Blueprints for Violence Prevention Series (D. S. Elliott, Series Editor). Boulder, CO: Center for the Study and Prevention of Violence, Institute of Behavioral Science, University of Colorado.

Gresham, F. M. (1989). Assessment of treatment integrity in school consultation and prereferral intervention. *School Psychology Review, 18,* 37–50.

Gresham, F. M. (2002a). Responsiveness to intervention: An alternative approach to learning disabilities. In R. Bradley, L. Danielson, & D. Hallahan (Eds.), *Identification of learning disabilities: Research to practice* (pp. 242–258). Mahwah, NJ: Erlbaum.

Gresham, F. M. (2002b). Social skills assessment and instruction for students with emotional and behavioral disorders. In K. L. Lane, F. M. Gresham, & T. E. O'Shaughnessy (Eds.), *Interventions for children with or at risk for emotional and behavioral disorders* (pp. 242–258). Boston: Allyn & Bacon.

Gresham, F. M., & Elliott, S. N. (1990). *Social Skills Rating System (SSRS).* Circle Pines, MN: American Guidance Service.

Gresham, F. M., & Kendell, G. K. (1987). School consultation research: Methodological critique and future directions. *School Psychology Review, 16,* 306–316.

Gresham, F. M., Lane, K. L., & Lambros, K. (2000). Comorbidity of conduct and attention deficit hyperactivity problems: Issues of identification and intervention with "fledgling psychopaths." *Journal of Emotional and Behavioral Disorders, 8,* 83–93.

Gresham, F. M., & Lopez, M. F. (1996). Social validation: A unifying construct for school-based consultation research and practice. *School Psychology Quarterly, 11,* 204–227.

Gresham, F. M., Sugai, G., Horner, R., Quinn, M., & McInerney, M. (1998). *Classroom and school-wide practices that support students' social competence: A synthesis of research.* Washington, DC: Office of Special Education Programs.

Griffin, K. W., Botvin, G. J., Nichols, T. R., & Doyle, M. M. (2003). Effectiveness of a universal drug abuse prevention approach for youth at high risk for substance use initiation. *Preventive Medicine, 36,* 1–7.

Gunter, P. L., & Denny, R. K. (1998). Trends and issues in research regarding academic instruction of students with emotional and behavioral disorders. *Behavioral Disorders, 24,* 44–50.

Hammil, D., & Larsen, S. (1996). *Test of Written Language–3.* Austin, TX: Pro-Ed.

Harcourt. (2008). *AIMSWeb.* San Antonio, TX: Author.

Hatcher, L., & Stepanski, E. J. (1994). *A step-by-step approach to using the SAS system for univariate and multivariate statistics.* Cary, NC: SAS Institute.

Hawkins, R. (1991). Is social validity what we are interested in? Argument for a functional approach. *Journal of Applied Behavior Analysis, 24,* 205–213.

Henggeler, S. (1998). Multisystemic therapy. In D. S. Elliott (Ed.), *Blueprints for violence prevention.* Boulder, CO: Center for the Study and Prevention of Violence, Institute of Behavioral Science, University of Colorado.

Hinshaw, S. P. (1992). Externalizing behavior problems and academic underachievement in childhood and adolescence: Causal relationships and underlying mechanisms. *Psychological Bulletin, 111,* 127–155.

Horner, R. H., & Billingsley, F. F. (1988). *The effect of competing behavior on the generalization and maintenance of adaptive behavior in applied settings.* In R. H. Horner, G. Dunlap, & R. L. Koegel (Eds.), *Generalization and maintenance: Lifestyle changes in applied settings* (pp. 197–220). Baltimore: Brookes.

Horner, R. H., Carr, E. C., Halle, J., McGee, G., Odom, S., & Wolery, M. (2005). The use of single-subject research to identify evidence-based practice in special education. *Exceptional Children, 71,* 165–179.

Horner, R. H., & Sugai, G. (2000). School-wide behavior support: An emerging initiative to identify evidence-based practice in special education. *Exceptional Children, 71,* 165–179.

Horner, R. H., Todd, A. W., Lewis-Palmer, T., Irvin, L. K., Sugai, G., & Boland, J. B. (2004). The School-wide Evaluation Tool (SET): A research instrument for assessing school-wide positive behavior support. *Journal of Positive Behavior Intervention, 6,* 3–12.

Hunter, M. (1991). Generic lesson design: The case for. *Science Teacher, 58,* 26–28.

Individuals with Disabilities Education Act Amendments of 1997. Public Law No. 105-17, Section 20, 111 Stat. 37 (1997). Washington, DC: U.S. Government Printing Office.

Individuals with Disabilities Education Improvement Act of 2004. 20 U.S.C. 1400 *et seq.* (2004). (Reauthorization of Individuals with Disabilities Act 1990).

Information Please Database. (2007). A time line of recent worldwide school shootings. Retrieved February 13, 2008, from *www.infoplease.com/ipa/A0777958.html.*

Isakson, K., & Jarvis, P. (1999). The adjustment of adolescents during the transition into high school: A short term longitudinal study. *Journal of Youth and Adolescence, 28,* 1–26.

Jones, K. M., Wickstrom, K. F., & Friman, P. C. (1997). The effects of observational feedback on treatment integrity in school-based behavioral consultation. *School Psychology Quarterly, 12,* 316–326.

Kaminski, R. A., & Good, R. H. (1996). Toward a technology for assessing basic early literacy skills. *School Psychology Review, 25,* 215–227.

Kamps, D. M., Wills, H. P., Greenwood, C., Thorne, S., Lazo, J. F., Crockett, J. L., et al. (2003). Curriculum influences on growth in early reading fluency for students with academic and behavioral risks: A descriptive study. *Journal of Emotional and Behavioral Disorders, 11,* 211–224.

Kartub, D. T., Taylor-Greene, S., March, R. E., & Horner, R. H. (2000). Reducing hallway noise: A systems approach. *Journal of Positive Behavior Intervention, 2,* 179–182.

Kauffman, J. (2005). *Characteristics of emotional and behavioral disorders of children and youth* (8th ed.). Upper Saddle River, NJ: Pearson Merrill Prentice Hall.

Kazdin, A. E. (1977). Assessing the clinical or applied importance of behavior change through social validation. *Behavior Modification, 1,* 427–452.

Kern, L., & Manz, P. (2004). A look at current validity issues of school-wide behavior support. *Behavioral Disorders, 30,* 47–59.

Kerr, M. M., & Zigmond, N. (1986). What do high school teachers want? A study of expectations and standards. *Education and Treatment of Children, 9,* 239–249.

Landrum, T. J., Tankersley, M., & Kauffman, J. M. (2003). What is special about special education for students with emotional or behavioral disorders? *Journal of Special Education, 37,* 148–156.

Lane, K. L. (1999). Young students at risk for antisocial behavior: The utility of academic and social skills interventions. *Journal of Emotional and Behavioral Disorders, 7,* 211–223.

Lane, K. L. (2002). *Primary Prevention Plan: Feedback Form.* Vanderbilt University, Nashville, TN. Unpublished rating scale.

Lane, K. L. (2004). Academic instruction and tutoring interventions for students with emotional/behavioral disorders: 1990 to present. In R. B. Rutherford, M. M. Quinn, &. S. R. Mathur (Eds.), *Handbook of research in emotional and behavioral disorders* (pp. 462–486). New York: Guilford Press.

Lane, K. L. (2007). Identifying and supporting students at risk for emotional and behavioral disorders with multi-level models: Data-driven approaches to conducting secondary interventions with academic emphasis. *Education and Treatment of Children, 30,* 135–164.

Lane, K. L., Barton-Arwood, S. M., Rogers, L. A., & Robertson, E. J. (2007). Literacy interventions for students with and at risk for emotional or behavioral disorders: 1997 to present. In J. C. Crockett, M. M. Gerber, & T. J. Landrum (Eds.), *Achieving the radical reform of special education: Essays in honor of James M. Kauffman* (pp. 213–241). Mahwah, NJ: Erlbaum.

Lane, K. L., & Beebe-Frankenberger, M. (2004). *School-based interventions: The tools you need to succeed.* Boston: Pierson Education.

Lane, K. L., Beebe-Frankenberger, M. E., Lambros, K. L., & Pierson, M. (2001). Designing effective interventions for children at risk for antisocial behavior: An integrated model of components necessary for making valid inferences. *Psychology in the Schools, 38,* 365–379.

Lane, K. L., Bocian, K. M., MacMillan, D. L., & Gresham, F. M. (2004). Treatment integrity: An essential—but often forgotten—component of school-based interventions. *Preventing School Failure, 48,* 36–43.

Lane, K. L., Falk, K., & Wehby, J. H. (2006). Classroom management in special education classrooms and resource rooms. In C. M. Evertson & C. S. Weinstein (Eds.), *Handbook of classroom management: Research, practice, and contemporary issues* (pp. 439–460). Mahwah, NJ: Erlbaum.

Lane, K. L., Givner, C. C., & Pierson, M. (2004). Teacher expectations of student behavior: Social skills necessary for success in elementary school classrooms. *Journal of Special Education, 38,* 104–110.

Lane, K. L., Gresham, F. M., & O'Shaughnessy, T. E. (2002a). Identifying, assessing, and intervening with children with or at risk for behavior disorders: A look to the future. In K. L. Lane, F. M. Gresham, & T. E. O'Shaughnessy (Eds.), *Interventions for children with or at risk for emotional and behavioral disorders* (pp. 317–326). Boston: Allyn & Bacon.

Lane, K. L., Gresham, F. M., & O'Shaughnessy, T. E. (2002b). Serving students with or at-risk for emotional and behavior disorders: Future challenges. *Education and Treatment of Children, 25,* 507–521.

Lane, K. L., Harris, K., Graham, S., Weisenbach, J., Brindle, M., & Morphy, P. (2008). The effects of self-regulated strategy development on the writing performance of second grade students with behavioral and writing difficulties. *Journal of Special Education, 41*, 234–253.

Lane, K. L., Kalberg, J. R., Bruhn, A. L., Driscoll, S. A., Wehby, J. H., & Elliott, S. (2008). *Assessing social validity of school-wide positive behavior support plans: Evidence for the reliability and construct validity of the Primary Intervention Rating Scale.* Manuscript submitted for publication.

Lane, K. L., Kalberg, J. R., Bruhn, A. L., Mahoney, M. E., & Driscoll, S. A. (in press). Primary prevention programs at the elementary level: Issues of treatment integrity, systematic screening, and reinforcement. *Education and Treatment of Children.*

Lane, K. L., Kalberg, J. R., & Edwards, C. (2008). An examination of school-wide interventions with primary level efforts conducted in elementary schools: Implications for school psychologists. In D. M. Molina (Ed.), *School psychology: 21st century issues and challenges* (pp. 253–278). New York: Nova Science.

Lane, K. L., Kalberg, J. R., Menzies, H. M., Bruhn, A., Eisner, S., & Crnorbori, M. (2008). *Using school-wide data to assess risk and identify students for targeted supports: Illustrations across the K–12 continuum.* Manuscript in preparation.

Lane, K. L., Kalberg, J. R., Parks, R. J., & Carter, E. W. (2008). Student Risks Screening Scale: Initial evidence for score reliability and validity at the high school level. *Journal of Emotional and Behavioral Disorders, 16*, 178–190.

Lane, K. L., Little, M. A., Casey, A. M., Lambert, W., Wehby, J. H., Weisenbach, J. L., et al. (2008). *A comparison of systematic screening tools for emotional and behavioral disorders: How do they compare?* Manuscript submitted for publication

Lane, K. L., Little, M. A., Redding Rhodes, J., Phillips, A., & Welsh, M. T. (2007). Outcomes of a teacher-led reading intervention for elementary students at risk for behavioral disorders. *Exceptional Children, 74*, 47–70.

Lane, K. L., & Menzies, H. M. (2003). A school-wide intervention with primary and secondary levels of support for elementary students: Outcomes and considerations. *Education and Treatment of Children, 26*, 431–451.

Lane, K. L., & Menzies, H. M. (2005). Teacher-identified students with and without academic and behavioral concerns: Characteristics and responsiveness to a school-wide intervention. *Behavioral Disorders, 31*, 65–83.

Lane, K. L., Parks, R. J., Kalberg, J. R., & Carter, E. W. (2007). Student Risk Screening Scale: Initial evidence for score reliability and validity at the middle school level. *Journal of Emotional and Behavioral Disorders, 15*, 209–222.

Lane, K. L., Pierson, M., & Givner, C. C. (2004). Secondary teachers' views on social competence: Skills essential for success. *Journal of Special Education, 38*, 174–186.

Lane, K. L., Pierson, M., Stang, K., & Carter, E. W. (in press). *Teacher expectations of students' classroom behavior: Do expectations vary as a function of school risk?* Manuscript submitted for publication.

Lane, K. L., Robertson, E. J., & Graham-Bailey, M. A. L. (2006). An examination of school-wide interventions with primary level efforts conducted in secondary schools: Methodological considerations. In T. E. Lane, K. L., Robertson, E. J., & M. A. L. Graham-Bailey. (2006). An examination of school-wide interventions with primary level efforts conducted in secondary schools: Methodological considerations. In T. E. Scruggs & M. A. Mastropieri (Eds.), *Applications of research methodology: Advances in learning and behavioral disabilities* (Vol. 19). Oxford, UK: Elsevier.

Lane, K. L., Robertson, E. J., Mofield, E., Wehby, J. H., & Parks, R. J. (2008). Preparing students for college entrance exams: Findings of a secondary intervention conducted within a three-tiered model of support. *Remedial and Special Education.*

Lane, K. L., Robertson, E. J., Parks, R. J., & Edwards, C. (2006, November). *Strategies for using school-wide data to identify students for secondary interventions: Illustrations at the elementary, middle, and high school levels.* Paper presented at Teacher Educators for Children with Behavioral Disorders, Tempe, AZ.

Lane, K. L., Robertson, E. J., & Wehby, J. H. (2002). *Primary Intervention Rating Scale.* Unpublished rating scale.

Lane, K. L., Rogers, L. A., Parks, R. J., Weisenbach, J. L., Mau, A. C., Merwin, M. T., et al. (2007). Function-based interventions for students nonresponsive to primary and secondary prevention efforts: Illustrations at the elementary and middle school levels. *Journal of Emotional and Behavioral Disorders, 15,* 169–183.

Lane, K. L., Stanton-Chapman, T. L., Roorbach, K. A., & Phillips, A. (2007). Teacher and parent expectations of preschoolers' behavior: Social skills necessary for success. *Topics in Early Childhood, 27,* 86–97.

Lane, K. L., & Wehby, J. (2002). Addressing antisocial behavior in the schools: A call for action. *Academic Exchange Quarterly, 6,* 4–9.

Lane, K. L., Wehby, J. H., & Cooley, C. (2006). Teacher expectations of students' classroom behavior across the grade span: Which social skills are necessary for success? *Exceptional Children, 72,* 153–167.

Lane, K. L., Wehby, J. H., Little, M. A., & Cooley, C. (2005a). Academic, social, and behavioral profiles of students with emotional and behavioral disorders educated in self-contained classrooms and self-contained schools: Part I. Are they more alike than different? *Behavioral Disorders, 30,* 349–361.

Lane, K. L., Wehby, J. H., Little, M. A., & Cooley, C. (2005b). Students educated in self-contained classes and self-contained schools: Part II. How do they progress over time? *Behavioral Disorders, 30,* 363–374.

Lane, K. L., Wehby, J. H., Menzies, H. M., Doukas, G. L., Munton, S. M., & Gregg, R. M. (2003). Social skills instruction for students at risk for antisocial behavior: The effects of small-group instruction. *Behavioral Disorders, 28,* 229–248.

Lane, K. L., Wehby, J. H., & Robertson, E. J. (2008). *Studying school-wide positive behavior support at the high school level.* Manuscript in preparation.

Lane, K. L., Wehby, J. H., Robertson, E. J., & Barton-Arwood, S. (2008). *Preparing for positive behavior support at the high school level: Implementation steps and outcomes.* Manuscript in preparation.

Lane, K. L., Wehby, J. H., Robertson, E. J., & Rogers, L. A. (2007). How do different types of high school students respond to positive behavior support programs?: Characteristics and responsiveness of teacher-identified students. *Journal of Emotional and Behavioral Disorders, 15,* 3–20.

Lanyon, R. (2006). Mental health screening: Utility of the psychological screening inventory. *Psychological Services, 3,* 170–180.

Leedy, A., Bates, P., & Safran, S. P. (2004). Bridging the research-to-practice gap: Improving hallway behavior using positive behavior supports. *Behavioral Disorders, 29,* 130–139.

Leff, S. S., Costigan, T., & Power, T. J. (2003). Using participatory research to develop a playground-based prevention program. *Journal of School Psychology, 42,* 3–21.

Lewis, T. J., Colvin, G., & Sugai, G. (2000). The effects of pre-correction and active supervision on the recess behavior of elementary students. *Education and Treatment of Children, 23,* 109–121.

Lewis, T. J., Powers, L. J., Kelk, M. J., & Newcomer, L. L. (2002). Reducing problem behaviors on the playground: An investigation of the application of schoolwide positive behaviors supports. *Psychology in the Schools, 39,* 181–190.

Lewis, T. J., & Sugai, G. (1999). Effective behavior support: A systems approach to proactive school-wide management. *Focus on Exceptional Children, 31,* 1–24.

Lewis, T. J., Sugai, G., & Colvin, G. (1998). Reducing problem behavior through a school-wide system of effective behavioral support: Investigation of a school-wide social skills training program and contextual interventions. *School Psychology Review, 27,* 446–459.

Loeber, R., Green, S. M., Lahey, B. B., Frick, P. J., & McBurnett, K. (2000). Findings on disruptive behavior disorders from the first decade of the developmental trend study. *Clinical Child and Family Psychology Review, 3,* 37–59.

Lohrmann-O'Rourke, S., Knoster, T., Sabatine, K., Smith, D., Horvath, B., & Llewellyn, G. (2000). School-wide application of PBS in the Bangor area school district. *Journal of Positive Behavior Interventions, 2,* 238–240.

Luiselli, J. K., Putnam, R. F., & Sunderland, M. (2002). Longitudinal evaluation of behavior support intervention in a public middle school. *Journal of Positive Behavior Intervention, 4,* 182–188.

Lynam, D. R. (1996). Early identification of chronic offenders: Who is a fledgling psychopath? *Psychological Bulletin, 120,* 209–234.

Maag, J. W. (2001). Rewarded by punishment: Reflections on the disuse of positive reinforcement in schools. *Exceptional Children, 67,* 173–86.

MacKinnon, D. P., Johnson, C. A., Pentz, M. A., Dwyer, J. H., Hansen, W. B., Flay, B. R., et al. (1991). Mediating mechanisms in a school-based drug prevention program: First-year effects of the Midwestern Prevention Project. *Health Psychology, 10,* 164–172.

MacMillan, D., Gresham, F., & Forness, S. (1996). Full inclusion: An empirical perspective. *Behavioral Disorders, 21,* 145–159.

Mastropieri, M. A., & Scruggs, T. E. (2007). *The inclusive classroom: Strategies for effective instruction.* Upper Saddle River, NJ: Prentice Hall.

Mattison, R. E., Hooper, S. R., & Glassberg, L. A. (2002). Three-year course of learning disorders in special education students classified as behavioral disorder. *Journal of the American Academy of Child and Adolescent Psychiatry, 41,* 1454–1461.

May, S., Ard, W., III, Todd, A. W., Horner, R. H., Glasgow, A., Sugai, G., et al. (2000). *School-Wide Information System (SWIS). University of Oregon, Educational and Community Supports.*

Mayer, G. R., Butterworth, T., Nafpaktitis, M., & Sulzer-Azaroff, B. (1983). Preventing school vandalism and improving discipline: A three-year study. *Journal of Applied Behavior Analysis, 16,* 355–369.

McCurdy, B. L., Manella, M. C., & Eldridge, N. (2003). Positive behavior support in urban schools: Can we prevent the escalation of antisocial behavior? *Journal of Positive Behavior Interventions, 5,* 158–170.

McMahon, S. D., & Washburn, J. J. (2003). Violence prevention: An evaluation of program effects with urban African-American students. *Journal of Primary Prevention, 24,* 43–62.

Mehas, K., Boling, K., Sobieniak, J., Burke, M. D., & Hagan, S. (1998). Finding a safe haven in middle school. *Teaching Exceptional Children, 30,* 20–23.

Menzies, H. M., Lane, K. L., & Kalberg, J. R. (2008). *Targeted interventions at the elementary school level: A forum for academic and behavioral support.* Manuscript in preparation.

Menzies, H. M., Mahdavi, J., & Lewis, J. (2008). Early intervention in reading: From research to practice. *Remedial and Special Education, 29,* 67–77.

Metzler, C. W., Biglan, A., Rusby, J. C., & Sprague, J. R. (2001). Evaluation of a comprehensive behavior management program to improve school-wide positive behavior support. *Education and Treatment of Children, 24,* 448–479.

Meyer, A., & Northup, W. (1998). *Responding in peaceful and positive ways (RIPP): A violence prevention curriculum for sixth graders.* Unpublished manuscript.

Miller, M. J., Lane, K. L., & Wehby, J. (2005). Social skills instruction for students with high incidence disabilities: An effective, efficient approach for addressing acquisition deficits. *Preventing School Failure, 49,* 27–40.

Miller, S. (2002). *Validated practices for teaching students with diverse needs and abilities.* Boston: Allyn & Bacon.

Molina, J., & Molina, M. (1997). *PeaceBuilders.* Long Beach, CA: Authors.

Morris, R. J., Shah, K., & Morris, Y. P. (2002). Internalizing behavior disorders. In K. L. Lane, F. M. Gresham, & T. E. O'Shaughnessy (Eds.), *Interventions for children with or at risk for emotional and behavioral disorders* (pp. 223–241). Boston: Allyn & Bacon.

Morrison, G. M., Robertson, L., Laurie, B., & Kelly, J. (2002). Protective factors related to antisocial behavior trajectories. *Journal of Clinical Psychology, 58,* 277–290.

Nelson, J. R. (1996). Designing schools to meet the needs of students who exhibit disruptive behaviors. *Journal of Emotional and Behavioral Disorders, 4,* 147–161.

Nelson, J. R., Benner, G. J., Lane, K. L., & Smith, B. W. (2004). An investigation of the academic achievement of K–12 students with emotional and behavioral disorders in public school settings. *Exceptional Children, 71,* 59–73.

Nelson, J. R., Martella, R., & Galand, B. (1998). The effects of teaching school expectations and establishing a consistent consequence on formal office disciplinary actions. *Journal of Emotional and Behavioral Disorders, 6,* 153–161.

Nelson, J. R., Martella, R. M., & Marchand-Martella, N. (2002). Maximizing student learning: The effects of a comprehensive school-based program for preventing problem behaviors. *Journal of Emotional and Behavioral Disorders, 10,* 136–148.

Netzel, D. M., & Eber, L. (2003). Shifting from reactive to proactive discipline in an urban school district: A change in focus through PBS implementation. *Journal of Positive Behavior Interventions, 5,* 71–79.

No Child Left Behind (NCLB) Act of 2001, Public Law No. 107-110, § 115, Stat. 1425 (2002).

Noell, G. H., & Gresham, F. M. (1993). Functional outcome analysis: Do the benefits of consultation and prereferral interventions justify the costs? *School Psychology Quarterly, 8,* 200–226.

O'Connor, R. E., Notari-Syverson, A., & Vadasy, P. F. (2005). *Ladders to literacy: A kindergarten activity book* (2nd ed.). Baltimore: Brookes.

Olweus, D. (2001). *Olweus' core program against bullying and antisocial behavior: A teacher handbook.* Bergen, Norway: Research Center for Health.

Olweus, D., Limber, S. P., & Mihalic, S. (1999). *The bullying prevention program: Blueprints for violence prevention* (Book 9). Blueprints for Violence Prevention Series (D. S. Elliott, Series Editor). Boulder, CO: Center for the Study and Prevention of Violence, Institute of Behavioral Science, University of Colorado.

Pentz, M. A., Mihalic, S. F., & Grotpeter, J. K. (1998). *The Midwestern prevention project: Blueprints for violence prevention* (Book 1). Blueprints for Violence Prevention Series (D. S. Elliott, Series Editor). Boulder, CO: Center for the Study and Prevention of Violence, Institute of Behavioral Science, University of Colorado.

Peterson, L. D., Homer, A., & Wonderlich, S. (1982). The integrity of independent variables in behavior analysis. *Journal of Applied Behavior Analysis, 15*, 477–192.

Peterson, L. D., Young, K. R., Salzberg, C. L., West, R. P., & Hill, M. (2006). Using self-management procedures to improve classroom social skills in multiple general education settings. *Education and Treatment of Children, 29*, 1–21.

Popham, W. J. (1999). Why standardized tests don't measure educational quality. *Educational Leadership, 56*, 8–15.

Quinn, S. R., & Poirier, J. M. (2004). Linking prevention research with policy: Examining the costs of the failure to prevent emotional and behavioral disorders. In R. B. Rutherford, Jr., M. M. Quinn, & S. R. Mathur (Eds.), *Handbook of research in emotional and behavioral disorders* (pp. 78–97). New York: Guilford Press.

Reid, R., Gonzalez, J. E., Nordness, A. T., Trout, A., & Epstein, M. H. (2004). A meta-analysis of the academic status of students with emotional/behavioral disturbance. *Journal of Special Education, 38*, 130–143.

Reimers, T. M., & Wacker, D. P. (1988). Parents' ratings of the acceptability of behavioral treatment recommendations made in an outpatient clinic: A preliminary analysis of the influence of treatment effectiveness. *Behavior Disorders, 14*, 7–15.

Reimers, T. M., Wacker, D. P., & Koeppl, G. (1987). Acceptability of behavioral treatments: A review of the literature. *School Psychology Review, 15*, 212–227.

Robertson, E. J., & Lane, K. L. (2007). Supporting middle school students with academic and behavioral concerns within the context of a three-tiered model of support: Findings of a secondary prevention program. *Behavioral Disorders*.

Rutter, M. (1967). A children's behavior questionnaire for completion by teachers: Preliminary findings. *Journal of Child Psychology and Psychiatry, 8*, 1–11.

Safe and Drug-Free Schools and Communities Act of 1994, Public Law No. 103-382, 4001-4133, 108 Stat. 3518 (codified as amended at 20 U.S.C. 7101–7143 [2000]).

Satcher, D. (2001). *Youth violence: A report of the Surgeon General*. Washington, DC: U.S. Public Health Services, U.S. Department of Health and Human Services.

Schumm, J. S., & Vaughn, S. (1995). General education teacher planning: What can students with learning disabilities expect? *Exceptional Children, 61*, 335–353.

Scott, T. M. (2001). A schoolwide example of positive behavioral support. *Journal of Positive Behavior Interventions, 3*, 88–94.

Scott, T. M., & Barrett, S. B. (2004). Using staff and student time engaged in disciplinary procedures to evaluate the impact of school-side PBS. *Journal of Positive Behavior Interventions, 6*, 21–27.

Scott, T. M., & Caron, D. B. (2005). Conceptualizing functional behavior assessment as a prevention practice within positive behavior support. *Preventing School Failure, 50*, 13–20.

Shinn, M. R., Tindal, G. A., & Spira, D. A. (1987). Special education referrals as an index of teacher tolerance: Are teachers imperfect tests? *Exceptional Children, 54*, 32–40.

Simcha-Fagan, O., Langner, T., Gersten, J., & Eisenberg, J. (1975). *Violent and antisocial behavior: A longitudinal study of violent youth* (OCD-CB-480). Unpublished report of the Office of Child Development.

Skiba, R., & Peterson, R. (2003). Teaching social curriculum: School discipline as instruction. *Preventing School Failure, 47*, 66–73.

Snyder, H. N., & Sickmund, M. (2006). *Juvenile offenders and victims: 2006 national report*. Washington, DC: U.S. Department of Justice, Office of Justice Programs, Office of Juvenile Justice and Delinquency Prevention.

Sprague, J., Walker, H., Golly, A., White, K., Myers, D. R., & Shannon, T. (2001). Translating research into effective practice: The effects of a universal staff and student intervention on indicators of discipline and school safety. *Education and Treatment of Children, 24,* 495–511.

Stanford Achievement Test Ninth Edition, Form T. (1996). San Antonio, TX: Harcourt Brace.

Sugai, G., & Horner, R. (2002). The evolution of discipline practices: School-wide positive behavior supports. *Child and Family Behavior Therapy, 24,* 23–50.

Sugai, G., Horner, R., & Gresham, S. (2002). Behaviorally effective school environments. In M. R. Shinn, H. M. Walker, & G. Stoner (Eds.), *Interventions for academic and behavior problems: II. Preventive and remedial approaches* (pp. xx–xx). Washington, DC: National Association of School Psychologists.

Sugai, G., Horner, R., Sailor, W., Dunlap, G., Eber, L., Lewis, T., et al. (2005). *School-wide positive behavior support: Implementers' blueprint and self-assessment.* Washington, DC: Office of Special Education Programs Center on Positive Behavior Interventions as Supports, 2001.

Sugai, G., & Horner, R. H. (2006). A promising approach for expanding and sustaining school-wide positive behavior support. *School Psychology Review, 35,* 245–260.

Sugai, G., Horner, R. H., & Todd, A. W. (2003). *Effective Behavior Support (EBS) Self-Assessment Survey Version 2: Educational and community supports.* Eugene: University of Oregon.

Sugai, G., Lewis-Palmer, T., Todd, A., & Horner, R. H. (2005). *School-wide Evaluation Tool Version 2.1.* Eugene: University of Oregon.

Sun, W., Skara, S., Sun, P., Dent, C. W., & Sussman, S. (2006). Project Towards No Drug Abuse: Long-term substance use outcomes evaluation. *Preventive Medicine, 42,* 188–192.

Sussman, S., Dent, C. W., & Stacy, A. W. (2002). Project Towards No Drug Abuse: A review of findings and future directions. *American Journal of Health Behavior, 26*(5), 354–365.

Sussman, S., Rohrbach, L., & Mihalic, S. (2004). *Project Towards No Drug Abuse: Blueprints for violence prevention* (Book 12). Blueprints for Violence Prevention Series (D. S. Elliott, Series Editor). Boulder, CO: Center for the Study and Prevention of Violence, Institute of Behavioral Science, University of Colorado.

Sutherland, K. S., Adler, N., & Gunter, P. L. (2003). The effect of varying rates of opportunities to respond to academic requests on the classroom behavior of students with EBD. *Journal of Emotional and Behavioral Disorders, 11,* 239–248.

Taylor-Greene, S. J., Brown, D., Nelson, L., Longton, J., Gassman, T., Cohen, J., et al. (1997). School-wide behavioral support: Starting the year off right. *Journal of Behavioral Education, 7,* 99–112.

Taylor-Greene, S. J., & Kartub, D. T. (2000). Durable implementation of school-wide behavior support. *Journal of Positive Behavior Support, 2,* 233–235.

Tingstrom, D. H., Sterling-Turner, H. E., & Wilczynski, S. M. (2006). The good behavior game: 1969–2002. *Behavior Modification, 30,* 225–253.

Todd, A., Haugen, L., Anderson, K., & Spriggs, M. (2002). Teaching recess: Low-cost efforts producing effective results. *Journal of Positive Behavior Interventions, 4,* 46–52.

Torgesen, J. K., & Bryant, B. R. (1994). *Phonological awareness training for reading.* Austin, TX: Pro-Ed.

Turnbull, A., Edmonson, H., Griggs, P., Wickham, D., Sailor, W., Freeman, R., et al. (2002). A blueprint for school-wide positive behavior support: Implementation of three components. *Exceptional Children, 58,* 377–402.

Umbreit, J., Ferro, J., Liaupsin, C., & Lane, K. (2007). *Functional behavioral assessment and function-based intervention: An effective, practical approach.* Upper Saddle River, NJ: Prentice Hall.

Umbreit, J., Lane, K. L., & Dejud, C. (2004). Improving classroom behavior by modifying task difficulty: The effects of increasing the difficulty of too-easy tasks. *Journal of Positive Behavior Interventions, 6,* 13–20.

Wagner, M., & Davis, M. (2006). How are we preparing students with emotional disturbances for the transition to young adulthood? Findings from the National Longitudinal Transition Study–2. *Journal of Emotional and Behavioral Disorders, 14,* 86–98.

Walker, B., Cheney, D., Stage, S., & Blum, C. (2005). Schoolwide screening and positive behavior supports: Identifying and supporting students at risk for school failure. *Journal of Positive Behavior Interventions, 7,* 194–204.

Walker, H. M. (2003, February 20). *Comments on accepting the Outstanding Leadership Award from the Midwest Symposium for Leadership in Behavior Disorders.* Kansas City, KS: Author.

Walker, H. M., Block-Pedego, A., Todis, B., & Severson, H. (1991). *School archival records search.* Longmont, CO: Sopris West.

Walker, H. M., Hops, H., & Greenwood, C. R. (1993). RECESS: Research and development of a behavior management package for remediating social aggression in the school setting. In P. Strain (Ed.), *The utilization of classroom peers as behavior change agents* (pp. 261–303). New York: Plenum Press.

Walker, H. M., Horner, R. H., Sugai, G., Bullis, M., Sprague, J. R., Bricker, D., et al. (1996). Integrated approaches to preventing antisocial behavior patterns among school-age children and youth. *Journal of Emotional and Behavioral Disorders, 4,* 193–256.

Walker, H. M., Irvin, L., Noell, J., & Singer, G. (1992). A construct score approach to the assessment of social competence: Rationale, technological considerations, and anticipated outcomes. *Behavior Modification, 16,* 448–474.

Walker, H. M., Ramsey, E., & Gresham, F. M. (2004). *Antisocial behavior in school: Evidence-based practices* (2nd ed.). Belmont, CA: Wadsworth.

Walker, H. M., & Rankin, R. (1980). *The SBS inventory of teacher social behavior standards and expectations.* Eugene: University of Oregon.

Walker, H. M., & Rankin, R. (1983). Assessing the behavioral expectations and demands of less restrictive settings. *School Psychology Review, 12,* 274–284.

Walker, H. M., & Severson, H. (1992). *Systematic screening for behavior disorders: User's guide and technical manual.* Longmont, CO: Sopris West.

Walker, H. M., & Severson, H. (2002). Developmental prevention of at-risk outcomes for vulnerable antisocial children and youth. In K. L. Lane, F. M. Gresham, & T. E. O'Shaughnessy (Eds.), *Interventions for children with or at risk for emotional and behavioral disorders* (pp. 177–194). Boston: Allyn & Bacon.

Walker, H. M., Severson, H., Nicholson, F., Kehle, T., Jenson, W. R., & Clark, E. (1994). Replication of the Systematic Screening for Behavior Disorders (SSBD) procedure for the identification of at-risk children. *Journal of Emotional and Behavioral Disorders, 2,* 66–77.

Walker, H. M., Severson, H., Todis, B. J., Block-Pedego, A. E., Williams, G. J., Haring, N. G., et al. (1990). Systematic Screening for Behavior Disorders (SSBD): Further validation, replication, and normative data. *RASE: Remedial and Special Education, 11,* 32–46.

Walker, H. M., Zeller, R. W., Close, D. W., Webber, J., & Gresham, F. (1999). The present unwrapped: Change and challenge in the field of behavior disorders. *Behavioral Disorders, 24,* 293–304.

Wehby, J. H., Falk, K. B., Barton-Arwood, S., Lane, K. L., & Cooley, C. (2003). Impact of comprehensive reading instruction on the academic and social behavior of students with emotional and behavioral disorders. *Journal of Emotional and Behavioral Disorders, 11,* 225–238.

Wehby, J. H., & Lane, K. L. (in press). Classroom management. In A. Akin-Little, S. Little, M. Bray, & T. Kehle (Eds.), *Handbook of behavioral interventions in schools.*

Wehby, J. H., Lane, K. L., & Falk, K. B. (2003). Academic instruction for students with emotional and behavioral disorders. *Journal of Emotional and Behavioral Disorders*, *11*, 194–197.

Witt, J. C., & Elliott, S. N. (1985). Acceptability of classroom intervention strategies. In T. R. Kratochwill (Ed.), *Advances in school psychology* (Vol. 4., pp. 251–288). Mahwah, NJ: Erlbaum.

Wolf, M. M. (1978). Social validity: The case for subjective measurement or how applied behavior analysis is finding its heart. *Journal of Applied Behavior Analysis*, *11*, 203–214.

Wong, H., & Wong, R. (1998). *How to be an effective teacher: The first days of school*. Mountain View, CA: Wong Publications.

Woodcock, R. W., McGrew, K. S., & Mather, N. (2001). *Woodcock–Johnson III Tests of Cognitive Abilities*. Itasca, IL: Riverside.

Yeaton, W., & Sechrest, L. (1981). Critical dimensions in the choice and maintenance of successful treatments: Strength, integrity, and effectiveness. *Journal of Consulting and Clinical Psychology*, *49*, 156–167.

Index